Passive Nihilism

Passive Nihilism

Cultural Historiography and the Rhetorics of Scholarship

Sande Cohen

St. Martin's Press
New York

ISBN 0–312–21362-X

Library of Congress Cataloging-in-Publication Data
Cohen, Sande.
    Passive nihilism : cultural historiography and the rhetorics of Scholarship / by Sande Cohen.
        p.   cm.
    Includes bibliographical references and index.
    ISBN 0-31232162-x (alk. paper)
    1. Historiography.   2. Nihilism (Philosophy)   3. Rhetoric.
I. Title.
D13.C593   1998
907'.2—dc21   98–15518
                                                                   CIP

Internal design and typesetting by Letra Libre

First edition: August, 1998
10   9   8   7   6   5   4   3   2   1

Contents

Acknowledgments

Thanks to Hayden White and John Tagg who read the first draft of this book in 1996 and made many suggestions for revision. I am grateful to the reader's reports at St. Martin's Press for their careful intellectual perspicuity, for readings in a "nonmoral" sense. Norman Klein and Dick Hebdige, colleagues at CalArts, offered valuable and generous advice. Kriss Ravetto offered sharp readings of these essays, so numerous as to be entangled with this text. Wulf Kansteiner raised a number of questions about historiography and I am grateful for conversations with him. Thanks to Andrea Loselle for a critique as well as for many conversations concerning critical theory. The students at CalArts patiently let me try out the ideas in chapters 2 and 5, and I am indebted to them. Thanks to Max Cohen and to Maura Burnett at St. Martin's Press. Thanks to all new Asian friends, in Taipei and Taichung, Taiwan, especially the teachers, for extending the experience "when one no longer has any idea how old one is or how young one will yet be," *Joyful Wisdom*.

This book is dedicated to Fong-Shing Chang and Mario Biagioli, whose rigorous threading of friendship and criticism, pleasure and intellectual intensity, found its way into these essays—"shaken in common by the winds, the trees of my garden and of my best soil," *Thus Spoke Zarathustra*.

A section of chapter 1 appeared in *Clio,* Fall 1996, v. 26, n. 1. Part of chapter 2 appeared in *Studies in History and Philosophy of Science,* June 1997, v. 28, n. 2 and a briefer version of chapter 4 was published in *Storio della Storiografia* 30 (1996).

Introduction 🔳

Passive Nihilism
as Historical Culture

In a world in which success means saving time, thinking has only one disadvantage, but it is an irredeemable disadvantage: it makes you waste time.

—Jean-François Lyotard

From the Textual Wars

These essays bring skepticism to scholarly texts. Skepticism is triggered as soon as a reader notices contradictions between scholarship's discursive structures: that they make aesthetically and morally satisfying thoughts and advance epistemically dubious and politically suspicious ideals and models. The skepticism offered here focuses on intellectual politics created by scholarly "truths," by scholarship's discursive assimilation of things, its substitutions of rhetoric for experience, rhetorics circulated as intellectually necessary.[1] Socially important concepts such as "history," "necessity," "truth," "possession," "original," "derived," "network," and "code" are some of the products of scholarly work, products embedded in all sorts of discourse.

Why skepticism toward scholarship? While it is open as to what makes a text scholarly, the ones analyzed offer acute mixtures of *fashion* and *overcoding;* they offer the *timely* and the *necessary thought,* and will be read as continuous with problems of intellectual credibility. One reads scholarship for resolutions (answers, better models, stronger connections), but if such discourse, "timely" and "necessary," does not in fact as much settle things as preserves a right to settle, what are we to make of that? More precisely, these essays focus on textual aggression, how specific scholarly texts "border-patrol" (Nietzsche), how they "read for" rival claims, absorb them, displace them, and engender signification as a public meaning. These texts or authoritative models give significance to time and culture, and will be read for their uses of language in making new models of credibility and plausibility, new instructions for the future.

To articulate this skepticism, radical conceptions of language are put forward, drawn from sources such as Gorgias's fragment on the "abductions" (forcible capture) of language, the rigors of Deleuze and Guattari, with stopovers at sites such as the writings of Vico, Nietzsche, de Man, Lecercle, Wittgenstein, and others. These sources are steeped in the history of discursive conflict between "norms" of language and culture and skepticism toward language. This conflict indicates the degree to which culturally supervising texts, authoritative instances of words of determination, persistently idealize connections between reference and a reader's intuition. "Supervisory" texts render language as answer to perplexities rather than adding another perplexity to our answers, hence giving readers secure instead of disruptive thoughts. To paraphrase Paul de Man, it is the "privilege" of scholarly writing to employ prosopopeia or imaginary references that create all sorts of subjects that can then be represented (for example, a "self in crisis," a "dazed public"), buttressed by the collection of events called *research*. And it is the curse of scholarship that such rhetorical imagination presented as "fact" and structure must deny what it affirms, namely that scholarship has no distinctive claim on epistemic truth; its truths are language, but not just language. Could it be that theories that insist that the present is a time of "abjection" or "trauma" or "emergence of hybrids" mistake the intellectual/laboring conjunctions of scholarly *work* for conditions of society?

The texts criticized below model conflicts in which desire, language, cultural disagreements, and senses of history collide. These collisions are resolved by supplying "brakeshoes" (Nietzsche) on the production of sense and meaning, using concepts against the proliferation of concepts. Such texts eliminate improprieties of thinking. They bring "must" to the status of encoding the unsupervised, the discrepant, the errant, the "floating" (Barthes), and insofar as such texts support transforming existing contentions into necessities, they belong to genealogies of conflict between the affirmation of nihilism—the logic of affirming the least negative of choices—and resistance to nihilism's "presently powerful intuitions" (Nietzsche). The various affirmations of the negative constitute the intellectual nucleus of these essays.

The writings selected for analysis are from different areas of the humanities—cultural and science studies, neopsychoanalysis, curatorial and art discourse, and models of history. They have had influence in their respective areas, and were chosen because they textually show how scholarly writing reinvents *cultural historiography*. This construct refers to the uses and abuses of history brought to various cultural functions, such as making hierarchies (of time, telos), ideals, judgments of taste, political filiation, and more. The argument throughout actively focusses on the effects that cultural historiography has on *cultural timings,* language based senses of urgency, slowdown, disruption and equilibrium, in other words, codes of fashion. In chapter four, a critique is made of the "voice" of a professional historian rendered as a cultural ideal: the connoisseur as a transhistorical figure of cultural divination. Connoisseurship is thus turned into proper intuition, with special rights. The time of the connoisseur—its "eternality"—is instead analyzed as the historian purified of a mixed genealogy, a model that resonates with exclusions, disjunctions, fantasies, and commands. Cultural historiography refers to American scholarship's self-application of European-derived notions that preserve scholarship's language as untouchable.

It has been argued in science studies that scientific disputes are resolved with "blackboxed" or replicable skills transferred to wider audiences, "skill" serving as connective tissue between experiment (or text) and result (social outcomes). Science "moves" in relation to contests over the introduction of new skills, a model suggesting that criticism of written texts should pursue how a text works as an "experiment" (in making a model). The difference is that criticism of written texts asks how such texts *obscure their skill,* how they obscure their use of language—rhetoric, logic, grammar, syntax, sense—in making ideals, political values, or metaphysical positions that cannot be directly stated. [2] This dimension of a text's "skill" is not its unconscious, or its propositional "truth," or its sociological determination. While such dimensions are important, the readings given here stress the "virtue" a text gives itself so as to make its way aggressively in a highly competitive system of text production. Such "virtue" (e.g., raising a judgment to a model, appearing timely, of necessity) will be interpreted as pragmatic instructions for the shrewd and the competent, a restricted textual economy but one with universalist demands.[3] Perhaps one is gathering something like a "fall" of high scholarship's self-deception, the impossibility of not using language to install epistemically dubious models. And perhaps this overall project is still too dependent on certain texts, certain limitations in which case "fall" certainly cannot have merely one meaning. [4] How do such texts produce meanings for a present in relation to the persistent failures of such meanings? The question asks about the credibility of texts when it can be argued that they presume a reader's naivete in treating concepts and descriptions of imaginary realities as if they were stable cognitive objects.[5] In chapter two, for example, it is asked how a progressive model of multiculturalism transforms negative realities, a new cultural historiography based on antirape and antiracism, into the condition for a positive historical model. Why is such multiculturalism still using Hegelian codes to recast the negative into affirmed necessities, the latter then insisted as the basis for academia's own passage to the future?

Beginning with the *nonseparability* of epistemology, language, cultural artifacts, politics, and metaphysics, the purpose of the criticism offered here is to challenge what Nietzsche called *passive nihilism,* or reactive thinking. Passive nihilism can be thought of as an effect of a near overdose on order-words, a frenetics of paralysis. Oscillating between norms overvalued and skepticisms blindly affirmed, the passive nihilism of discourse pertains to the suppression of linguistic unreliability rendered in certainties, inadvertent oxymorons. J. Hillis Miller gives a cogent summary of this when he says that nihilism comes into being "when the highest values are devalued by the vanishing of what had seemed their necessary transcendent ground."[6] The texts analyzed valorize models such as "the expert," the "connoisseur," the "mediator," the "psychoanalyst," new "artists of the mud," (that is, anti-Conceptualists), which are rendered institutionally and economically viable and intractable as they suppress their own potential groundlessness or recourse to political authority. Passive nihilism means we go on and on trying to extract some "surplus" (here, of language and power) instead of radically transforming the way we do such work. In trying to activate a type of criticism based on textual evidence of intellectual overcoding and domination, in which the textual evidence is taken seriously as already achieved institutionalizations of discursive models, these essays clear a space, as Nietzsche put it, for that "third ear" that fosters abundance in matters of reading and writing and creates more critical choices for thinking about such matters instead of defensiveness, reaction, and idealization.

Now let me specify what is involved in this kind of criticism. Consider two texts, which at face value are antithetical, the first from one of our last "avant-garde" writers, the second a piece of traditional historical analysis. In his recent *Specters of Marx,* Derrida insists there is such a thing as a human "impulse" to ghostly communications, unrecognized until now. This "impulse" can, it is said, come into its own with what he calls a "new scholar" who can nonmetaphorically "herald" and "promise" a special knowledge of "the dead [who] must be able to work . . . a mode of production of the phantom . . . As in the work of mourning, after a trauma."[7] In the name of the "history of the specter," today must be a time of *spectering,* this "ecstatic" thought cast in the syntax of the messianic, an order-word "("the dead are speaking—listen"). Here, intellectual work must be done in the name of the dead and with the dead. Could one not read these phrases of *Specters of Marx* as at once avant-garde and reactionary—setting terms for the future and invoking a figure of communion by closing the circle of life and death?

Now consider a text written by Joyce Appleby, president of the American Historical Association. In a review of the "history wars" (the Smithsonian's representation of World War II [1994–1995]), she notes a conflict between "experts" (historians and curators) and veterans or subjects of historical commemoration. Her review associates the "fidelity and comprehensiveness" of scholars with a "distinguished record of sober analysis" by "experts." The veterans, who are surely "eyewitnesses," are dismissed, for the terms of comparison are good historians versus an "indifference of the public" as well as Congress' miserliness toward historical commemorations. Ominously, her essay makes one other point: "historical revisionism and elite deconstructionists trivialize the serious issues involved here." As an expert historian, professor Appleby, president of the AHA "knows" that to connect "revisionists," of whom the most notorious is Faurisson for his denial of the Holocaust, with deconstructionists, creates a monolithic and venal idea of deconstruction coded simply by the conjunction "and," a refusal to qualify, to specify.[8] The space Derrida reserves for "new scholars" is occupied here by "expert"—who is also said to embody a feeling of contact with that redoubtable human "craving" for historical memory, the historian having a special faculty "for touching lives long past."[9]

Textually considered, despite their differences, we have reliance upon conventional notions of "expert" and calls for a "new" type of scholar made continuous with the historiographic presencing of "spirit." Both are united in aim, divided only by rhetorical device: one ecstatic, one moralizing, but both joined in the belief that language can bring such intellectual "possessions" to readers, a language purified of contestation, removed from an impure genealogy. Derrida's writing excludes any mode of *ressentiment* and moves away from ideas of immanent causality, while according to the historian, historiography is a transcendence of politics. Each text works by negating so as to affirm a model not fully discussed. Each model has adherents to whom it "sounds good." These texts may well exemplify a unified "cultural logic" *of the vicarious,* differently rendered yet connected to the politics of textual authority. The historian trashes deconstruction while Derrida deconventionalizes historiography: but *both* evoke an ideal rendered immune to skepticism. Both employ order-words to make commanding models. In different ways, these texts restore historical sense as the power to install arrangements of writing as cultural determinants, worthy of being subsidized by present institutional arrangements. Derrida's "new scholar" involves no institutional transformation, nor does Appleby's "expert" entail any change of circumstances for historical writing (the research ideal is left intact). The concept of *cultural historiography* will be used to evoke relations between discursive orders and cultural ideals, although it is to be readily admitted the phrase pertains to no conceptual immobility or purity.

Evoking history suggests decisions about continuisms and breaks; language refers us to figurations and models; and cultural politics regularly announces selective and hierarchical linkages of history and language, suggesting a conjunction of *fashion* and *orders* in systems based on the signifier.[10] Expressed in syntaxes transacademic and "popular," words such as "endowment," "legacy," and "spirit" come to mind. In the two examples given above, the respective models use language to periodize—now the "new scholar" can come; now the historian can sort public debates about the past.

What happens when reflection leads to the consciousness of a redundancy and repetition performed by the language of "normal" criticism, conventional and unconventional? Associating *revision* with right wings and deconstructionists and insisting upon the "dead at work" are both instances of "normal scholarly discourse." It will be stressed that both texts evince something "mad," dissociative, but certainly not the same "mad"— the historian's defense of the "expert" is not the same as Derrida's call for a "new scholar"—and yet both excessively prune for cultural ideals, reinstall two forms of political liberalism, and make entries to the future. Is all this simply "ordinary" scholarly work? Is scholarly discourse "ordinary"? Is the "ordinary" ordinary?

Thematic Concerns:
Repetition, Deconstruction, Close Reading

Notice the words above that create different senses of *re:* so many re's indicate that today is a time of intellectual *abbreviations,* shortcuts, in which the configurations of re are an important *re*source in how scholarship recodes what Nietzsche calls its "rank and reverence," its escape from politics and obsolescence. The textual frequency of *re* is like a wave moving across the disciplines of historiography, science studies, psychoanalysis, multicultural theory, and more. *Re* pertains to passive nihilism, for it makes things "come back" (*return*) in words, an event that both separates (proper words from improper ones) and unifies (as in making a model). Is *re* a logicorhetorical quality of idealist discourse? The contemporary success of *re* will be interpreted not as an unavoidable intellectual connection as in "return of the repressed," but as a default at the center of intellectual work. *Re* marks out a territory within criticism, which the following essays challenge. *Re* is a concept that renders continuity instead of incommensurability between readers and texts; in this sense, the texts analyzed below are all instances in which, in Deleuze's words, "the world has become chaos, but the book remains the image of the world," the book subverting our work with chaos.[11]

Such texts are read for the sense they make out of present intellectual dilemmas and in doing so, how they reject any influence deconstruction might have in those same areas. Deconstruction is used here to register the recoding of "normative" cultural historiography's making the present "historically" recognizable and suitable for appropriate misrepresentation. But deconstruction is also complicated by reading. For example, in chapter one it is argued that Derrida's version of deconstruction has shifted from avant-garde criticism to an extreme messianism that reads as a reactionary demand, as spirit-talk. The "fate" of deconstruction is not used here as a standard of measurement but only as a fulcrum to isolate certain problems. In relation to texts that soothe the mind as they raise issues undeniably fascinating (who speaks for the dead, what are the limits of psychological models, why is today another "rush" to the past, or is this an assault on the future?), deconstruction is used to specify zones of intellectual conflict, scholarship's wars with language, culture, and history.

The tribulations of deconstruction in America show one of the "guardrails" surrounding the scholarship considered here. It is impossible not to notice that deconstruction became a scapegoat, a resistance to intensive critical analysis. For example, Alice Kaplan's *French Lessons* (1993) supposed that de Man's subjective desire led him to Fascism and then to deconstruction. Kaplan's book, widely reviewed by leading liberal and conservative journalists, is written in such simple sentences that the writing takes on a scary presence. Here is some of what *French Lessons* asserts:

> Romanticism was the key to his [de Man's] thought . . . Romanticism was at the root of fascism—giving one's self to the revolution, linking aesthetics and politics. He [de Man] was working through his confusing relationship to European culture . . . De Man failed me . . . [12]

> De Man would have been a better teacher if he had given more of his game away. He was Belgian. . . . The root of de Man's intellectual questions was in his own experience and pain. . . . [Deconstruction's] rigor about language constrained our imaginations. [13]

Romanticism is reduced to Fascism and vice versa, an equivalence that destroys the very "historical knowledge" *French Lessons* claims to give its readers. Knowing that de Man's field of expertise was precisely the history of Romanticism's variegated connections with multiple ideologies, the reduction seems particularly nasty. To then say that de Man was "working through" his own "confusion" is to immerse deconstruction in the history of the confusion between Romanticism and Fascism. As people were "tricked" in the past by both Romanticism and Fascism, deconstruction's emphasis upon figural "tricks" must also repeat the original confusion, that of desire with revolution. Further, and particularly insinuating, de Man was looking for figural "tricks" because he, in his own person, must have been a "trickster." As de Man went looking for the "tricks" of language, well, then, he must have been involved in "tricking" everyone. Romanticism—at the "root"—makes the conjunctions organicist, that is, de Man wanted to achieve a sense of identity between himself, Romanticism, and Fascism. The "historical lesson" *French Lessons* gives is really the ordinariness of a rhetoric (here, an *ara*) that destroys its own credibility—but it "reads well." Of course it confirms de Man's argument: language is brought under control by simultaneously personalizing and historicizing it, or by reducing the realm of the conceivable to the personal.

Similarly, in a text that gives a historical critique of modern "denigration of vision" purportedly carried out by French intellectuals, Martin Jay tries to establish that this "ocularphobic discourse has seeped into the pores of French intellectual life."[14] The fifteen or so intellectuals analyzed by Jay for their contribution to skepticism concerning sight have made the relation of ocularphobia a bad force. Jay writes the negation of antiocularism, urging an appeal as to the necessity of not abandoning an Enlightenment heritage. It reads smoothly—that is, until reflection sets in. "Seeped . . . pores" makes French skepticism ("fifteen intellectuals") toward vision an insinuating event, raising the projection that these fifteen intellectuals might "dominate" with their own dis-ease with ocularity. Jay's "seeped . . . pores" is not a metaphor: It is somewhat paranoid, a warning to its audience, and displaces analysis of the self-contradictions of Enlightenment, although it hardly seems possible that Bataille and company are going to destroy mass-based ocularity. The antiforce of "seeped . . . pores" expends its energy in working as a blocking effect, and an attentive reader cannot miss the sense of the writing's issuing injunctions: the "French will not get through," "the doubting of vision goes too far," "our cultural allegiances will be threatened."

These are some of the implications of Jay's proposition, once the proposition is evaluated as a historicosemantic event embedded in and mixed with institution (instruction, order), with a collective organization of sense. "Seeped . . ." already connects, materially and practically, with a matrix of language-institution, if only in the mode that antiocularity is so dangerous that controls should be placed on its normalization within university life.

"Seeped . . . pores" is simultaneously word-existence (the words them-selves) and an event or action in and of itself, an intervention on its reader, saying that antiocularity might drown our Enlightenment model.[15] This incorporeal transformation, what "seeped . . . pores" does without saying what it is doing, indicates that "one does not speak of things or states of affairs, one speaks in the midst of states of affair" (Deleuze). Close reading explores the mechanisms in which texts make new orders of intuition for readers, as Kaplan and Jay have done. Hence the readings made in the fol-lowing essays will then sound counterintuitive: texts are models of their own unmodeling when skeptical readers apply close reading to a text's command functions.[16]

Nietzschean Labor

The conceptual syntax of cultural historiography in its eerie, unbounded and ubiquitous presence is not uncanny. Rather, cultural historiography is a textual function in which language makes orders for time: continuities, rankings, necessities and tasks, obsolescences and emergences making the present bearable, smoothing conflict, encoding time to words. What are "order-words"?[17] An order-word is a synthesis of an idea of time, culture, and subject that culturalizes and temporalizes at once. It is exemplified in the statement of one of our leading philosophers, who argues that even if "nothing is immune from criticism [it] does not mean that we have a duty to justify everything" (Rorty). The statement asserts acceptance of present realities, "solidarity," one's *acquisitions,* as it gives continuity against the pos-sible disruptions of criticism by others.[18] Invoked in the essays below is a "dark side" to contemporary historiography, an "abuse" of history, because historiography is one of the resources used by discursive systems to reduce "can" to "must." Rorty's text makes present and past mutually support a present discourse that renders substantive limiting intuitions about the pre-sent. In this sense, such texts give themselves over to the violence of de-mands, instructions for dismissing skepticism.[19] Against this, critique draws from skepticism so as to maintain pressure against the "historical sense": from the critic who called Herodotus the "father of lies" to Nietzsche and beyond. Such a critique no doubt strikes many as arcane and impossible. For what discourse can dispense with historiographic needs? What ge-nealogy of a counterintuitive reader can compete with authoritative schol-arly writings?

Close readers can understand how a text *uses rhetoric to make epistemic claims as to what should be known, studied, pursued,*[20] where the writing's mastery gives way to the reader's sense of repetition of language instruc-tions and commands. Such texts signal complexes of aesthetic comfort by removing cognitive dissonance and swerving from multiplying contradictory implications. A *je ne sais quoi* goes hand in hand with satisfying intuitions that assert the propriety of scholarship. In relation to such impositions, a skeptical reader responds to these texts as if texts were the equivalent of their teachings, their interpretations, making readings that refuse to concede epistemology to the sciences or wisdom to humanist scholarship. The texts of Carlo Ginzburg and Bruno Latour, analyzed in chapters two and four, insist that future cultural analysis belongs to the "mediators" (Latour) and not political contestants, that the "connoisseur" is a metahistorical role (Ginzburg) and hence unalterable. Their writings are partisan because they endorse disciplinary trainings in the order-words and times that result from such models, bursting out of words like *mediator* and *connoisseur.* These texts issue commanding models while giving themselves immunity from analysis. Such scholarly mastery, as a writing up of judgments of authority, might be compared to a machine where passive nihilism uses prosopopeia in making overcoded and overdetermined texts, flawed in demand insofar as figures are offered that cannot support the claims made for them.[21] Because such writings often strive to neutralize their own hallucinations, there is a "chase" between a text's model-making capacity in which its referential function tries to outwit its linguistic structures or referential truth is played out in the mode of dramatic error. While the analysis here is textual, it should not be thought of as separate from other critical perspectives.

The epistemics of criticism from a Nietzschean perspective operates as an outbreak within "high culture," since its objective is not to critique the masses for lack of anything, but to critique the elite acceptance of "acceptable metaphors of social consolation." This project involves, as Nietzsche saw, a politics of the educated proletariat taking up the language of the "chair" in its own library.[22]

The fact that Nietzschean ruminations are brought to the realm of cultural analysis suggests to many critics that notions of language and culture involves an acceptance of the Tower of Babel, of precluding the "public." One of our most visible intellectuals, Cornel West, rejects Nietzschean based critique for "the trashing of mediation, the valorization of difference . . . the decentering of the subject," a trinity of sins because it rejects liberal scientism (in the long run, technology is good), conservative hallucinations of tradition, and Hegelian Marxism, with its emphasis upon "dialectics."[23] But a Nietzschean take on West's discourse notices at the outset that "mediation" is often sacralized and that "trashing" is already dominant in the accusative discourse of professor West. What then is the significance of "mediation" in a culture in which the "public" already exists as object of desire and control, excuse structure, ideal? Nietzsche called such verbal concoctions *equations,* making "mediation" a measure of something else (conflict), but what measures mediation as measure? "Mediation" sometimes authorizes the passive embrace of the "smallest superiority" in the face of intractable realities, wrote Nietzsche, where all of us "juggle a little with names" so as to "rechristen . . . a benefit, a comparative happiness" for "objects which [we] hated." Idealizing discourse brought Nietzsche to the critical ledge where language that appears to "benefit" us should be thought a "consolation" for our collapse into self-serving language, removal from the danger of staying with language.[24] Nietzschean labor suggests one might make language dangerous instead of "friendly."

Vicissitudes of Criticism: Demands and Resistance

Specific conditions of intellectual work in the United States shape the "background" built into these critical essays. The texts analyzed below have been professionally received as "timely"—they satisfy a projected "need" and interest—and thereby put in place an articulation as perplexing as it is institutionalizing (as psychoanalysis, according to Deleuze, passed from a contract to a statute). Has the promise of criticism become part of the minimum social transformation of institutional arrangements, a maximizing of the minimum? Collectively, our academic disciplines keep "chasing" evaporating names: sexuality, class, race, technology, information, etc. Each "chase" adds a few concepts that appear to be indispensable, but set within an overall process of recoding, the application of "brakeshoes" to discursive sense. Just as Paul Valéry argued that the "flowering" of "high historiography" between 1850 and 1914 did nothing to prevent World War I, so too present scholarly writing more and more merges with consumable products, the text as a "tie-in," a ubiquitous antirelation.[25] If writing is one of "the wheels of the world" (Nietzsche), who can ask that it "shakes us to our depths" (Heidegger)? In the recent formulation of History Standards (1995) discussed by the U.S. Senate, a spokesperson defended "historical knowledge" on the basis of its providing "bittersweet" concepts to school-children.[26] How ironic: Children need "history" for the lesson of irony. From *Artforum* to *Critical Inquiry* to *Rolling Stone,* from the *Los Angeles Times* to government reports, from high scholarship to the most mundane and accessible texts, has a bad aura of satisfaction settled on criticism and scholarship in their "mainstreaming" of passive nihilism, an endless task of making the negative something to be affirmed? We cannot finish with "pasts which are not past," as in the case of modern German historiography, but what kinds of social dangers might be said to matter here? We are all fascists—can Fascism never happen again?

Nietzsche warned that fresh doses of asceticism are required to sustain the negative energy of protecting worn-out, inherited ideals. One can speak of a hardening of "ideals," that is, a *reinsistence* of them to satisfy contemporary arrangements. Yet if writing is a resource, then can't it be used up in such endeavors? A leader in "mutant theory" speaks of cybernetics in exactly the terms once reserved by conservatives for their cultural treasures, where enthusiasm overruns sense: " . . . on the Net . . . people are forced to construct a more complex, satisfying interaction out of the limited materials supplied."[27] The phrase "people are forced" involves terror and violence, summoning Nietzschean asceticism, but as this cannot be raised in a discourse of enthusiasm, we obtain virtue from necessity.

Paul de Man fretted over the incapacity of Westerners to live with the "destructiveness of unmediated truth" (for example, there is no such thing as a social contract), in which a "morality of deceit" is paper-named with metaphors that help us "forget the lie that the metaphor was in the first place."[28] Endless papers surround us announcing the destruction of every ideal and function of mediation, but what would it take for intellectually based and critical work to disturb our own passive and nihilist functions, since destruction fuels the processing of nihilism? De Man continued a line of argument started by Gorgias in his "Encomium on Helen" (550 BCE), warning of the power of language to cast spells, mixtures of prosopopeia, passive nihilism, psychologization, intellectual aggression, and order-words. What does one say then, when the literary critic, Fredric Jameson, insists (1993) that intellectual work is materially impossible unless we enact a "single white lie," a "lie" without which intellectual work would lose its distance from the social? It is worth pausing over this claim, because it says so much about writing today. Jameson valorizes criticism as one with the "very real truth . . . of the intellectual as observer . . . that status . . . that intervenes between the object of knowledge and the act of knowledge." Here is a key passage in which object and act are united in the *separation* of the observer from the social, intellectuals from society:

> . . . that such lucidity as to the real mechanisms of social relationship demands the price of a *single white lie,* a strategic blind spot in the area of the intellectual, the occupation of everything that is social about our own observer's viewpoint itself, the renunciation of social commitment, the attempt to surrender social knowledge from action in the world, indeed the very pessimism about the possibility of action in the world in the first place, will come to seem an act of atonement for this particular (structural) sin. For the intellectual is necessarily and constitutively at a distance. [29]

It is claimed that as intellectuals we must not only renounce activism but willfully embrace that "single white lie" (only one?), our own "original

sin," that we should submit to Sartre's choice, becoming an "objective traitor" to class origin and class affiliation so as to break off from the activism
of militants. This is worded by Jameson as an "impersonal and uninten-
tional Stalinist crime for which no solution can be found, but only expia-
tion or bad faith." This "observer" encoded as Stalinist releases rigid
order-words against criticism. There are no Pascalian choices for intellectuals. We cannot "wager" over intellectual work: Critique of distance is futile. The only choice open to an intellectual is religious: unless we affirm
negation (envy and loathing), we will become what we must avoid; intellectuals who celebrate mass culture or popular culture or writing itself will
end up like Edward Curtis who slipped away from the propriety of distance for wanting to "participate . . . in the dances and solidarity of the
ethnic tribe itself." Atonement and sin figure forth the supreme negative
idealization of intellectual work as unworthy yet necessary, a paradox unnoticed by Jameson. Since he puts down Foucault's notion of the "specific
intellectual" as "trivial" and the Maoist solution as a "tragic impossibility,"
can we not say of Jameson's own program that it is majestically catholic
and reactionary, that is, that it has "one lie," the observer who is released
from metaphor? And isn't this Marxist version of blindness to language
complementary to those of conservatives such as Appleby and Derridian
progressivists? More specifically: can such a default to a political morality
of the observer come forward as psychoreligious and responsible truth? Is
this possible?

One reads today of the demand for linguistic clarity ("swiftly from one
surface to another" [Nietzsche]), but the demand guarantees aggression toward reading, for how can we tolerate writings that take too much time?
The demand has institutional weight, as it feeds a new anti-intellectualism
of the academy itself, issued in the order-words that shelter academe from
confronting its own fate, the fact of its own steady disappearance.[30] More
fine books and articles than ever are being written, but subverted, for criticism yields to new powers, especially those of the network, threaded to
budgets, or the power to select and spend, the intertwining of economics
and discourse, which were never separate in the first place.

Today it is demanded of "public intellectuals" that they make interpretations that are accessible, available, kept in circulation. Reading and writing must give us *faces,* recognitions, even if a defacing. This demand belongs
to a cycle of *re*curring ideals and their *re*petitive collapse, then *re*coding yet
again. In this process of asking about the value and force of criticism, historiographic or not, we can't avoid thinking what concept formation really involves for the discourses of the humanities, in which concepts and
their articulations are sabotaged by the pull of institutions, by market values, and by the lure of professional recognition. For twenty-five hundred

years, Westerners have continuously made the case that prose criticism is something more than a way-station for idealisms of the word. How can there be that "dialogue" demanded of us in an era of such vast precensorship that scholars often calibrate even their endnotes so as to avoid offending some more powerful reader? In short, what are the goals that pertain to a will to read and to write?

Mode of Presentation

In chapter one, three texts are analyzed that show the historians idealizing their return to the "history fort" after having vanquished the onslaught of deconstruction, especially in the territory of the popular media. This "return" is then juxtaposed with Derrida's *Specters of Marx,* and a surprising convergence appears, for Derridian deconstruction also "returns" to notions of historical thought that are utterly traditional, its avant-garde or "shock" value part of its *re*activation of eschatology. On the basis of these texts, perhaps the idea of the difference between historicity and deconstruction can receive some fresh discussion. Both traditional historiography and Derrida's counterhistory deploy the syntax of idealism, what the intellectual historian G. A. Kelly called the labor of ideas of reason, at once political and chimerical, which activate the intellectual and political dissolution of "otherness." [31] Anti- and prodeconstructive positions can accommodate the chimera of a reason that *sounds rational precisely when it eliminates difference.* [32] Chapter one concludes with a counterintuitive model reader, who leaves off from idealisms of such "last readers" so as to affirm an "excessive reader" in search of reading spaces where skepticism toward writing is affirmed as a positive value.

In chapter two, arguments for neohistoricism and neoanthropology are analyzed by addressing the claims made for a multicultural historiography and a resuscitated anthropology that would *re*fold historiography, giving it powers of affirmation against the destructiveness of modernism. The argument here is that historiographic and cultural intersections are textually engineered so as to resolve the politics of difference (multiculturalism) and the epistemological suffering caused by modernism (the writings of Bruno Latour).

In chapter three, focus shifts to the oxymoronic elevation of the negative as neopsychoanalysis arranges the unconscious as a confirmation of failure. Love of failure is another mode of affirming passive nihilism. This is related to the idealization and appropriation of the category of the "adolescent" in the work of the Los Angeles based artist Mike Kelley. This chapter also examines connections between the triumph of the Lacanian model (Zizek) and the artistic/curatorial discourse wherein art language presents something called "the American psyche." The popularization of neopsychoanalysis has become reactionary, and in relation to this turn, Judith Butler's idealization of the concept of *rearticulation* which she opposes to psychoanalysis, is critiqued as a "blind-spot" of the opposition to neopsychoanalysis. Must criticism completely sever itself from psychologization? This chapter concludes with an expansion of the Jameson example above, noting that his insistence upon the negative, religious basis of cultural analysis has the effect of foreclosing cultural criticism as something active.

Chapter four asks what the effects are when "historical" scholarship embeds cultural idealism in the very act of narrating and modeling its own relation to the popular. The cultural/historiographical texts of Carlo Ginzburg are read as high academic political writings that remove any strong genealogy of the scholar in the production of a model in which the scholar is given only positive relations to objects of study. Such a picture is impossible. Ginzburg's writings indicate, in fact, that only a counterpolitics of reading the-high-reading-the-low has any chance of proposing an alternative to this scholarly policing, the real objective of Ginzburg's cultural writings, since they relentlessly eliminate all but the most refined sense of the historian's "taste," moving such "taste" a million miles beyond epistemology.

All of the writings analyzed insist that answers to palpable intellectual problems are to be found in a unity of historical knowledge and language, accomplished by the recoding of scholarship, a unity that turns out to be a political category as much as anything else.[33] In chapters one to four, then, readings are made that come up against the entanglements of writing and scholarship, politics and cognition: how can scholarship offer responsible synthesis if it *is* politics (of language, culture, and history)?

Finally, chapter five considers three countermodels to normal critical discourse, derived from the texts of Wittgenstein, de Man, and Deleuze and Guattari. This chapter is a dialogue with Nietzsche's great essay "Truth and Lie in a Nonmoral Sense" and offers positive differences from the kinds of texts analyzed. In setting forth Wittgenstein's dynamic of the said/shown, Deleuze and Guattari's theory of incorporeal transformations, and de Man's scrutiny of the impositionality of meaning, an existentialism of language is suggested as an alternative to overcoded discourses. Language is the impossible object that resists and precludes our attempts to "possess" ordinary concepts of subjectivity and language. The materials and ideas in chapter five are based on the presupposition that normal criticism is chimerical, and affirmative alternatives to the couple avant-garde/ reactionary are achieved not by opting for some middle distance, but by drawing out initiatives of discourse, discourse as productive of paradox, immediacy, and dissonance.

Chapter One ▨

Is There Postconventional Historiography?

Now an intellectual case that texts can be analyzed through constructs such as order-words and time demands must be "proved." These concepts are working tools yet also textual objects, syntactic organizers, not only instrument-concepts for analysis but textual relations. The working concepts of the following analyses are quasi-metalinguistic theories as well as discursive modes, which is to say that prose writing is a thing yet subject to interpretation by other word-things.[1] One can argue their existence only by first naming them in their functional sense. The objective of the readings given in this chapter is to specify these textual dimensions, and the strategy is to connect historiographic writings thought to be antithetical. Texts that reconventionalize are brought into comparison with a lengthy analysis of Derrida's *Specters of Marx* treated as a *de*conventionalization of cultural historiography.

Keith Jenkins's recent *On 'What Is History?'* directed to students who can read it in "four or five sittings," offers the writings of Richard Rorty and Hayden White as replacements for those of G. R. Elton and Edward Carr, whose impact on postwar British historiography has been extensive. The modernism of the latter (emphasis on history as politics) is obsolete, and the postmodernism (liquidation of foundations) of the former is now "our fate."[2] The "jaded and/or nostalgic reassessments" offered by Elton and Carr are unsuitable for present societies "which have no legitimizing ontological or epistemological or ethical grounds . . . beyond the status of an ultimately self-referencing (rhetorical) conversation." The holisms of modernism are dead: Jenkins's writing is part of the grave digging of that tradition. One question: Did modernism have "ultimately self-referencing (rhetorical) conversation[s]?" How could this be proved or disproved? The linguistic "turn" of writers such as Rorty and White will support an enlarged social "conversation"; historiography must now abandon the articulation of history-as-such in favor of making the "histories one is getting clean and 'upfront'."[3] "Clean and up front"—the students of our histories will be able to read "history" without suspicion toward the texts. In the name of separating from objectivist illusions, "clean" takes on a scary presence, for it involves purification—an eliminative aim.

The antidote to modernist false objectivism is a rhetoric that returns to the autobiographic as a better mode of such "dialogue" and "conversation," in which the expression of the "subjective position of the author" is made the minimum condition for even imagining the "objective" and the critical.[4] Stunningly, autobiography is not "read" in Jenkins's model as a mode of writing, as syntaxes and meanings that might be discrepant with author, but is maintained as a mode of writing purified of difficulties. The conflation of actual subjectivity with authorial text, mixed with what is "clean and up front," recalls modern lyric poetry's elimination of the object as constitutive of the real, of history, but without the radical sense of a Mallarme, for whom language's sense of subject was "impersonal, disincarnated, and ironical."[5] Let us call this example an instance of extreme reconventionalization: it saves the subject in its contemporary experiences, "free" to imagine "history" without the conventions of earlier texts, such as those of British historiography with its incessant commitment to political meanings.

In her introduction to *The Persistence of History,* Vivian Sobchak insists that we are living in an era in which the ironies and playfulness of a film such as *Forrest Gump* point the way to a "postconventional historiography," an imagination of historicity no longer bound to history with a capital H as inclusive coherence, but one at peace with "the breakdown of the segmentation that, in a previous age, secured for us the borders and value between 'significant' and 'trivial' events, between fact and fiction."[6] Like Jenkins, history is at best today histories, specific stories. Whether the unity of history is found in the historian's training, outlook, or function or is given up is not considered. For Sobchak, we are all living in the "metahistorical" world in which, as with the fictional film *Forrest Gump,* every standpoint "on history" is potentially outside every other standpoint, each one of these "outsides" ("others") said to converge "on the conflation of the personal and historical, trivial and significant." The present is conceived of as a swamp, figured forth as "history happens" just as "shit happens."[7] This is an *exergasa,* a proclamation of an all embracing ethos, a zeitgeist that reinstalls history with the vengeance of irony.

This is because *Forrest Gump* gives us "metahistory" or posthistorical consciousness in the form of a super self-consciousness, said to be the very

condition for a "novel 'readiness' for history among the general population."[8] After a discussion of the Disney dispute over "malling history," issues about national history "standards," and the O. J. Simpson case, the text
reaches a conclusion as to this "qualitatively new self-consciousness about
history." This gives rise to a virtual millennialism:

> a moment marked by a peculiarly novel "readiness" for history among the
> general population . . . people seem to carry themselves with a certain re-
> flexive phenomenological comportment toward their "immediate" immer-
> sion in the present, self-consciously grasping their own objective posture
> with an eye to its imminent future possibilities for representation (and com-
> modification) as the historical past.[9]

The present has a "unity" owing to this projection, such unity found in the
sense of tacit irony in which each present is squeezed into material for
judgments of rank and success, of recognition of desire, even of an extreme
"anticontext" in which no action goes unnoticed as a possible tactic
against others. Everyone acts with full consciousness of the evaluations and
judgments to be rendered in the future. The ironic is assumed to be the
truth condition of present future. The present is sentenced, literally and fig-
uratively, in its own name, to acts that maximize future choices, which
seems Darwinist and not "ironic," drained of precise and specific determinations. *Forrest Gump* signifies a vehicle for mass desire presumed satisfied
with the present ironic culmination of modern history, it being an axiom
of collective life that the audience of the film is "already in on the joke of
Forrest Gump," namely that everyone must "act" for how he or she will be
"seen" by "history." There can be no resistance to irony. Historical self-
consciousness is here a positioning for re*vision,* riding on the back of the
supposed traumas of modern loss (of security for middle-class Americans),
a boundless revisionism, as Sobchak insists, that "seems to happen right
now—is transmitted, reflected upon, shown play-by-play, taken up as the
stuff of multiple stories and significance, given all sorts of 'coverage'." History is everywhere—but one acts with an another "eye" on how one's past
will look in someone else's *mediatized* future, the present terroristically
smothered in fear of producing ineffective futures. What could be construed as a new terrorism, that of acting now to protect a future, is made
over into a new universal condition: a "hunger for history" (what Sobchak
calls a "search for a lost object" or the consciousness of the sufferings
brought about by Modernism).

Sobchak terms all this a need for a "usable" past. It reads as therapy of
the present. I have suggested that it is a question of the conjunction of
terror/territory of and as irony. The old theme here, from the history of

Protestantism, of why take the trouble to do something significant now if it comes to an ironic outcome, is shunted onto a "joke" we are all in on, a new "equality" of irony. Presented in a mode acceptable to "everyone," its discursive enthusiasm occludes its dubious epistemic assumptions, an extreme example of professional writing as *deesis,* submission to a projected audience's possession of universal truth.

Two Kinds of Convention, or *Reaction* in Motion

Jenkins and Sobchak's respective discourses are but samples in a literature without boundaries. They offer notions of cultural historiography that make it workable for present use-value. The actively pursue the elimination of rival claims, if only by omission, perhaps the most common tactic in setting aside contradictions at the level of concepts, ambiguity at the level of syntax. Such texts cleanse the present, making it suitable for articulation as a space of subjective expression or objective condition. They reach into the idea of an avant-garde, signaled here by their insistence that convention does not work, is obsolete, and immediately reconventionalize the coming future, where the respective order-words indicate the political and cultural syntaxing involved: a historiographic defense of specific present experiences (what autobiography and "shit happens" connote), the fragmentation of history as metanarrative and reconvened as condition, multiple yet isolated self-consciousnesses in need of subjectivity and an all-pervasive irony of the real become "filmic." These new conventions vindicate the present at the level of sensory experience (Jenkins), at the level of self (Sobchak), where vindication means a new solidarity of the neoliberal type: the present is settled insofar as it is forced into a pattern of continuity, a recoding of Rorty's premise, cited in the introduction, in which a genetic pattern undercuts criticism of the present.

I would like now to compare in some detail two texts, the first of which returns historiography to a model in which picturing rather than writing makes up its basic performance, the other of which drastically purifies the discipline of all but conventional "experts." These texts were chosen because they run so close to the line professional historiography gives itself, the line that encloses it from discursive contamination. After that, Derrida's more unconventional *Specters of Marx* is analyzed as to the status of an avant-garde historiography.

The recent *A New Philosophy of History,* edited by Frank Ankersmit and Hans Kellner, devotes considerable space to Ankersmit's argument that textual models of historiographic works should give way to visual models. He takes Hayden White's elaboration of the historical text to be a culmination of modernism's suppression of the metaphor of the "picture of historical reality." Modernism has made text-as-picture a "naive and misleading" schema. The text model of historical writing has repressed visual models. To reestablish the ties between picturing and truth or reliable representations of the past, Ankersmit wishes to defend the claim that a historical text "assumes the form of a 'picture' of the past," in which the historical models for this are said to be figurative and landscape painting.[10] Historical texts should appeal to their reader's sight, where the separate statements of an historical text receive their sense from the picture given by a text, so there is said to be parallelism between text-as-picture and world-as-picturable. As an idea of the historical text, this is a reworking of Kant's theory of the beautiful with its spontaneous harmony of judgment and sense. The premise assumes ordinary language is *secure* in its competency to picture the past.

Ankersmit's model is certainly provocative—it brings back Plato's Cratylian notion of a coincidence between signifier and signified (in which the *r* of *rhein* [flow] represents "flowing," an identity of sound and concept), the spatial restored to priority over the temporal, a mimesis called rapprochement between word and picture. Leaving unanalyzed the disjunction at which the metonymic (contiguity or temporal dismemberment) is absorbed by the metaphoric (mimesis), escaping the gap between word and picture, the historicity of the priority of word over picture is to be challenged. This project requires the restoration of the visual/metaphoric equivalence that will undermine "the distinction between resemblance and convention" (217). Now this is potentially radical, since two systems are to lose a "distinction." And to bring "resemblance" and "convention" together is certainly to imply that nonresemblance (not-history?) and nonconvention go together, as a definite position to avoid. To make convention the resemblance of what? Of experience, hence lessening the distance between subject and artifact as well. These are extremely strong, inclusive claims, registered in a few paragraphs.

The claim, then, is that convention and resemblance are not only not in opposition but are in fact parallel, and so a powerful identity obtains between them. Here is the key example: The chemical name *1,2-dimethyl enzene* immediately gives the molecule of which it is the name; the name gives us "the thing" because semantic and syntactic conventions "determine the combination of these elements [name and entity], this name is in effect a pictogram, a verbal model, indeed, a verbal picture of the molecule in question" (218). Signs do not merely stand for things or resemble the objects they name; naming effectuates picture when someone takes the name as picture; hence, naming is a success of familiarization, a process that

Ankersmit unfortunately omits from his account of picture over text. How a convention is made is obscured. Who can deny the familiar? The mushroom cloud over Hiroshima as pictured in a photo, a drawing, a moving image, a verbal description, subject to all the rules of projection and distortion, may well render cultural concepts of "disaster," but such concepts are dynamic interpretants rather than "icons."[11] The example drawn from chemistry relies upon an overcoded definition treated as the verbal sign. That is to say, the analogy between the discourse of chemistry and historiographical description breaks down as soon as one asks in what ways are nonchemical things molecules? What could be the molecules of, say, the history of ideology in America? Rom Harre has said that chemistry is the exemplary classificatory practice, which seems then an odd model for narrative motions. Even more: "molecular" is potentially misleading—isn't description operative on every level but the "molecular," in the sense that descriptions are often molar—imprecise and incomplete?

These "molecules" are then linked to semantic conventions that are said to "determine reference," and indeed they do, but the conclusion is drawn that names are conventional pictograms, a "verbal picture of the molecule in question," effecting "resemblance between word and reality which we intuitively reserve for the relations between picture and reality. Convention and resemblance (as models for the relation between representation and what is represented) are parallel, not opposite, paradigms here" (218). A sentence is a picture, a transparency of language. I should like to note that Ankersmit draws on Wittgenstein here, but only to affirm that true sentences equal pictures of reality, omitting the dynamics of how sentences *show* their sense as they are also partially false, senseless, tautological. But this transparency brings its own strangeness, for, as in the citation above, it is threaded to "intuitively reserved" schemas without which cognition would dissolve. At any given moment sense with others is guaranteed by what we already know—there is uncontested background knowledge such that differences between a sense of history, present, and future need not be manifested. In the terms proposed by Paul de Man, such "intuitively reserved" schemas can also be considered those interpretations that are modes of resistance to new information and difficult complexes of thought.[12]

Citing Leibniz from the seventeenth century and a passage from Foucault elaborating the Renaissance episteme as encoded by "sympathy," the argument also relies upon passages from the *Tractatus* where verbal conventions and reality share a structure, so that the "very distinction between word and picture should lose its meaning" (219). Words are to be thought of as pictures, but pictures are irreducible to words. This is an old see-saw. Hence the confidence we feel about the *difference* between word and picture is unreliable—the "biased neutrality" of considering convention to be resemblance gains for us "realistic representations" which "conform[s] to the existing pictural *conventions*" (221). The "density" Ankersmit attributes to pictures and the "articulate disjointedness" of words is a difference rendered inoperative by narrative substance, a text's sense of totality, which "cannot be divided into a part that refers and a part that assigns a predicate. The narrative substance always comprehends *both*" (226). Like pictures, the historical text resists "the differentiation between subject and predicate." If I understand this correctly, it lays out the formal basis upon which historical statements should be understood—they are analytic statements or names at which subject and predicate coalesce. At a certain point, the names of things at once classified and narrated (since pictures at least do both) are beyond analysis by a reader.

For all intents and purposes, names are substantialized. This is a synthesizing operation devoted to a code of command: Ankersmit calls it a "short-circuiting" of the word-picture difference and making "historical truth" a question of picturing, not writing (213). But getting "names" wrong, by omission, by neglect of predicates, bias, and so forth, is also part of the game. None of this can surface in Ankersmit's essay, as the encoding turns historians into makers of formulae, where interpretation by readers is kept to the minimum *executive* dispositions.[13] That is to say, the model reader of an historical text is imagined as a reader who can apply the narrative substance to the writing's specific sentences and make the right calculations, a reader who does not challenge picturing. The historian's actual text is mimetic, from documents referenced to reader's responses, so that one might say that resemblance mediates between word and past, but is itself without mediation once accepted as "intuitive." If intuitive schemas hold between exterior reality and word-pictures and readers' sets of expectations, is this not an imaginary space, a fiction? When Ankersmit insists that "representative codes" are the means that "we should give to the content of our thoughts when we wish to express them," that "the represented code establishes which form matches which content," the rhetorical and logical are forgotten and repressed. They are ordered out of the "room." The historian invents nothing consequential; the writing apparatus is rendered unobtrusive. This is too "good" to be true, a concept made intuitive.

The rhetoric of logical coding that sustains Ankersmit's model, where form and content are said to be independent, and where resemblance obtains when "the historian has found the *correct* form for the content presented," is rigorously aestheticist. Citing Buffon as the authority that "the historical text as a whole . . . cannot be reduced to the truth of the separate descriptive statements which make up the . . . text," this sense of a "harmony" from out of musical "tone" precludes the close reading of any particular text. Close reading is bad taste insofar as such reading might pull on a concept and find that it cannot support other textual claims, other cognitive senses. "Exemplification" is the ideal of writing history, for the reader's judgment need not be awakened: to exemplify renders the historian as someone who gives a "determination" of content. When one reads, say, a narrative of World War II that gives an account of the "end" of the classical "German tradition," one's "intuitive schemas" should share the writing's schemas, which are said to be congruent with the facts. The "right form" gives the proper measure of necessity. Tocqueville's use of paradox to narrate the "centerlessness" of American democracy "agrees with the content of his views on democracy." The job of historiography then is manifestly not to undermine what historians do, but only to scrutinize when a particular narrative has slipped out of the mode of "exemplification" and into that of ideology, where form overwhelms content. What some of Wittgenstein's arguments in the *Tractatus* did to philosophy's relation to science—stopping philosophy from meddling in the hard work of science—historiography is to do for history. The writing of history is *reautonomized* in the name of the visual arts as literary theory is set aside. Literary theory is not itself the right discourse, for the "historical text" is said to be the prototype of the novel just as historical "inquiry" has logical precedence over literary theory, for the latter "is a reflection on an evolution which started only *after* historical research and literature in its many forms went their separate ways and little is to be expected from this reflection for the understanding of the historical representation of reality" (238). And what of the visual arts which are non-representational or entirely unstable (for example, T. J. Clark's analysis of postimpressionism)? Premodernist in its invocation of parallel, harmony, and aesthetic/logical unity, antimodernist in its examples of history writing and art, Ankersmit's model belongs to a politics of the signifier as "classical" transparency.

Ankersmit's elegant model excludes the possibility of a close reader, that is, readers for whom written significations give visual stimulations not separate from rhetoric and syntax. Written signifiers are always voluntary, whereas visual stimulations are often involuntary.[14] The model also presumes that a historical text is self-explanatory, there being no outstanding epistemic problematics to its writing. This is of a piece with the claim, found in a "Bibliographical Essay" at the end of *A New Philosophy of History,* that one should take the "self-interpretation of historians more seriously than the high-handed approach of the deconstructivists would ever be prepared to do" (280). But the aestheticist coding given by his text accounts precisely for this rejection of deconstruction. Indeed, in the same essay, interest in questions of the "presence of the historian" is said to be of importance, a concern raised as "intransitive writing," and abruptly coded as a "form of literary or historical writing in which the author 'writes himself' just as the neurotic 'speaks himself' . . . and where . . . the self of the historian obtains a hitherto unparalleled predominance" (238). Arguments from Hayden White and others that the historian might experiment with writing by means of probing "intransitive" modalities are acknowledged and removed by the equation that the "neurotic 'speaks himself'." Historiography should protect history-as-picture while experimentation with forms of representation is kept away. Deconstruction should not speak of historical texts; encoded above as "high-handed," isn't this to reject it as having a "right" to closely read an historian's text? There is something strange when close reading becomes a threat to the written text.

The second text in this rearticulation of convention, *Telling the Truth About History* (1994), written by three distinguished historians, opens with the sentence: "More people in the U.S. have been to college or university than was the case in any country at any time in the past."[15] Filled out, this narrative result is called a positive outcome and, as it is not contradicted by other "facts," it is systematically misleading: 50 percent of students admitted never complete degrees, many go to schools at which teaching assistants make up the majority of instructors, this in a profession of 600,000 college teachers, 45 percent of whom teach part-time. Student debt levels are punishing and set up subservience to employers, and the diversity of what American students "know" always confronts an excessive division of labor such that many students are unable to deploy their own education. Such facts disrupt, or perhaps denarrativize *Telling the Truth About History.* Indeed, removing contradictory effects, *Telling the Truth* eschews analytic thought. Identifying with "women, minorities, working people," voiced by historians who entered the profession when there was still explicit discrimination, these once-upon-a-time "barbarians" (their term) have become "gatekeepers" (my term), for they come to restore what is "lost" (their term):

> the philosophical foundation that had underpinned the confidence of educated people. . . . Skepticism is the order of the day . . . Our central argument is that skepticism and relativism about truth . . . have grown out of the insistent democratization of American society. The opening of higher education to nearly all who seek it, the rewriting of American history from a variety of cultural perspectives, and the dethroning of science as the source and model for all that is true are interrelated phenomena. (7)

Democracy breeds skepticism, today is an interregnum. No progress can be achieved with too much skepticism: there is today a void instead of accepted criteria by which "history" can provide the tracks of this progress. And this interregnum is unacceptable: "the cynicism and nihilism that accompany contemporary relativism" have become "complete skepticism . . . debilitating, because it casts doubt on the ability to make judgments or draw conclusions," and so requires new orders to restart the "engines" of history and proper judgment.

The most extraordinary "reading of history" these authors make is when they turn relativism and skepticism into antecedents of Nazism:

> The experience of World War II with its horrendous new weaponry and the genocidal policies of the Nazi regime temporally forestalled the progress of skepticism and relativism. The killing of the Jews seemed to show that absolute moral standards were necessary, that cultural relativism had reached its limits in the death camps. But the lull was only temporary. (7)

This passage links the highest levels of professional historical writing about culture with a thesis supplied by historical fable. The story: skepticism and relativism were progressing and halted by Nazism—used here as the "truth" of skepticism's "progress." Nazism reveals the previous failure to stop skepticism and relativism, the conclusion of which can only be some present fright: "if the lull is temporary and there is too much skepticism, do we face a Nazi future?"

What is relativism here that makes it the object of such equations? It is the widespread belief that the "truth of a statement is relative to the position of the person making the statement?" No consideration is given to work on incommensurability of perspective and point of view, the discourse rushing on to assert that relativism "questions . . . the ideal of objectivity" (7). Hence relativism and skepticism must be controlled. In the past they were uncontrolled, the horror of "cultural relativism" becoming ("reached its limits") death camps. These historians are narrativizing present day relativism and skepticism, inserting present cultural conflicts in a story that warns of repetition. The rhetorical coding is that of glooming the present. The *associations* are reactionary, conveyed by an idealist discourse, the rhetorical device of *apophasis* denying anything but predetermined connotations. Historiographically, we have a story of horror with the cultural analogue that it is the end of us if we keep up our skepticism and relativism, both rendered in the language of fact. The historical thesis that loss of foundations leads to right-wing solutions seems to be a staple of contemporary, professional neoliberal/conservative/progressive "crossover," making equations between left and right or the maintenance of the right as sheer devil and terror. The narrative presumes an outcome instead of entering into analysis—it issues a demand in the mode of story.

Contradictions flourish:"standpoint" is denounced, yet we are to accept that "workable truths appear as the result of messy, ideologically motivated, self-absorbed interventions undertaken by myopic people whose identities may be vastly different and distant from one's own." (192) Nowhere is this flourishing clearer than in their treatment of deconstruction.

Their central exhibit against deconstruction wrenches out of context Foucault's extensive writings and reduces his work to the cliche "no truth outside ideology." Nazis become postmodernists who have targeted "the nature of historical truth, objectivity, and the narrative form of history." They encourage the belief that historical knowledge is nothing but ideology having acquired the signs of reason. Lyotard is excoriated for his writing's "fury of negation." *Apophasis* soaks *Telling the Truth's* writing yet again, asserting that the "discipline of history does not disengage its practitioners from the politics of politics," while they denounce Nietzsche and Heidegger as antidemocratic, anti-West, antihumanist, culminating with present-day intellectuals whose "disillusionment" goes too far and for whom society is "driven by the desire to discipline . . . control the population in the name of science and truth." (206) The concept of control is definitely one of the tabooed subjects of contemporary scholarly writing—one can scarcely raise it without inviting the name of paranoiac. Yet the history of criticism of elites did not start with Nietzsche. These historians wish to remove historical writing from politics, using political rhetoric all the way through. Nietzsche's texts are cutoff from any semblance of analysis, the vast literature on Nietzsche reduced to "knowledge . . . [as] an invention that masks a will to power," where "claims for truth . . . [are] only dissimulations," and where Nietzsche approached "the morally repugnant" (209). As hundreds of fellow university experts have argued, Nietzsche's writings can only be reduced by the very political drive that has wanted, and still wants, to get rid of them—the drive for writing as a spiritual satisfaction, or "priestcraft."

The postmodernists have "pitched out" causation from "history"; their writings release a "murkiness" in which "reality is the creation of language" (212). Convicting postmodernism of crimes against reason, they conclude that it is cultural studies, with its incessant analysis of language (untrue), that shows what is wrong with the postmodernists, for whom "reality is always shrouded by language, and the workings of language are in turn veiled by the operation of cultural codes" (213). Postmodernists (read: deconstructionists) are always "killing" language, their ultimate target the undoing of "cultural codes." What is it about analysis of such "cultural codes" which makes it so poisonous? And why is it associated with the crisis of social history, its capacity to provide synthesis? Knowledge of culture-as-code threatens to turn the gains of social history into raw material of "interpretive mechanisms and value systems"—that is, emphasis upon culture is itself ruination, especially if it leads to the (anti)perspective that languages are "incommensurable," for if they are, how could one possibly narrate/synthesize them? "When swimming in culture, neither causes nor effects could be distinguished." (223)

Cultural analysis is the negated object here. The lineage of Nietzsche to Lyotard empties into the desert where "women and men are stripped of the meaningful choices whose reality had once served to distinguish human beings from animals." (224) So deconstructionists even move toward the *bestial,* an evocation whose standpoint is absolute, indeed ahistorical. For once culture is judged to be "textual," it can be more ruthlessly criticized—"If postmodern theories are taken seriously, there is no trans-historical or transcendent grounds for interpretation, and human beings have no unmediated access to the world of things or events." (225) Is this to say that the "mediations" of historical knowledge give *immediations*—pure cultural truths—here and now? As a demand, it is extreme, but the demand is there as an order-word: postmodern theories should be rejected.

What has happened in the thinking of our historians that they could equate cultural analysis with such devils? The answer is found in their historicization of capitalism. Asserting that there were "distinctive American roots for the capitalist economy," cultural analysis threatens such roots. Cultural analysis has replaced Marxism as the radical. They insist that one has to separate capital as an economic activity from the sphere of cultural activity—they note that the concentration of economic power is at odds with democracy, that there is "ambivalence" about this, but they immediately sever any such complication from what is uncriticizable, the conjunction of a national culture and "capital":

> Far different is what might be called the subliminal culture of capitalism—those images of individual fortitude, prosperity, agricultural abundance, open opportunity, hard work, free choice, inventive genius, and productive know-how . . . The culture of capitalism has thoroughly permeated the nation's historical consciousness . . . This self-understanding has played a critical role in promoting actual capitalist development. (119)

Thus, "our culture acts as the invisible engine driving the free market." The bringing to "cultural codes" of analysis threatens the subliminal and the invisible, that "holistic" sense of culture that "Americans" have created, which requires acceptance of "our" current arrangements. This is a neonationalism of neoliberalism.

Further, this citation has it that "Americans" have created a benevolent "sublime" ("images of"), a contradiction in terms. At some point, such a "sublime" has become willed—the implicit presupposition being that Americans have chosen this "sublime." Determinism is thus severed from culture, a division that at once elevates a particular cultural standpoint as the model before which all else is fragmentary and partial. This standpoint is none other than the perspective of the "expert" historian who has rendered the judgment that present-day culture is legitimate, not subject to analysis, postmodernism's "ironic voice" removed from overshadowing "the historian's wonder." Critique will not overshadow narrative: "We are emphasizing the human need for self-understanding through a coherent narrative of the past." (229) That is a deeply anti-intellectual order-word directed against the very idea of critique.

Textually considered, Appleby, Hunt, and Jacob make their most extreme exhortation when it comes to giving an *ontological* requirement for narrative, which is essential in securing "identity," and which makes "action in the world possible. [Narratives] make action possible because they make it meaningful." As subjects already think "historically," historians are continuous with such *true* subjects, those who think historically, a blind tautologism. Nietzsche thought that in advanced societies definite "goals are missing," an opportunity for experimenting with different desubjectivizations. Instead, our historians insist that archives are "laboratories" and offer a "glimpse" into a world "disappeared," where the historian "uncovers evidence" and "touch[es] lives long passed," the historian an anti-existentialist par excellence, since achieving presence with the dead is affirmed. Offering an inchoate primordiality as the ultimate resistance to cultural analysis, real subjectivity is given only to those who desire to be historical:

> History fulfills a fundamental human need by reconstituting memory. Memory sustains consciousness of living in the stream of time, and the *amour propre* of human beings cries out for the knowledge of their place in that stream. (258)

What delirium delivered in the rhetoric of aggression! The primordiality of *amour propre* and the phrase "cries out" obliterates cultural analysis of these constructs. These concepts are antitextual (anti-intellectual), and operate at the same level of "purity" as Ankersmit's sense of "harmony," Jenkins's "clean" autobiography, and Sobchak's sense of the present-future as "shit happens." Differences between memory, history, and writing are collapsed in favor of giving culture a "history" it can use. (One can add that amour propre derives from seventeenth-century French elites and the defense of privilege, thus "democratized" here, an interesting suggestion of recoding).

"Westerners have learned how to externalize this curiosity about the past." So say Westerners! This ideal of learning finalizes the inchoate and primordial: "craving for insight into what it is to be human." Does this mean that ahistorical discourse cannot achieve "insight," this visual tag turning its readers from text to picture? "Craving for insight" invites analysis as to its effects and plausibility. "The human intellect demands accuracy while the soul craves meaning." Such a thing as the "human intellect" may or may not exist in the ideal sense given here, but what matters is the reiteration of "soul craving." It makes the historian continuous with the human as such, ontology giving way to theology: "History ministers" (262). *R*evision is controlled by a special emotion of the historian, who "reinvests," as they put it, past accounts with "contemporary interest." (265) Hence their call for "new definitions of truth and objectivity" is chilling given what they lay claim to in their possessive model of culture and memory. To read that "peer review, open refereeing, public disputation, replicated experiments, and documented research . . . make objective knowledge possible" and cancels relativism and irony is to enter the twilight of historiography—for each of these terms is a mountain of concatenations of semantic and emotional and political selections, overcoded in every conceivable manner. The temporal marker "sometimes" has been obliterated by their discourse.

Specters of Marx and Recoding Differance

The examples given so far indicate how convention is reestablished today. Insistence on a model is maintained by metaphysically expressed cultural discourse: In the first instance, resemblance brings identity, aesthetics reautonomizing the historical text as something which can give pictures, analytic philosophy of history separated from historical writing; in the second instance, a direct political discourse, endlessly narrativizing, purifies true historians by cursing the present when it is said to be under the control of unrestrained skepticism. This is performed in the name of an historical result—that of the accumulated expertise of the historians in a war against relativism.

Here, an analysis of Derrida's *Specters of Marx* and its claims that historiography matters in terms of present-day culture and language may be useful. There is very much at stake about this text, given the usual sense of antipathy between deconstruction and historicism. After this analysis, there follows a discussion of historiography's uneasy relations to language, framed by a consideration of modes of reading, what I call "last" and "excessive" readers.

The dedication to *Specters* plunges its readers into a Gnostic "exordium": "Someone, you or me, comes forward and says: *I would like to learn to live finally.*" This urgent question and demand inaugurates the discourse and allows the writing to proceed with insistencies: the question is called a "magisterial locution," it "would always say something about violence," it is an expression of "ethics itself," and "to learn to live finally" is such that it "cannot be *just* unless it comes to terms with death."[16] The writing arrives at the destination of a synthetic command utterance:

> If it—learning to live—remains to be done, it can happen only between life and death. Neither in life nor in death alone. What happens between two, and between all the two's one likes, such as between life and death, can only maintain itself with some ghost, can only *talk with or about* some ghost. So it would be necessary to learn spirits. (xviii)

In the space of a few sentences, language is yoked to the grammar of insistence, to urgency concerning the logic of mutually implicating doubles, and to specters. How strong is the philosophic claim that binarism, dualism, "two's," can be absorbed by this "to ghost"? The analytic value of Derrida's version of deconstruction, where binaries are merely simulacra of limits within language, is reiterated, but the sentences imitate the idea of *différance,*[17] they read as ghostlike meanings, not *différance,* but an Idea of it. There *are* ghosts, it says, but it does not say: language is spectral and ghostly in its ability to install the unnamable. The ghost is not language at work; rather, *Specters* insists that ghosts *are.* Or at least this will be the English-speaking world's version.

Hence, *Specters* makes enormous claims: to learn to live, or to become, requires one learn to live with ghosts, to learn that History has always been a matter of ghosts, hence an identity or continuous line between any past and any future. History is subject to a reiteration that completely outstrips itself:

> The time of the "learning to live," a time without tutelary present, would amount to this, to which the exordium is leading: to learn to live *with* ghosts, in the upkeep, the conversation, the company, or the companionship, in the commerce without commerce of ghosts (xviii).

There are no present models for life/learning, there has never been such a model, and this "never has been" is delivered over to the infinitive mode: "with ghosts" is what has not happened, at once absence, command, and necessity. For without ghosts, there will be no social conversation at all. The phrase "commerce without commerce" means no reciprocity "with ghosts": We need to "be" with them, but we can make no expectation of reciprocity (a freedom of ghosts—they can do as they please). Ghosts, like

God, may or may not care about us. "*With them,*" *Specters* calls out, and it is a chilling demand:

> . . . no *socius* without this *with* that makes *being-with* in general more enig-
> matic than ever for us. . . . And this being-with-specters would also be, not
> only but also, a politics of memory, of inheritance, and of generations
> (xviii, xix).

Historiographically considered, History has never happened because being-with-specters has not happened. A complete nothingness of History must be thought. This figure converges with historiographic fables of loss, like those of Pierre Nora, in which "memory installs remembrance within the sacred," set against the relativizing tendencies of an unlimited histori-cal consciousness. For Nora, ghosts belong to memory, signifying "silence of custom" and "repetition of the ancestral."[18]

Responsibility and respect for justice concerning "those who *are not there*" alone makes possible any relation of future/past. We are in that con-ceptual/mystical territory that Benjamin, after Lotze, Goethe, and many Europeans, outlined as precise intellectual work, a response to the disasters of modern history (for example, culture as allegorical ruins, failures of a collective intelligentsia, mass behaviorisms). This responsibility *repeats* the displacement of intellectual work as a confrontation with actual social structures, since it calls for a deepening of a special kind of memory, one available only to inscribers: "to be just: beyond the living present in gen-eral—and beyond its simple negative reversal. A spectral moment, a mo-ment that no longer belongs to time" (xx). This "spectral moment" recodes *différance,* for "beyond reversal" and "out of time" raise intellectual work to the realm of "to differ and to defer." To Derrida, *différance* means "spectral" and both terms belong to the category of the Same by comparison to what they are "beyond"—opposition and criticism entombed in time and re-versal. Derrida calls this special attunement of the intellectual an axiom, a dignity (from Kant), and is not answerable to any living present. *Specters* registers the objection to this, but insists that in the face of present life, em-pirical or ontological actuality, there is something beyond:

> a *living-on* [sur-vie] . . . a survival . . . to disjoin or dis-adjust the identity to
> itself of the living present . . . There is then *some* spirit" (xx).

Yes: intellectual work is directed against presencing, a basic premise of Der-rida's *oeuvre,* but this suspicion is *presented* as a command utterance—"Spir-its. And *one must* reckon with them. One cannot not have to" (xx). Clearly the negation of presence is accomplished by a greater presencing—of what is not present (spirit, ghost). The syntaxes of paradox and negation dominate here, and it is not unfair to say that the gesture of writing with disjunction functions as another mode of junction. The writing can be considered schizophrenic—it affirms what it denies, in the name of a specific mode of intellectual practice, a theologization of cultural warfare(s). For the *survival* of disjunction carries with it a stronger injunction: the ghosts of history matter. The denial of conjunction in the name of a transcendental injunction is a continuation of the project of *differance,* but the latter has now become the installation of being-with-specters. And this continuation is also the *persistence* of the intellectual/scholar as possessed of a special faculty of continuism with the dead, a connoisseurship of the netherworld.

The Historiography of Being Haunted

From Pascal, who insisted that there must be no sleeping with Jesus in agony, to Benjamin's delirium of the passage to a messianic instance shattering present negative forces, intellectuals have set up communication with the dead as a transcoding of religious precepts. There's nothing strange about this until it is made a "stake" in the ability of intellectuals to work, once such demands are normalized and institutionalized as work or writing permits. Hardly anyone can publish on Benjamin without demonstrating his or her commitment to "spirit." So too with Derrida: *Specters of Marx* will circulate as a raising of the ante of historiographic discourse on account of its dramatistic (in Kenneth Burke's sense) and opaque phrases taken as signs and signals of a "higher reflection" in the scholarly endeavor to install a taste for "spirit."

"Haunting," *Specters* insists, "would mark the very existence of Europe. It would open the space and the relation to self of what is called by this name" (4). This "haunting" has nothing to do with such traditional historical subjects as European venality in the Opium Wars or the French treatment of Algeria in the nineteenth and twentieth centuries. Instead, haunting belongs to an equation: historiography and haunting are one and the same. Haunting stands in for the "uncanny" and irrepressible past of Europe, those aspects of European historicity as yet narrated. The discourse presupposes that there are still mysteries to be said or written about the history of Europe. But even if no decisive historical judgments can be rendered at the level of the significance of Europe, it does not follow that there are any outstanding problems to be addressed. A "haunted existence" attributed to Europe could be seen as something else: a way for a European intellectual to maintain the openness of the European past, a way of giving historicity back to Europe, or at least reclaiming a historicity never settled. An infinite rereading of European history is thus made possible as recoding through the haunted. This recoding, which claims to upset the chronicity of names, also makes for a more inclusive successivity, for the specter can be figured forth not just as a way to dislodge the dominance of presence but also as a device for continuity: the specter "interrupts here all specularity . . . it recalls us to anachrony . . . we do not see who looks at us" (7). Inclusively, the specter is always "here." Anachrony does not mean just out of time or the untimely or disjunction, as Derrida insists; it also means what is *invisibly continuous,* a supercontinuity such that History is subject to a new *law:* "all semanticization is given over to *mourning,* to the voice, and to the work of the 'spirit.' The question 'Whither Marxism' whispers to us to *follow* a ghost" (10). Historiographically, then, the function of the "ghost" is to return a historicity to Europe, stripped of the semantics of conflict, in which none of the narrative models available to ordinary historiography are of use; the new terms of continuity are posed by hauntology.

This hauntology, which operates in the same manner as the concept/nonconcept of *différance,* replaces ontology and the metaphysics of historiography. For this hauntology already "harbors within itself . . . eschatology and teleology themselves" (10). The discursive aspect of historiography, semantics, its incessant return, recalling and recoding of the past, all the work of *re,* finds itself absorbed by this model, for *Specters* is adamant that this absorption is a case of justice, not discourse. Hauntology would "comprehend them [eschatology and teleology], but incomprehensibly," for the "ghost" has been deferred, and repetition is such that the specter "*begins by coming back*" (11). Contact with "ghosts" precedes discourse with them. The scholar who "knows" of this return/repetition has not yet existed, for "there has never been a scholar who really, and as scholar, deals with ghosts" (11). The scholars of historiography have been unable to listen to return/repetition, but there is another voice that calls the scholar from afar, the literary figure Marcellus from *Hamlet,* who

> . . . anticipat[ed] the coming, one day, one night, several centuries later, of another "scholar." The latter would finally be capable, beyond the opposition between presence and non-presence, actuality and inactuality, life and non-life, of thinking the possibility of the specter, the specter as possibility. Better (or worse) he would know how to address himself to spirits. He would know that such an address is not only possible, but that it will have at all times conditioned, as such, address in general (12).

A certain scholar can "address himself to spirits"—but who or what is the *ancestry* of this special power (of course, a "power beyond power")? Noth-

ing other than the specter itself, which has always "at all times conditioned" such address—a metahistorical axiom, an urgency of continuism.
Marx's texts are absorbed into this new responsibility, which, as we will see
in a moment, jettisons oppositionality: "There will be no future without
this. Not without Marx, no future without Marx, without the memory
and the inheritance of Marx" (13). The historiographic notions of diagno-
sis and prognosis, intertwined since antiquity, are overthrown by the
rhetoric of an obligation to an impossible debt. Are these terms both reactionary and avant-garde?[19]

Specters of Marx thus disconnects historicity understood as continuity in
favor of continuity understood as a metahistorical identity of the repres-
sion/repetition of specters and ghosts. The scholar/intellectual is turned
from opposition (criticism, disruption) in favor of confronting the specters
internal to scholarship, the scholar into an actant who can find the words
to grasp the *secrets* of Marx's writing, "which says 'read me, will you ever
be able to do so," a scholar pledged to the word of "deferring just so as to
affirm, to affirm *justly,* so as to have the power . . . to affirm the coming of
the event, its future-to-come itself" (17). Affirmation stamps out opposition; the time is "out of joint" (which recodes the archaic historiographic
notion of a period of transition), and in the face of this "time without certain joining or determinate conjunction," opposition is judged detrimen-
tal to intellectual work. But is it so that today is a time without
"determinate conjunctions"—this said in the face of extreme concentrations of wealth, authority, value, and choices? The affirmation negates any
sense of an historiography that takes up opposition and disjunction and
works these concepts up as something that matters. The scholar's time is
transcendental to opposition/disjunction. To say that "time is out of joint"
and that Marx's writings cannot be historicized—"read me, will you ever
be able to do so"—involves accepting that Marx cannot be *outwritten*—but
under which conditions is this plausible? The affirmation of a disadjusted
time that must not lead back to critique of "injustice," a "mere" ontological relation, a relation of chronicity, means emphasis by intellectuals on "injustice" is an affirmation of the *wrong time,* the time of vengeance, of
righting wrongs. In lieu of this, intellectuals must sever any connection
with critique/opposition. *Différance* stamps out criticism.[20]

The disjunction of injustice and the infinite asymmetry of the "place of
the other" are the terms of a temporality "out of joint," but the space
opened by "specters" must not call for

calculable and distributive justice. Not for law, for the calculation of restitu-
tion, the economy of vengeance or punishment . . . Not for calculable
equality . . . [or] accountability or imputability of subjects and objects, not

for a *rendering* justice that would be limited to sanctioning, to restituting, and to doing right but for a justice as incalculability of the gift and singularity of the an-economic ex-position to others (23).

How *unscholarly* to ever connect criticism and justice! Notice how quickly the language smears justice with the direct predicate of "vengeance." And notice just how quickly, how rapidly the text moves to the "incalculable" of the gift. "Incalculable" means the transcendence of what humans must not ask for. The text associates this "gift" with "a musical or poetic work" (26) as well as the messianic: "the coming of the other, the absolute and unpredictable singularity of the *arrivant as justice.* We believe that this messianic remains an *ineffaceable mark* . . . of Marx's legacy, and doubtless of inheriting" (28). The historiography of this scholar of the "gift" levitates out of the world of violence and contradiction into the smooth celestial air of the scholar's ability to receive the gift, this ability complementary with the metahistorical framing of the "specter." The language is firmly lodged within the register of revelation and grace. The scholar is modeled as the medium for the passage to the transcendent. To say, for example, that one-third of the world's actual population has no daily, reliable, source of potable water would, for the imagined scholar here, regress to the level of "calculable justice," outlawed by the new law of transcendence enunciated here: only the mystique of *re* matters. There must be "alliance of a rejoining without conjoined mate, without organization, without party, without nation, without State, without property . . ." (29). The intellectual must not be caught speaking for an interest that can be returned to actualities fraught with conflict and social danger.

What is said to matter is the reading of Marx's texts with their "irreducible heterogeneity, an internal untranslatability" (33). Something was said in those writings that is far more important than a message or code, and *Specters* isolates this as the "testamentary dimension." This sense of the "testamentary" is the true historiographic legacy. "*There must be* disjunction, interruption, the heterogeneous if at least *there must be,* if there *must be* a chance given to any 'there must be' whatsoever, be it beyond duty" (35). The desperation signaled in the repetition of so many "there must be's" will not connect with any existential historicity other than that of the impossible: the "testamentary" is beyond history, it is "a matter of linking an *affirmation* (in particular a political one) *if there is any,* to the experience of the impossible, which can only be a radical experience of the *perhaps*" (35). The "inheritance" of Marx's writing is reduced to the vicissitudes of the empty desert of "perhaps," "perhaps" itself a recoding of the famous historiographical notion of necessity, which cannot be addressed here except as the "impossible." The avoidance of actual determinations, how the social is put together, its rules and mechanisms, are squeezed out by the "perhaps" of metahistory. Again, textually considered, it is not the form of Marx's writings that outstrip the content; rather, it is that they offer to Derrida's version of deconstruction a pledge and a promise, a *re*iteration of hope.

Now modern historiography shows definite vacillation over the language of means, ends, goals, directions, and outcomes. The polarities of determination (*of* history) and surprise (*by* history) are but two terms in a seemingly endless list of substitutions in modeling historicity. Any contemporary American feminist could easily assert that the "right to choose" abortion is both a positive means in women's self-determination and a valuable end insofar as liberal notions of subjective value are enhanced; yet many (or some) feminists would also acknowledge what is positive as abortion may have other social consequences, namely, that such choices are class-bound and subjective and harm the chances for developing new modes of collective association. With Derrida's text, all these questions pertaining to the language of telos and outcomes are set aside in favor of the language of eschatology:

> Is there not a messianic extremity, an *eskhaton* whose ultimate event (immediate rupture, unheard of interruption, untimeliness of the infinite surprise, heterogeneity without accomplishment) can exceed, *at each moment,* the final term of a *physis,* such as work, the production, and the *telos* of any history? (37)

"Messianic extremity" evokes the idea of a historiographic avant-garde, but the question form—"Is there not"—demands the question be refuted instead of moving toward answering its own request. The *eskhaton* has explicit bases in religious desires and needs, including the modern historian's obsessive question, "how shall we go ahead," a topic as much of prophetism as prognosis, and the idea of the *eskhaton* is inseparable from the related notion of *telos* inasmuch as it "also articulates and fulfills a . . . process of history . . . by a definite goal."[21] So while teleology may well be nearly unthinkable today given the shattering of metanarrative models, why is eschatology favored as the medium of this deconstruction of Marx and Marxism? How can the *eskhaton* be discussed if there are no examples of it that are not also instances of teleology? *Specters of Marx* writes itself into a vicious circle: in speaking against telos, against the history of outcomes, it retreats to a metaphysical positivism, an "impossible" affirmation of the messianic, the greatest hope against all actual empirical measures, the greatest duplicity as it maintains the interminability of our waiting for deliverance.[22]

Haunting and Meta-metahistory

Specters of Marx delivers itself over to supercontinuity. Textually, this is issued as the insistence that communism "presents itself only as that which could come or could come back," as the pledge to not slip into the dualisms that account for its own self-suffocation. For example, *Specters* insists that between 1848 and 1994 there is continuity in terms of the "specter" treated as a threat, this negative continuity first linked to the reality of the hegemonic, then shifted into a question that evokes the superhistorical: "What is the time and what is the history of a specter?" (39). If concepts such as hegemony keep us focused on successivity and substitutions (replacement of equivalent forms, for example, from repression to consumerist terror), the question asked here would make of hauntology something *timeless* but a force nonetheless (like the concept/nonconcept *differance*). Derrida calls this a "spectrality effect," or hauntology in operation, and it is meant to undo "this opposition, or even this dialectic, between actual, effective presence and its other" (40), and as with *differance,* this specter conjures (a ghost) by putting "to work and to produce, without any possible reappropriation, a forever errant surplus value" (40). Wasn't *differance* once the ideal errancy of language, in that it was offered as production and surplus melded together? Or to put this directly in historiographic terms: if "metahistory" refers to the conditions of possibility in the writing of a narrative (selection criteria not directly themselves "historical"), then isn't haunting "meta-metahistorical," precisely because, with *differance,* it not only controls the field of representations but is always there, timeless, that is, the condition of conditions? If you believe in history as haunted, then you must believe in meta-metahistory, or the doubling of the doubling of historical reflection as a way of keeping historical reflection *open* to re.

And what does all this have to do with Marx? Following the literary exemplum of Shakespeare's *Timon of Athens,* Marx conjured money (and religion) as a social disaster as much spectropoetic as critical and historical. He showed that the State employs "magic" when it makes paper into value, just as religion does in making another world valuable, or when language conjures definitions that are socially delirious. And while Marx does not want to believe in specters and ghosts, he "thinks of nothing else" (47). Marx, like his adversaries,

> will have tried to conjure (away) the ghosts *like* the conspirators [conjures] of old Europe on whom the *Manifesto* declares war. However inexpiable this war remains . . . it conspires *with them* in order to *exorc-analyze* the spectrality of the specter. And this is, today, as perhaps it will be tomorrow, our problem (47).

As Marx came to repeat what he contests, we cannot do without a contest with Marx's writings. Marx and Marxism are folded in repetition, but not a return to the merely historical. The repetition involved must submit to the *failure* of Marx, that his language was bound over to the logic of negation and opposition, to conjuring and exorcising "formulae" that resulted in "putting to death" his rival's positions, hence a writing that "phantomalize[d] itself" in a demand for effectivity. The "heterological tauto-ontology" of Marx's texts, with their demand for presence (of the revolution), is subject to mourning.

"The time is out of joint": Derrida's writing gives this construct something other than the highlighting of differences on either side of the "joint." That is to say, while *Specters* certainly does not posit any such "time" when "time" was not out of "joint," the problem it evokes is to make "time out of joint" a condition of timeless ahistoricity. The writing thus slips into eternalizations: it evokes "to be present" and this presence "is not a *mot d'esprit* but *le mot d'esprit,* the word of the spirit, it *is* its first verbal body" (50). Presence restored in the name of the elimination of presence. What is affirmed is that "the time is out of joint" is always true, hence the present is always nonpresent to itself, yet present to itself in exactly that way, therefore always related to spirits and specters, which are the indices of what will not go away. This is the presencing of meta-metahistory: The "spiritword" precedes all other determinations as to "history." There *is* something.

Derrida is certainly correct that Marxism is always conjured away by rivals. The conjuring-away of Marxism is linked to the call for a "new international" and sounds politically correct. He insists on this "international" because of the displacement of politics by the media, by its own forms of "spectralization," but the question not asked is: when did the "media" not do this?[23] What is gained by insisting that the media "mediatizes"? Current institutions of discourse—political, media, and academic—have merged, he insists, "as . . . never done before" and this "conditions and endangers any democracy" (54). Does he have an ideal of democracy in mind? Convinced that the ongoing repression of specters and ghosts is the most vital intellectual project and that spectral powers, apparitions, simulations, and prosthetic images are rampant, Marxism can be embraced only if it places on the "drawing board" (a figure academic unto eternity) "life-death beyond the opposition between life and death" (54).

To summarize: *Specters* traces a beyond to opposition, a "meta-metahistory" that is also a historiography of transcendence. "We are in mourning" for specters, for this "beyond," the writing cries out, in mourning for the "to be" of Marxism. Mourning is the way in which History is possessed and "inherited." Here the dimension of the *testamentary* is elevated to the purity of the superhistorical: "the being of what we are is first of all inheritance, whether we like it or know it or not . . . we can only *bear witness* to it."

Why is such regression to an identity before opposition called a "critical inheritance?" Why are we to speak of domination and conflict but "without necessarily subscribing to the concept of social class" (55)? What is it then that transcends the edginess of class conflict, this concept that at least indicates a high degree of social control and differentiation? It is nothing other than the "irreducible genesis of the spectral." Derrida gives as his chief example of this "spectral" beyond class the "worldwide historical stakes" of the Middle East conflicts, an example so highly *dramatistic* as to call into question the writing's sense of judgment. In the Middle East, three messianic ideologies mobilize "all the forces of the world," a colossal synecdoche, such forces said to be archaic and futuristic. "The war for the 'appropriation of Jerusalem' is today the total war," a proposition numbing in its active elimination of places such as Zaire or Rwanda, Bosnia, or any suffering American inner city. The constative form allows no disagreement; no one must say that the religious zealots of the Middle East are all equally political and invoke "history" as a tactic of destroying the other. Are such Middle Eastern ideologies messianic, telic, or suicidal? The text falls silent. Nonetheless, this "singular figure" of "time out of joint" is precisely singular—of no relevance whatsoever outside of the dramatistics of the writing. Marxism, it insists, will have a future only if it accepts such "religious ghosts" (58) and presumably views all social relations as if they were the Middle East.

This historiography of haunting reaches its most insistent, self-consumptive dimension in affirming that messianic eschatology, common to religion and to Marxism, must not renounce

> a certain experience of the emancipatory promise; it is perhaps even the formality of a structural messianism, a messianism without religion, even a messianic without messianism, an idea of justice—which we distinguish from its current concept and from its determined predicates today (59).

An "idea of justice" is more important than "determined predicates." The impossible matters more than any actuality. In relation to the three institutions of discourse (politics, media, academia), to the false "good news" of neoliberalism, Derrida has found the true matter of historiography: a "democracy *to come,* not a *future* democracy in the future present," which would be the site of conflict (over means, ends) but an historiography of infinitive, logical syntax, which is not "a *future present,* of a future modality of the living present."

Historiography would then be completely recast according to the entangled logics of *differance*, messianism, and specters (or ghosts). *Specters of Marx* promises that once we affirm "the absolutely undetermined messianic hope . . . [an] eschatological relation to the to-come of an event and of a singularity, of an alterity that cannot be anticipated," we can be freed from dead-end conflict (65). The messianic reads as a performative in announcing the deliverance that death can claim "from which one will not ask anything in return and who or which will not be asked to commit to the domestic contracts of any welcoming power (family, State, nation, territory, native soil or blood, language, culture in general, even humanity)." At this threshold of meaning, metahistory is broken off, since metahistory involves claims as to signification and representation, and something else takes over: a language that is no longer of language but is of and for death, devoted to death. Such is the *trace* of the meta-metahistorical.

Historiography without History

Nearly every convention of historical thought is set ablaze by *Specters,* and because of that it does not support identification with the conventions of historical understanding. Such non-identification will account for its being cited as an important document in the scholar's genealogy of avant-garde hope, rupture over continuity, rupture attached to the "eternality" of metaphysics. No doubt hauntology will be used to uproot historical identities of all sorts. But the larger problem is that it sabotages its own nonidentification in favor of another identification: the convergence of *differance,* messianism, specters, and death. This identification is given further textual solidity or figuration when *Specters* gives name to its affirmative projections, calling for a new historiography predicated on "*just* opening . . . a hospitality without reserve, which is . . . the condition . . . of history" (65). How can this be? The text insists that if history can be thought, it must be thought through the sense of "this strange concept of messianism without content, of the messianic without messianism, that guides us here like the blind" (65). "Like the blind" stands in for the religious tradition of *grace* in which, as Karl Lowith remarks, the Cross and Resurrection were the very pattern of "the transformation of the realm of necessity into a realm of freedom," the medium of the "messianic vocation." *Specters* embraces Jewish prophetism and leaves Greek tragedy behind; the messianic is severed from pagan belief in "historiconatural forces" and is still within the arc of the linearity and time-cut of Christianity.[24]

Normative historical thinking must emphasize the successivity of events; it pays little attention to the gaps and spaces between events of thoroughly different orders. Derrida's antidote, this "messianic without messianism," falls back on a historiographic category that is as dubious as anything he critiques. This fallback is the concept of a latency period: What occurred between an event "heralded" (before) and its result (after) is figured forth not as connected to a "temporal medium" but as a "mutation" which, it is asserted, "perturbs the onto-theological schemas or the philosophers of technics" (70). The idea of a latency period, obviously telic, substitutes for the concept of a *period of transition,* a historiographic theory long rejected for its antiphenomenological bias (that is, for whom is there a "transition"—the narrators or the agents of an event?). In specifying there was such a period preceding the fall of communist Europe, the writing recodes a staple of conservative historiography: study is called for as to the neglected *in* its latency. "How did an unexpected X come about?" is the same question Derrida asks along with the historians he so fervently rejects.

Historiography without history summarizes its own delirium: *Specters* insists that Alexander Kojeve was correct in rendering a "task and a duty for the *future* of post-historical man . . . Posthistorical man *doit* . . . for eternities of interpretation, there is an 'it is necessary' for the future" (73). Kojeve's *mana* word—there is a "must"—is offered as simplicity itself, and *Specters* has it that what Kojeve has given us is nothing less than "*this 'it is necessary' is necessary, and that is the law*" (73). The sense of this is mad, of the same order as Appleby, Hunt, and Jacob when they tie skepticism to Nazism. *Specters* makes time mad especially by figures such as this: "It is this law that dislodges any present out of contemporaneity with itself." Each of these sentences kills any figuration of temporality, the grammar of insistence overriding thought. Now a reader can grasp that Derrida's historiography ushers in a sense of life without history: obligations without any sense of reciprocity are installed. "*It is necessary*" repeats the continuism of the word as *portent,* a "magic power" of words that is "mysterious, fatal, and decisive."[25] In this sense, *Specters* passes over to the syntax of the divine.[26] This is not, as with Appleby et al., using a psychology of the subject (the "soul" craves narrative clarity) but rather making an absolute ("it is necessary") the condition for any thinking (subject) at all.

This priestly writing enables *Specters* to move out from Kojeve's *doit* to the insistence that the "historicity of history [now] begins," an inscription of presence boggling in its implications (can "now" really begin "now" given what *différance* involves?), this because the temporality of "to herald" and "to promise" are affirmed as the necessary frames of any posthistorical thinking. "To herald" and "to promise" are Heideggerian trumpets announcing the "infinite responsibility" of a new "historicity of history." Since history deals with choices and outcomes, the affirmation of the messianic and the promise of emancipation will separate from "new history" and "new historicism" still enmeshed in ideas of telos, finality, and context. Such is the historiography of the void, for only the empty is real, only the emptiness of the messianic releases us from interests, desires, and existential submersions. But who is this "us" freed for the work of the void—who is its addressee?

If we focus on the notion of telos, we can see just how extreme and reactionary Derrida's model really is. Telos, it is asserted, does not work: "the world has more than one age . . . Neither maturation, nor crisis, nor even agony. Something else" (77). But are we to confuse telos with a sense of determinations, of the entanglements of choices and decisions made and in the making? *Specters* rejects any "unfolding of a normal, normative, or normed process" (78), yet accepts that the world is "going badly . . . almost black." While the equation between "badly" and "black" is an unfortunate conjunction, this "blackboard picture" makes use of the phrase "wearing down beyond wear" to characterize the collective narrative process of the world. How is this not telic? The writing acknowledges the "new unemployment" or the social inactivity of our "new era," but is the "ruthless economic war," which is said to "control everything," not utterly continuous with the persistence of an ever-operative neocapitalism? Omitting to analyze such new solidities as the middle class hatred for politics, or the academization of criticism, *Specters* leaves out any structural modulation that might implicate its own writing in inextricable social problematics. Focusing on the dramatics of "interethnic wars" with their "primitive conceptual phantasm[s]," as are said to inform the structure of conflict in the Middle East, is of a piece with the superdramatization of posthistorical necessity, of the divinity of *doit:*

> For above all, above all . . . international law and its institutions . . . [with their] fortunate perfectibility, despite an undeniable progress,

offer the only model of a valid "to come"—

> Justice demands . . . that one pay tribute to certain of those who are working with [international institutions] in the direction of the perfectibility and emancipation of institutions that must never be renounced. . . . We should salute what is heralded today in the reflection on the right of interference or intervention in the name of what is . . . called the *humanitarian,* thereby limiting the sovereignty of the State in certain conditions (84).

One has to ask about this extreme affirmation. On the one hand, *Specters* finally acknowledges the obvious horrors of the world but on the other it moves to a celebratory discourse on the management of the least negative. When the United Nations finally intervened in Bosnia, it was only after continued slaughter there would harm its own survival. Where *Specters* thus denigrates "mere" law and rights and elevates an institution that makes internationalism look beneficial, it lapses into the self-same liberalism it otherwise tries to distance itself from. To say again that international law is a positive "link of affinity, suffering, and hope, a still discreet, almost secret link, as it was around 1848," means that *Specters* presupposes historical continuity and identity: a "new international . . . calls to the friendship of an alliance without institution" (86). This is to make the global traffic in artists and intellectuals (remember "traveling theory"?) a synecdochic ideal rather than what it often is, a highly overcoded mode of the self-same "media-tele-visibility" syndrome denounced by *Specters.*

Historiography without history is given a "post" or place of duty: "to sort out, critique, keep close by, and allow to come back" all the specters, a "watch [that] itself will engender new ghosts." There are no actual historical determinations that matter by comparison to keeping "watch" for the specter's return. The intellectual is returned to the job of "bear[ing] witness, at least, to the justice which is demanded." As witnesses of the ideal, the scholar will of course continue to speak for and about others. The witnesses "witness" in the zero figure of "pure formality," of the "messianic spirit" rendered as a "gesture of fidelity," an "imperative," a "priority," all this for "a new Enlightenment for the century to come." Thus, telos is restored by *Specters* as it denounces the very idea of the telic. One could say that Derrida's sense of deconstruction has fallen into the ruses of historical thought.

Historiography has many examples of the dead conjured so as to be images and literary figures of the not-dead. Much of modern social history, with its emphasis upon the neglected and anonymous subjects of vast historical processes (whose traces are rendered in diaries of crossing the plains), or Carlo Ginzburg's insistence that ancient peasant messianism was "echoed" in the words of a fifteenth century miller, has tried to make the dead not-dead in the form of *ekphrasis,* or vivid retellings and accounts. To make vivid in the minds of present readers is a highly prized value today. Historiography has never been separable from *ekphrasis* and the "not-dead dead," despite the internal wars over questions of signification (for example, positivism and the rule of fact, Hegelianism and possessing the "spirit of an age"). What *Specters* brings to the table of historiography is entirely within what one can legitimately call the implicit *madness of possession:*

> . . . we know better than ever today that the dead must be able to work. And to cause to work, perhaps more than ever. There is also a mode of production of the phantom, itself a phantomatic mode of production. As in the work of mourning, after a trauma . . . (97).

" . . . the dead must be able to work"—the sense is not figural and imaginative, but literal. And when we ask after this intense insistence, we read that it is true because mourning "is work itself, work in general" (97). *Differance,* rolled into being-with-specters, today annihilates any sense of experience that dares to say the difference between mourning and, say, positive forgetting. Trauma negates politics. Are the neoconservatives of the American Democratic Party "haunted" by the ghost of Roosevelt? *Specters* has it that active politics is a matter of politicians not able to face their ghosts, turning lethal in the repression of the ghostly, as if politics had nothing of material interests, social choices, the chance to choose existential possibles. Historiography without history comes to mean that the ghosts already among us have absolute precedence.

Now come *Specters's* urgent demands. The assertion of the "density of death" is not for *Specters* a powerful reaction determined by convention, language, inertia, repetition; it is one with a debt: "*to answer for the dead, to respond to the dead" (109).* This debt is the greatest of all presences: "nothing is more serious and nothing is more true, nothing is more exact [*juste*] than this phantasmagoria" (109). Historiography without history would then issue an identity between historiography and death, for it is the specter of debt/death that "weighs" on the scholar. Life must justify itself to the face of history, except it is now a *historiospectography* that determines, as presence, the "rights of succession." If you do not agree to engage with the specters already inside you, you cannot participate in this new "law of the fiduciary" (109).

Historiography goes the way of a "fantastics" that is "as general as it is irreducible," in which all temporal convolutions go the way of an impossible temporality, a "disadjustment which will no doubt ever end," since specters are interminable. *Specters* demands one reading: that "the figure of the ghost is not just one figure among others. It is perhaps the hidden figure of all figures" (120). In a stunning piece of writing, haunting is so transcendental that it alone eliminates a relation with language: "There would be no metarhetoric of the ghost" (120). With this, the age-old dream of religious historiography is achieved—the secret is out, for now "no metarhetoric of the ghost" can only mean no theory, no hypothesis, no consideration, no signification figured in language matters by comparison to death-as-ghost.

Historiospectography

Specters of Marx has it that the masterpieces of historiography can be read under the framework of a "eucharistic Narcissus," where readers of Marx will notice that Marx was fooling himself in a truly sophisticated way: he did believe that his writing captured the real presence of the proletariat. Marx and nineteenth-century rivals such as Max Stirner did practice writerly techniques to make their thoughts "seen by ghosts," conjuring phantasma for consciousness that would provide them with criticisms of existing negative phantoms (for example, Stirner evokes self-consciousness to ward off the bourgeois Other). But to say, as *Specters* does, that "*The ghost, always, is looking at me,*" that "the phenomenal form of the world itself is spectral [and that] the *phainesthai* itself . . . is the very possibility of the specter, it brings death, it gives death, it works at mourning," pushes the void into language. It announces the replacement of historiography by historiospectography, a mad word, no doubt, but so is self-terror (don't ever forget your "ghost"). *Specters* is not shy about this replacement:

> Humanity is but a collection or series of ghosts . . . since everyone reads, acts, writes with *his or her* ghosts, even when one goes after the ghosts of the other" (138–39).

The reduction of "is but" is chilling: It gives essence. And there is a curious return and repetition to this move or shift to the eternality of specters and ghosts. It seems that historiospectography actually belongs to the oldest of family routines:

> . . . words always cause to come back, they convoke the *revenant* that they conjure away. Come so that I may chase you! You hear! I chase you. I pursue you. I run after you to chase you away from here. I will not leave you alone. And the ghost does not leave its prey, namely, its hunter. It has understood instantly that one is hunting it just to hunt it, chasing it away only so as to chase after it. Specular circle . . . The *long time* is here the time of this distance *hunt* . . . lure and prey (140).

Is this not amazing? "lure and prey"—the hunt—becomes the h(a)unt, a congruence with the most severe of Derrida's European readers.[27] H(a)unting comes before history, before social determinations, before language, before—haunting is the before of "before," and this satisfies Levi-Strauss's great challenge to the history of historians: history leads to nearly any relation so long as you leave it. Haunting produces its own elementary social relation, that of collusion, which is what connects the "self-protection" of any ego as a "unique living-ego" with "the other within . . . before language" (141), and this collusion is also nothing less than "spectral survival" (148). It is not rhetoric that ensures the survival of specters, fetishes, religion, or ideology, but the ghost itself that is the "invincible force and the original power" (148). *Différance* gives way to historiospectography, an effect of the eternal presence of this "force" and "original power."

From history to historiography to historiospectography—such is the narrative of the "new scholar" unrolled by *Specters of Marx* as it moves away from the marks of successivity to nonsuccessivity, as it mixes traditional notions of avant-garde and reactionary scholarly writing. Just as the commodity is held to be an ever-present mark of human sociality, so too is the specter:

> This double socius binds *on the one hand* men to each other. It associates them insofar as they have for all times been interested in time . . . the time of the duration of labor, and this in all cultures and at all stages of techno-economic development . . . which itself would not be possible without surviving and returning . . . (154).

From eternity—the affirmation of "all times" is the moment that all Western historiography had fantasized as pure revelation and disclosure of the nonsecret of secrets, an effacement of differences. This effacement takes the form of a particular trope, that of *apophasis*. In saying that Marx left the concept of use-value intact, which repeats Baudrillard's argument from the 1960s, *Specters* urges that if use-value is not "pure," that is, self-same,

> then one would have to say that the phantasmagoria began before the said exchange-value, at the threshold of the value of value in general, or that the commodity-form began the commodity-form, itself before itself . . . A culture began before culture—and humanity. Capitalization also. Which is as much to say that, for this very reason, it is destined to survive them (160).

The "must be" of Kojeve here becomes "there always was" and "there always will be," Bible Studies 101. The phantasmagoria of exchange comes *first*. History-as-such comes before, as haunting, ghosts and specters. "To haunt does not mean to be present, and it is necessary to introduce haunting into the very construction of a concept" (161). Answers before questions: and historiography must then have as its sole important object the definite nonpresent presence of a mysticism that precedes all precedence. "Everything begins before it begins" (161). Repetition is history; history is repetition. But timeless and before. Anti-existentialism is therein completed.

Ghosts and specters come before every "before." The "fabulous" search for the origins is settled by *Specters of Marx* and the origin is nothing other than the hollowing-out of language by phantoms such that there is an *absolute history* far more tyrannical than any ever conceived by the idealism of historicism. This is the tyranny of the ghosts who are waiting for us to elicit them (and a recoding of Walter Benjamin's fantasy about the dead as victims of present domination). What critics have fretted over, Derrida's writing as Mandarinism, is resolved by *Specters* in the modes, carried as rhetoric, of *exergasa* (*différance* is the specter, the specter is exchange, exchange is the origin) and prosopopeia, where the reification of an imaginary subject is said to be nonimaginary (the repetitions of "there must be" of *Specters*). The writing is "miraculating," it makes "miracles."[28] De Man's notice of Derrida's reading of Rousseau as a "modernist," which allowed *Of Grammatology* to have no "precursors," gives way to the textual destruction of any sense of periodization—but without this leading to any existential "charging" of the present. In demanding that "phantasmorization" alone is without limit, this type of deconstruction opts for the satisfactions of aesthetics: to say that "one has to realize that the ghost is there" is to eliminate what *différance* has supposedly been all about.

The single most disturbing sentence of *Specters of Marx* comes precisely at the end of this text: "we are wagering here that thinking never has done with the conjuring impulse. It would instead be born of that impulse" (165). Here is the retreat to idealism and psychologism: primordiality, inchoateness, and "new scholars" who alone can speak of such places. "Impulse" announces regression to neohumanism's belief in language that can save the self.

Finally, there is the issue of why the desire for the messianic comes today, now. "The messianic, including its revolutionary forms . . . would be urgency, imminence but, irreducible paradox, a waiting without horizon expectation" (168). But there is no paradox here—just the insistence of what the messianic is said *to be*. In refusing to think through the messianic, that it is a specific discourse with specific textual and social effects, *Specters of Marx* shows a high degree of intellectual fear that the messianic will go the way of the telic (into unlimited social disagreements). There is a textual hysteria that the messianic has already been made an *obsolete* term of relation. Is it a literary or textual default that *Specters of Marx*, in a passage as silly as it is eloquent, insists that Marx came upon "it ghosts" and while he rejected this, it is Freud who holds the secret: "Marx—*das Unheimliche*"? What does it say that we must affirm Marx's texts as "uncanny"? Haunting, with messianism, "before life *as such,* before death *as such,*" is given the most commanding *continuism* imaginable; for *Specters of Marx* closes with the injunction that "if he loves justice at least, the 'scholar' of the future, the 'intellectual' of tomorrow should learn it and from the ghost" (176). The scholar of historiospectography is then the only figure of history who matters—which is what (some) scholars have been saying since writing was commandeered for the purposes of priestcraft, now become the dismissal of the present in the face of what is eternal and catatonic.

On Force and Language

The texts analyzed so far grant themselves remarkably similar privileges: They accede to the impossibility of rendering history as objective process while readers are assumed to be interested in securing access to "historical meaning," text and subject mobilized by means of ideals of form (Ankersmit), psychology (Appleby et al.), and, unconventionally, the dynamics of "spectering" (Derrida). These texts are *suppliers* of meaning structured so as to forestall passive nihilism as a recognizable existential relation. In other words, these texts "save the subject" of historical meaning by making this subject into a psychological effect of ideal and "spirit."[29] The cultural condition of nihilism appears as an "undefined agony of meaning" (for example, Appleby *et al.* and the anxiety over a "fall" of the expert; Derrida's insistence, blindly aggressive, on divination) in which textual recoding makes models in which the reactive is affirmed, whose "cargo" adds to the stock of passivity. To "save the expert" or give "birth" to a "new scholar" characterizes model readers, or what I prefer to call "last readers," existential correlates of the order-words and other syntaxes involved, or readers of whom very little interpretation is expected. In Umberto Eco's terms, such texts appeal to the "intellectual indolence" of their readers,[30] a "'sabbatical' beatitude . . . in the shadow of perfect nihilism . . . to rest in the certainty of the *unum necessarium*."[31] Epistemically, the writings offer subjective attractions by which reactivity is given orders for taming existential excess, displacing and reversing forces for outcomes entirely fictional. Language is coded so as to reestablish debts and contracts, what we "owe" to Marxism given over to spectering, what we "owe" to irony's enveloping ether, what we "owe" to the "expert," what is "owed" to convention, each of these ascetic ideals displacing existential conflict (between a reader and his or her modeling of future), the displacement making bearable the crushing weight of "history."[32] The "crisis" that Ankersmit claims as necessary for convention (analogy), where picturing requires suppression of text, uses that theoretical fiction to politicize against close reading. The use of such fictions effects a blindness created by the force of its own error: Derrida's celebration of "ghosts" collapses onto an "impulse," which displays the dubiousness of the project of "ghosting."

The claim, then, is that such textual semiosis depends upon intellectual and political considerations, in particular the idea of passive nihilism. In Deleuzian terms: these writings obey their own order-words and in that way close divergence between sign and meaning, accomplished by a saving elevation: return to convention, maintenance of the office of the "expert," a "new scholar" capable of spirit talk. The porosity of historiography may well be exposed in the differences between texts, but so is the identity of idealism and orders. There seems to be a deep affinity between such textual "blackboxing" and "last readers," which involves readers presumed to desire the satisfactions of "knowing about historical culture" in a model that severs ideal from skepticism.

Now, for the sake of analytic playfulness, another notion can be opposed to such "last readers." The readings made so far have presumed the idea of an *excessive* reader who moves between a text's aesthesis of cognition and cognition's promotion of intellectual choices. This reader is collective in a way unthinkable to the writings made for "last readers," for this reader (Nietzsche's "educated proletariat"?) is someone who "scrambles" a text's concocted "marching-orders," its instructions for reception.[33] Texts produce their "last readers" when they appeal to resolving ideals. But excessive readers wonder how these texts eliminate collision between their own production of cultural ideals and discrepant language, or language's instances of serious implausibility. Does this just restate that all prose criticism, historical or not, is subject to "blindness," "ideology," "repression," "idealization," figures of limits? That would simply give us a new universal of the negative in writing. Of course every text is *datable,* an intertextual product structured by the politics of its orders; but the point is to specify how texts create passive nihilism as a counterforce, a real presence of writing. Passive nihilism's resistance to intellectual upheaval is accomplished by language that rejects that "signification is unstable," and such nihilism blocks the activity in which

> the subject of discourse . . . [is] transformed into an impassioned subject that disrupts its own cognitively and programmed statements . . . [and] such a discursive subject can also interrupt and shift its own narrative rationality, and follow a passional pathway, or it can even perturb it with discordant pulsations.[34]

Why use "excessive reader" to imagine readers who notice the presence of writing's own resistance to disruption? The "excessive reader" is alone with the text but reads against the antiforce of the text's consolidation of meaning. Such a reading notices, as in the examples above, the devices of argument by analogy, by sheer demand (relativism leads to Nazism) and by the repetition of "must," which already begin to account for the text's self-integration of what might undo it. The "excessive reader" is, paradoxically, the "producer of the text" insofar as such a reader has some criterion by which to recognize the text's solicitation, its "plasticizing" of a singular system, which makes its own nominations subject to the command or order of "not being forgotten."[35] In the conventional and postconventional examples of reestablishing a cultural historiography that "matters," an attentive reader could notice coded satisfactions of modeling, contradictions and multiplicities denied.

Is all this a question of the professionalization of writing about cultural historiography, an "academic mode of text production"? Orders for the "shrewd and competent," as was stated in the Introduction? Is it a question of scholarly text purification, in which the modes of historiographic formalism, the politics of experts, going "spectering," resubjectivizing autobiography, and ironizing "shit" show how the present is "cleared" as a site capable of receiving the "charge" of cultural historiography? No doubt these texts, which cannot escape entanglements of figure and epistemology, are part of that ceaseless erection of an inner world described by folk psychology,[36] where knowledge is a moral purification; such beliefs and demands "hide" as much as possible their commitment to conceptual presuppositions. This "hiding" is in no way contrary to aggressive modes of writing. In this sense, attention to the purifying functions belongs to a tradition of analysis whose modern incarnation is at least partially indebted to Nietzsche's insight that language, like capital, is resolute in channeling effective choices into tight spaces—work, leisure, family, reputation, sense, meaning, and figure. The new scholarship analyzed above is inseparable from models of purification in the service of "recovery"—their purpose is to "foreground" reactions that "pulluate," language near exhaustion, eliciting the "predictive indolence" of readers.[37] All of the text's analyzed figure forth the vicarious as condition, fact, reality.

The linguistic function that is correlated with passive nihilism is the imaginary grammar of a third-party perspective from which, in addition to the "sufferer and the spectator," the third person considers experience for the advantage to be gained from presenting it: scholars give us the truth, the clergy soothes the way, etc. This third party, figure of mediation and transition, connection and network, installs within discourse a "brakeshoe," as Nietzsche put it, or the discussable reduced from speakers to observers: "the person who does not act considers that he possesses a natural light over action, that he deserves to derive advantage or profit from it."[38] Last readers are writers who want the "brakeshoes" applied. If Ankersmit's ideal reader is the connoisseur, Appleby's the "sober analyst," and Derrida's a medium between life and death (someone who can speak to harmony of form and content, someone who can pronounce satisfaction with the "expert," someone who can speak to "spirits"), then such mediations are also the places where the text shows more than it says.

The thoughtful work of Brian Massumi on active and passive language is exemplary in this context. In Massumi's evaluation and selection from Deleuze and Guattari's *Capitalism and Schizophrenia,* passive nihilist texts bring an idea of unity together with an idea of authority, an instance of which is the explosion of the name "hybrid," now a small industry of writing. To produce an effect of power and authority, a text must capture a ground, hold a territory, maintain its borders. But considered actively, another concept, that of force, emerges when we think about a text's "angle of application."[39] A teacher's form of expression (that is, a technique of imparting what is to be learned) and a given student's form of content (in which he or she "becomes" able, say, to perform research) wear down their separate "edges" (little of the surprising occurs), yet indicate reciprocal presuppositions of the form of content and the form of expression. Massumi puts it this way:

> the "hand to hand combat" of energies comes to a head when the plane shaves the wood [form of expression over form of content]. But many things intervene . . . a boss, a body, hands, technique, intentions, the handle of the tool [form of expression] . . . a piece of wood, a customer order, rain, trucks, delivery, a tree [form of content].[40]

Language, power, and force are always brought together at a number of acute intersections: commands with operative penalties, in which the form of expression, the order, brings about a change in content (from accused to prisoner); poetic stimulations, with indeterminate consequences; a term that upsets an opposition (for example, agitation irreducible to a polarity); dramatization, suspenseful knowledge-to-come; even grief, in which the form of content overwhelms the form of expression.[41] Any mode of expression, even ones saturated with power, can be dismantled for the purposes of other forces.

So to speak of force and power in terms of analyzing texts is first to affirm that texts are irreducible to any of their self-givens (that is, they are continuous neither with sense-data nor with their own concepts) and they articulate a contest between power and force. The question as to what textual force is "like" amounts to "What is the language of force?" And what are the forces of language? Think of how elusive is the sense of "need," instantaneously passing from the psychological ("one needs satisfaction"), through cultural politics (marginal groups "need" representation), via a social detour (society "needs" its margins to reflect its norms), only to be restored to the collective psychological ("societies need ____"). Such constructs very effectively operate as "power surges" that mobilize linguistic resources especially as they have the most varied relations with extra textual realities. In a review of Francis Fukayama's book *Trust,* Richard Kaplan paraphrases Fukayama's assertion that in contemporary world-conflicts, "cultures where suspicion reigns cannot create the necessary organizational links that fuel economic growth. Japan's industrial policy . . . derives organically from Japanese culture." Evaluated as to the force involved in grasping this syntagm, one notices immediately a vast but simple assertion: No culture has a future if it is suspicious, a rationalization for the suppression of suspicion![42] Evaluation thinks to the power of installing passive nihilism. The incredibly shaky rationalization proffered by Fukayama is normalized by the syntax of acceptance ("derives organically"). New redundancies of the obvious, new concentrations of language shore up existing powers.

Power, then, affects language at any one of its points of application (logic, grammar, rhetoric), where aggression and defensiveness have overrun thought, whereas the concept of force is able to affirm thoughts open to more distinctions and more choices, more evaluations and more connections, more illuminations and metamorphoses. The reading of these textual installations of modes of power involves a destruction of "ordinary" reading.[43] An "excessive" reader is perforce destructive. As the arguments of J. J. Lecercle suggest, self-dispossession of linguistic reactivity involves challenging ordinary language along each of its axes. Consider the most ordinary of phrases, "the man is silent," which can be made to pass from statement to subjectification ("he is a silent man"), the adjectival into the attributed generic, a perception into a quality, hence a grammatically encoded and logically valid slot, for example, "the silent majority." What governs such activities is language as will to reactive power, that is, language as allowing for our possession of anything whatsoever, maintaining substitutions for the breakdowns of language, recoding pathways of identification (for example, if our historian-as-expert begins to break down, it becomes historian-as-"inspired," etc.).

Lecercle, following Deleuze and Guattari, argues that propositions can do at least three things: they can designate truth and falsity; they can manifest a proposition and the subject who utters it, which includes shifter relations or pronouns (voices of a speaker); and they can signify interdependence between words and general concepts. Designation presupposes manifestation or signification (concepts), but sense—what Hjelmslev called "purport"—is what a proposition expresses, an incorporeal event, irreducible to the terms of the propositions (significations), to the designated state of affairs, to the beliefs manifested, and to the concepts signified. This expressed of a proposition, its sense, might be conceived as part of paradox and incompletion. For the expressed is "there" as the ever virtual about to be said, called into being sometimes by anger, by curiosity, by a delirium over terms, by the multiplication of evaluations, as well as by impossible objects, absurd or self-contained propositions. Words and things, propositions and states of affairs, always combine both "making sense but being nonsensical itself." There would then be implied in even the most rigid order-words a force that is not symbolic, conveyed sometimes by designation, by manifestation, by signification, but more actively construed as a "differential element" in which a nonmetaphorical activity of *selection* really matters. Why selection? Because force brings selections that always enter from somewhere else, someone else's writing, one's own writing of the reading of the writing. . . . An excessive reader works at the edges of all this, slipping out of order-words, but to where?

Conclusion

On the level of manifest content, I would argue that cultural-historiographic thinking cannot get beyond convention to postconvention because it is not the type of discourse that can ever do anything but "start all over." Back to convention, to the "expert," or forward with the "new scholar" are really the same thing, in one way—textualizations of passive nihilism, which precisely now means: elimination of forces, removal of claimants, a high degree of idealization, the aestheticization of the ordinary, and denial that language is a contestable medium. Despite all differences, reconventional and post-conventional texts participate in and draw a share from the agreement that language poses no insuperable barrier to threading present cultural configurations to time-orders. They give Ideas of culture once the capital H of History has become shaky, but they still figure forth inoculations in which the capital C of culture will not be undone by analysis. Considered at the level of power, the insistence by Ankersmit that convention is more than adequate in representing the past as picture has to make experimental historical writing "neurotic"; *Telling the Truth About History* insists we already live in a culture freely chosen in all essentials, so its power lies in a future that will confirm this shape of the present; Derrida's appropriation of Shakespeare and of his own idea of *différance* are the ways in which contestation is removed.[44] The writings analyzed are trying to formalize desires and ideals, and it cannot be done other than by presupposing some "primitive agreement" that undermines the very intent. In this sense, "historical" language is one of the great intellectual chimeras. It is crucial, then, that attempts to establish historiographic language on some foundation or other like "communication," "persuasion," "syntax," "form," "unity" be seen as political impositions, with cognitive determinations, emotional affects, and cultural reverberations.

All of this is said to emphasize the overlap between the reactivity of language with idealist cultural models, for example, of the type the "nightmare of history" or "fear of relativism" or, more generally, models that positivize resubjectification. Created by language, these models let us stabilize our possession of what we want language to do *for us.* How can a discourse such as historiography, which has many centers or no one center, not then subject itself to a spiraling repression of itself as writing?[45]

Nietzsche reminds us that historiography is most interesting when it allows us to evaluate how culture and language are made to interact in an oscillation between aestheticism and enigma, and what is made of such conjunctions is already political, intellectual, cultural. What seems eerie about the historiography of the present is that even an avant-garde notion about the messianic is soon routinized, just as the reaction against relativism crosses swords with a deconstruction it has more in common with than it can acknowledge.

Finally, Nietzsche's ruminations on language and force oppose the symmetrical metaphysics of desire and demand, the wish to make peace with language instead of effecting "new laws of motion of force."[46] A consistent suspension of the satisfactions of writing seems necessary in order to break and rebreak the spells of language, to break with the agreement to read and write in the passive-aggressive mode. A reading that lets the excess of writing be discussed draws out the negating power of the reactive so as to recognize its shape and form, its insinuations and possessions, appropriations, within language. It makes the evaluation that it is better to work this way through language than it is to remain in language's columbarium or vault in which language is an urn holding the ashes of cremated sense.[47] Grim, Stoic, anarchist, and who knows what else, this mongrel—Nietzsche's "educated proletariat"—has strange thoughts about what "orders" the order-words in any given situation. But this reader wants to exceed negation of "imitation of temporal, spatial, and numerical relationships in the domain of metaphor."[48] For the excessive reader has a sense of "pairing the most alien things and separating the closest," offering the most "unheard-of combinations of concepts," criticism irreducible to an imitation "of the impression of the powerful present intuition."[49] Even a writer as provocative as Derrida assumes the truth of a present intuition ("ghosts are," "there must be one word") instead of disturbing one.

Chapter Two ▣

Neohistoricism, Science Studies, and Violence toward Deconstruction

The Concept of Transition

Neohistoricism refers to textual practices in which the historical profession legitimizes concepts of historical transition. In this chapter, two versions of this, multiculturalism and modernism, are analyzed. The issue is how these writings operate the levers of organizing and consuming such dizzying master-periodizations, these cultural supercomplexes. As taken up by neohistoricism, multiculturalism and modernism serve as cultural and social means of integration, rendered necessary for understanding the present, the latter then transported to a future already recognizable. The concept of transition is about leaving and entering time; this concept is ubiquitous and because of that, it often slips out of notice in public discussions of forces of change. In a first example, multiculturalism is turned into a condition for "saving" historical pedagogy, while in the second focus is on how construing modernism as a "failure" encodes a neoanthropologic attempt to restart cultural historiography on the ground of principles like that of symmetry between nature and culture.

Jenkins and Sobchak's essays, cited in chapter one, were neohistoricist: their texts made models of cultural necessities, where "now is" the time for new autobiography, "now is" the time of super-irony, "now is" not the time of politically driven historiography, "now is" not the time of resisting the filmic. The "now is" of *Specters of Marx* turned on making an eternal "impulse" into the basis of a "new scholarship." Neohistoricism has many varieties, but the two read here assume the historical "end" of modernism;

they are eager to separate from what they call "excesses" of postmodernism, and construe the future of historical knowledge as mediation. Like the texts analyzed in the first chapter, the writings here use discursive modes that are commanding—in control, offering mastery—so as to give the present "space" in which the failures of modernism can be addressed and settled. The difference here is that the texts below avoid excessive reconventionalization and flirtations with notions like the messianic. They are texts of cultural historiography that are socially conscious: they account for their models by reference to what the present is "really like" rather than emphasizing what historiography itself is "really like." In these texts, the power of politics and networks set aside problems concerning culture and language. Again, the first section analyzes how a historian can make a progressive case for multiculturalism treated as a model of historicization, the second section giving a close reading of Bruno Latour's *We Have Never Been Modern* (1993). Both go out of their way to locate deconstruction as a threat to scholarship's autonomy. This chapter concludes by bringing forth some considerations of that excessive reader to the recodings and reductions of such transitions.

Recoding Historicism

After the vast number of words devoted to the topic, the historian Michael Geyer has it that multiculturalism supports the social space of "reconstituting cultural capital," which is, institutionally considered, a "capital" necessary for the political-economy of university-based education. Drawing upon two (re)sources, one attending to civil rights, democratic egalitarianism, the other a theorizing and intellectualizing associated with "French thought" (read: deconstruction) that is "much more limited and precarious" for present knowledge production, multiculturalism is offered as a "capital" infusion giving the academy "a recovery of submerged knowledge, a working through of the repressed."[1] Here, lifting the repression on multiculturalism leads to the concept of recovery. Two *re* in one. This proposition codifies a stereotype of idealism—"recovery" can begin only when repression is ended—and intensifies the agglutinative power of *re* in securing the new (re)sources that, it seems, can safely be folded into the rearticulation of the seriousness of education. A progressive model of history leads to a progressive model of pedagogy. It presupposes there is nothing repressive at all about multiculturalism.

Geyer's narrative model is a sophisticated defense of Ranke against Hegel, in which singularities matter, but it is Hegel who surmounts Ranke: "it is the memory of the bondsmen rather than the monuments of the masters that assures the survival of humanity." This is a straight coding of progressive Hegelianism, or neoliberalism. It is neither reactionary nor avant-garde. It supposes the truth of the master is "in" the "bondsmen's" empirical reality, and has very frequently come to mean that cultural analysis must never obliterate the perspective of one who has suffered life under the "master." There are vast literatures on this subject. But since deconstruction or "French thought" is not of the "bondsmen" sociological type, or because it has come from "masters," the insertion of multiculturalism in the context of the "bondsmen" gives it a claim of "historicizing the present." The analytic and critical implications of French thought could only be secondary to the political impact of "democracy" and its tribulations. The "limited and precarious" aspects of this French thought may provide (egalitarian) multiculturalism with a few devices for its passage to the future. The strategy of integrating multiculturalism is lifted from what Barthes called "inoculation," the feint of acknowledging a problem so as to escape from troubling thoughts concerning means of resolution. Whatever claims deconstruction has on our minds are tucked in a political envelope: multiculturalism belongs to democratization, while French thought should make us wary.

In Geyer's argument, the cultural wars over multiculturalism can revive historicism in providing the latter with an effective transition from a discredited universal history to that of "provisional histories," the present (but not presentistic) then "empowered" in semantic identifications that are figured by Geyer in this way:

> modes of inquiry . . . strategies of coping with the fear of otherness while honoring difference. Such strategies are familiar from a variety of therapeutic activities such as antirape or antiracist education.[2]

An older leftist tradition would notice that "antirape" and "antiracism" have replaced labor and class as foundational categories. While rape and racism are never less than terroristic, they are returned here as the basis for "inquiry" and, as "strategies," thus generalized to problematics between university and society and within knowledge production. How far do antirape and antiracism really extend as models of academic politics and the politics of delivering a "serviceable" education? Working through rape and racism reduces the social to the psychological; the first sentence of the quote marks out "fear" and "honor" as the polarity of the social as such. We suffer from too many fears of the other (race, homophobia, and identity) but these can be offset by inclusive politics of the victims, making their claims ours. What "French thought" might say about Geyer's instantaneous fusion of historicism, psychoanalysis, theory, problems, et al. is effaced by the signifier "coping," which affirms there are no critical strategies but those already *within* the transition. This is an extremely powerful settling of accounts. "Coping" should be understood as an order-timing: The text has already assumed as fact that coping is beyond analysis. To cope, infinitive mode, implies truths about the "dark sides" of modernity, its surplus negations, but made undiscussable here. The primary "move" of this neohistoricism aims at providing an objectivist referent (we live "in" this New World) with forms of our recognizing it; the new realities of world history have generated problematics, the solutions of which are also here now.

Geyer recognizes that his notion of multiculturalism is subject to absorption by a "plural middle ground" or "an administrative concept of 'diversity' and the scholarly praise for a new pluralism," of becoming yet another "debate" on objectivity versus relativism and explanation versus interpretation. The usefulness of his order-words within and as "transition" is legitimized by two world-historical processes that are said to make up the irreversible temporalities of present-future. The first is syncretism, the "fusion of dissimilar artifacts," and the second is creolization, or the "nonauthentic fusion of disparate elements into one among many microexperiences," which, taken together, are the "key expression of our time."[3] Syncretism can take a number of interpretations, from global commodification to networking of any type, depending on the politics involved (the middle classes of India have more in common with American salespeople than either group has with its respective "underclass"). Creolization, in receiving the quality "nonauthentic," is thereby denigrated, such discourses invented by oppressed peoples strangely *re*-repressed here.[4] It is not difficult to imagine that creolization simply stands in for those aspects of French theory that undermine identity politics—the politics of disputation rather than the politics of agreement.

Moreover, this historicizing of the present coincides with realizing history: the "history" of this New World and "to cope" recodes one of the earliest figures of historicization, that of "virtue through wisdom . . . for a worldly man."[5] Not only does it locate conflict in the past, it affirms that intellectual work has tasks and goals that are shot through with rationality inclusive of humanity, perhaps a "last referent" of our cultural system(s). If the victims can be said to offer a model of the way "progress" can be strengthened, then the "masters" have won by losing. The "cunning of history" is a wily effect.

Thus, as in most progressivist discussions concerning intellectual work, there is no denial of the structural "fact" of the ongoing reduction of the "general" in "general education" to intensifying "tutorial" functions, set amidst a furious proliferation of "education" proposals (but, tellingly, there is no consideration of the "historical" failure of past remedies). Geyer forcefully supports multiculturalism as "modes of inquiry" requiring "intercultural reading or explorations in symbolic exchange," as necessary complements in the study of "unsettlement" (for instance, diasporization) and how unstable groups "struggle to think and create orders and to provide meanings." These modes should enable an enlivened academia to stall the juggernaut of "compensatory education," the purgatory of multiculturalism (but "coping" is already compensatory). This "knowledge for a state of emergency" (cataplexis) sketches an opposition between "self-chosen *différance* [that] turns against or stands in contrast to a functionally selected and imposed diversity," an impasse between the elitism of French theory and the elitism of State imposition of educational standards. The third way is conceived as "transcoding," a term borrowed from Jameson, whose error of equating transcoding and reconciliation is freely repeated. For here it is transferred to the moral sphere: progressivist historicism wants "to acknowledge different referential universes and [. . .] does not abandon a sense of linkage and communality."[6] But to "acknowledge" the claims of others and accepting their identities involves no strong acceptance of the claims of *différance,* which is often about how to elude the traps of identity. And what is "communality"? It stands for something like no allowable fracture in the transition to the future. The historicism of "transition" is duplicated in the figure of moral renovation of the academic institution—a rediscovery of our "bewilderment," insisted as something "age old." Scholars make the transition only on condition of accepting this "third way."

The energies of transformation, transition, transcoding, "trans" as such, are yoked to injunctions of *re,* embedded in an intellectual structure at once an affirmation of negation (absorption of change, learning from horror) and a program of turning this into the "next" stage of intellectual work. In this way, neohistoricism will provide distance from the commodification of a popular culture (journalism, media) and that of corporate exclusionism, both of which threaten the future of institutions of knowledge.

Such are the salient encodings of Geyer's text: the language of a retreat to the future through a Hegelian recoding, the assumption of "two cultures" (democratic, theory), the resolutions offered. It reads as a "grafting" operation while it mimes bricolage: it is highly selective, indicating a certain edginess about it. Geyer's piece has prognostic value, that it says what is likely to happen (has happened) within the overall furious reconfigurations of "learning," encoding what is shaping up as fact; cast in the language of prognosis, it is already part of the language of the "master" within academic reculturation. Perhaps some aspects of multiculturalism are irreducible to the commodification of academic labor, but the academic organization (textbook production, new positions, images of value to the public, etc.) brings with it recoding, recentering, rearticulation, repetition, managerial bindings necessarily antireflexive toward situations as jammed as the present.[7] Embedding multiculturalism in the structural code of benevolence presumes agreement on the parameters of cultural discourse; it disallows improprieties of multiculturalism, repeating progressivism's uncomfortability with uncontrollable thought.

Second Reading

Reading can start again, this time with a tentative hypothesis about the first reading: French thought (deconstruction) is not very useful in helping the current "transition." It is not a good mode of time travel, of making transitions. At the same time, neohistoricism is narrated consonant with political idealism: It comes back as a timely discourse and "saves" us from confrontation with equivocation of meaning, what "to cope" installs as an order-word. We are rescued by "recovery" and avoid what (some) "French thought" has found in its ceaseless textualizations:

> language posits and language means (since it articulates) but language cannot posit meaning: it can only reiterate (or reflect) it in its reconfirmed falsehood. Nor does the knowledge of this impossibility make it less impossible. This impossible position is precisely the figure, the trope, metaphor as a violent—and not as a dark—light, a deadly Apollo.[8]

This version of French thought, de Man's, argues that sign and the meanings of signs diverge: meaning cannot be equated with sense, conclusion, evidence, theory, or any other conjunction; "to cope" just terminates potential misfiguration. As this "transition" is positivized by means of "to cope," potentially stronger feelings about the present (for instance, Nietzsche's sense of capitalism as a "noose") are forgotten, made inaccessible. But even "to cope" is a concept for which there is no correlative reality unless its model, rape/racism, is extended to all subjects, a destruction of the concept of victim. Transitions often occur in such discourses of convergence. Are the meanings of victim, trauma, mourning and the like generalizable? Stronger: aren't these generalizations what the writing gives as its resistance to its readers knowing? French theory, deconstruction, gives the kinds of ruminations about language/world and self/other that Geyer's discourse acknowledges and removes. It would be very beneficent if knowledge were like "to cope," as Geyer says, but it is precisely the comparison that elicits suspicion because one can readily think of knowledge in a multiplicity of senses, as necessary pain, release, or enigma, none of which is exactly "it" in any given case.

Moreover, the defamiliarizing of classical historicism performed by Geyer's arguments is not carried into academia as institution-signification, its overall operation of providing rational, possible choices through conceptual systems that are believed to be, if not the last word, appropriate as usable terms and concepts for tying this transition and others together. Geyer knows that academic discourse is threatened by any number of disturbing forces (the media is now a direct claimant/rival for all but advanced study), but Geyer strips any response to the bare minimum: his model promotes "intercultural reading" fit for and suited to what is embraced, humanism as "translation." The concept of translation promises so much, and in Geyer's model it is entirely convergent with the writing of the "transition." It promises the triumph of a usable identity—assuming that the "transition" is not fatal to the identities of numerous groups.

Further, the identity between "translation" and "transition" contains suppressed "frontier" elements, to use J. J. Lecercle's phrase, which gives language ambiguous and subversive meanings.[9] Is that what is bothersome about French theory, that it is not a "safe discourse," that it pursues these frontiers and produces ambiguity of proper discourse? Geyer writes, "The history of twentieth-century globalization is the history of the large-scale privatization of the global commons by incorporated, legal subjects rather than the constitution of a universal public sphere," a proposition whose criticism of privatization is completely at odds with the remedies offered. The Marxist nod to class gives way here to Hegelian synthesis, ambiguity of the public/private terminated. With extreme urgency, the progressivism with which Geyer systematizes the transition from the university as founded upon mediation, which he says is finished as an historical possible, to one of "making sense" of—the transition—succumbs to the "market" by urging that we build our own "market" out of the negative. The logic of identity drives the identity of opposition, of resistance only to the lowest common denominator (fear of the media). Here is acceptance of the logic of the least negative. In a crucial passage, Geyer acknowledges multiculturalism as part of a "thorough reworking of the institution of higher learning," and then, instead of focusing on proposals and claims concerning such "reworking," the writing swerves to make a threat:

> The sooner academia makes this turn, the better it will be able to avoid the fate of such Fordist troglodytes as the Detroit automobile industry. To this end, we need a radical reconsideration of the place, the subject, and the goal of general education as part of an entire reconfiguration of higher education.[10]

"Radical" and "reconsideration": this is thought stopped in its tracks. It announces the heavy hand of "fate" and is meant to scare: obsolescence is not very pleasant. Hence we must all reset our historical clock: modernize and contemporize—or disappear! Deconstruction can be avoided. "Reconsideration" has no proper counterclaimant, another spell in removing outbreaks of skepticism.

Geyer's notion of translation cannot seriously entertain conjunctions between modern "history" considered a disaster of capital, from factory to network (or disappear!), nor that the academic institution's "translation" function might be a power-play in the removal of dissident intellection. To consider, say, capital as less a challenge for recoding than as a "noose" (Nietzsche) is to consider something other than the construction of rationalizing discourse. This second reading grasps the politics of intellection as purification and in this sense intrinsic to the work of aggressive cultural historiography.

The historiographic problematic as set forth directly in the significations of "transition" is as old as Western writing. A new world is here, shaping the future as the past passes away, everyone slightly mad over how the past can stay. But that the concept of "world" might not apply to these "new" forces is often not considered by many contemporary critics.[11] Much university writing would forestall adding to the worsening of the negative processes we can identify (or mediate and purify, as Latour has it, on which more below). We are all "caught" in transition. As a corollary, this supposes that historical culture is stable enough to recode—possess the present in enough linguistic material so as to shape the future in figures, grammars, and logics consonant with pastness. Geyer's essay, rewritten countless times by all of us involved in questions of "historical rank and relevance," privileges the failure of modernism, but affirming the negative as avoidance of obsolescence. It is scripted according to Habermasian notions of communicative action such that contradictions, ironies, weirdnesses, and contortions are defamiliarized, this to oppose any dissident or extremist argument that deadly processes are at work too. The concept of perpetual recoding lends itself to aesthetics when it implies an intellectual comprehension forced back on Hegel and not the production of more puzzles and enigmas concerning all these supposed "transitions" and "translations." For why should one embrace "unsettlement" and "syncretism" and not, say, terror and enormous levels of professional incompetence as historical constants? A more penetrating analysis might co-implicate the writing of the transition in ways that Geyer's discourse simply blocks.

Science Studies and Order-Words:
A Critique of *We Have Never Been Modern*

Can science studies create concepts that are models of relation so as to resolve contradictions endemic to cultural analysis? B. Latour's *We Have*

Never Been Modern (1993) makes such claims, namely, that intractable problems of modern historicism (periodization) and interpretation (concerning hybrids and social repression) can be settled. Hybrids or unanticipated new beings, whether made out of machinic, biologic, cultural, or political combinations, have made historicism and even interpretation archaic, obsolete, modes of writing. Instead, *We Have Never Been Modern* (hereafter, WHNB) insists that the strangeness of relations as such, whose catch-all phrase is modernism,[12] requires the kind of sorting that only science studies can achieve because it is equipped with the intellectual tools that can forestall the disaster of modern cultural and intellectual separation, which drives hybrids into the netherworld. Historicism renders images of discontinuity (time separation) and hermeneutics often dissolves into special pleading (for instance, the incomparability of different orders). WHNB insists that science studies, on the basis of a reconceived anthropology—the conjuncture of knowledge, power and practices[13]—can provide a new monism capable of absorbing the world's proliferation of hybrids or unrecognized phenomena and bypass the quandaries of discursive cul-de-sacs. Outfitting itself in the categories and substance of holistic relations, it comes forward as a collective intellectual promise, entirely analogous to the "once upon a time" of psychoanalytic or Marxist literary studies: only truth is on its side.

The reading of WHNB will elucidate its intellectual force; specifically, focus is directed to: (1) how can science studies really use a "few sets of concepts sturdy enough" so as to synthesize incommensurable objectities, if one definition of a concept is its "unsturdiness," that is, its value as passage between differences?[14]; (2) can science studies really transcend the semantic problems which are endemic to critical studies? Can it, for instance, overcome that surprising unreliability of language to provide foundations, although no other discipline has as yet been able to develop a generally accepted metalanguage? And (3) Latour's version of science studies articulates proposals concerning intellectual and social violence, which are disconcerting. WHNB, it will be argued, lends itself to a suppression of social and intellectual violence. It makes it impossible to think violence in the intellectual space of its "network" model: "networks" require translators, which are coded very close to a new omniscience (3).[15] The negation of violence, through intellectual elimination, and the elevation of the "network" into the position of a privileged locus of intellectual inquiry turns intellectual work from analysis to management. Criticism is asked to sacrifice its "bite" so that intellectuals can once again be "helpers" of culture. This strange place or, better, nonplace of violence, calls into question the "network" model, exposing it as a political and idealist oversynthesis, a kind of Platonism of intellectual relations. For

WHNB, anthropology becomes the transcendent ideal which, because it is invisible, repressed by modernism, divides into the "good copy" of holism and the "bad copy" of deconstruction, that malevolent intellectual movement that will have nothing to do with transcendence.[16]

This critical reading of WHNB also continues the discussion, the unfolding, of an "excessive" reader, which suggests that a text will be taken as strictly equivalent with the production of effects where the text attempts to leave language behind so as to become institution, or language placed under control of its "few sturdy concepts." The critical guideposts, de Manian suspicion toward judgments which are in fact moralizing-aesthetic reductions and Deleuze's theory that language is a nonunified type of force and in no manner a substance or form, involve reading WHNB as it tries to cut itself free from the discursivity it employs. This reading strategy makes discussable the ways in which figurations are suppressed, how they resist the syntax and grammar in which they are cast. A de Manian reading treats language as performance, insisting that discursive figures, be they rhetorical, logical, or grammatical, are "text producing functions that are not necessarily patterned on a non-verbal entity."[17] Neither objective as a being to be perceived, nor nonobjective as a purely imaginary object, language is here itself a "disturbance of the cognitive field," and de Man emphasized its unsettling implication:

> it is not *a priori* certain that language functions according to principles which are those, or which are *like* those, of the phenomenal world. It is therefore not *a priori* certain that [prose] is a reliable source of information about anything but its own language.[18]

In treating science studies as if it was released from linguistic complications, WHNB elaborates political-ideological idealism, including an aestheticization of analytic critique. As before, the issue is to make a reading that wants to know how such important claims can be decided and selected, whether such claims of the writing can be addressed in analytic terms if they are figurations at once cognitive, moral, and aesthetic.

Epistemic Suffering

WHNB is suffused by a powerful interest in getting out of "history"—in favor of an ethnographic and anthropological mode that reveals the radical autonomy of Western "history" to be a modernist fantasy. The Western overvaluation of "difference" (for example, economic "take-off," revolutions of rising expectations, rejection of the archaic) is said to be identical to its historiographic illusions. Overemphasis on history as difference is rejected by a generational claim:

> Because we are the first who believe neither in the virtues nor in the dangers of science and technology, but share their vices and virtues without seeing either heaven or hell in them, it is perhaps easier for us to look for their causes without appealing to the white man's burden, or the fatality of capitalism or the destiny of Europe, or the history of Being or universal rationality. Perhaps it is easier today to give up the belief in our own strangeness. We are not exotic but ordinary. As a result the others are not exotic either (127).

This "first" does not want to ask questions already posed; it simply dissolves the contraries set forth so as to render its own demand, already a conclusion: "to give up . . . strangeness," which serves as the premise legitimation and deflates historiographic, sociologic, and philosophic models of collective modernism. Differences are negated: science studies rejects modernism as well as any metahistorical speculation.

This affirmation of identity grafted to submission ("give up") is a negation or move with radical implications. Science studies would suspend any causal-historical model that cuts off the "mediators," the "delegates and senders" "shuttling forth" between and amongst the "networks"; in a world in which everyone shares the same functions, it is not the "job" of knowledge to produce difference (articulation) as much as it is to acknowledge (reiterate) the already existing hybrids that are unrecognized:

> The human is the delegation itself, in the pass, in the sending, in the continuous exchange of forms. . . . Human nature is the set of its delegates and its representatives, its figures and its messengers. . . . We should be talking about morphism. . . . A weaver of morphisms—isn't that enough of a definition? (137–38)

"Delegates" and "representatives," "figures" and "messengers"—this mixture of knowledge and power, discourse and practice is synthesized as a "weaver-weaving" model whose associations are legion but one sense of which is literary, that of weaving as a substitution for the quest to have "totality" "epitomized."[19] The model claims that it will finally allow us to judge the mistakes of epistemology, social science, and philosophy (deconstruction). The as-yet mediated hybrids that the moderns have built, pulled out "by the roots" by epistemologists, by social scientists who "purify our network of any object" (for instance, make reified abstractions), and by deconstructionists who "purge . . . adherence to reality . . . or to power plays," are in a limbo of asymmetry, binarism, methodological individualism, and false relativism, which all attest to a collective intellectual life "out of kilter" (5) These discursive systems have been unable to grasp what is distinctively modern in the modern because they have missed "the delicate shuttle . . . [that has] woven together the heavens, industry, texts, souls and moral law— this remains uncanny, unthinkable, unseemly" (4). The philosophical series, for example, initiated in Boyle's distinction between eyewitness/experimental science as it was connected to Hobbes's defense of collective political authority, "classicized" in Kant's separation of faculties and Hegel's attempt at a dialectical resolution, became that intensified modernism of phenomenology's desperation for a transcendental guarantee (for example, Habermas's demand for agreeing on incommensurables), and has crashed in a (putative) nightmare of paralysis. In each series (literature, social demographics, etc.), the same pattern: epistemic deracination, the social sciences emptying the world of agents and agencies (intermediaries, messengers, passes, senders), resulting in a deconstruction/postmodernism that epistemologizes culture and thus separates it more than ever from other networks. The basic insistence is that epistemology makes us suffer, that it prevents us from "weaving," and which requires restoration of Ariadne's "thread." This insistence accounts for the book's audacity in allegorizing the "weaver" as the New Scholar of Return, an intellectual move that Vico, in his boundless skepticism over things linguistic, characterized as "the conceit of the scholars, who will have it that what they know must have been eminently understood from the beginning of the world."

Clearing the Space

> For twenty years or so, my friends and I have been studying these strange situations that the intellectual culture in which we live does not know how to categorize (3).

These "strange situations" are the "imbroglios" that have come from three centuries of producing hybrids. They are the uncategorized, the unmediated phenomena that surround us, whose "oddity" has been missed, neglected, repressed. Society is unconscious and unable to integrate these hybrids because the classical division between knowledge and power represses, yet presupposes, a larger or greater symmetrical relation of the social bond which is always torn between assimilation of the new and preservation of the old; here is a typical statement of how WHNB poses its resolution:

> [to] . . . retie the Gordian Knot by crisscrossing the divide that separates exact knowledge and the exercise of power (3).

Existing knowledge must then be suspended, its negations negated, while maintaining or conserving the modern narrative structure for future resolution:

> we have chosen to follow the imbroglios wherever they take us. To shuttle back and forth, we rely on the notion of translation, or network . . . the Ariadne's thread of these interwoven stories (3).

Humans, nonhumans, and society—formed and forming as associations, hybrids, collectives, and networks—are foregrounded simultaneously as objects of study, as new realities, and as object relations modern thought cannot handle. Expressed in the rhetoric of exasperation—"Is it our fault if the networks are simultaneously real, like nature, narrated, like discourse, and collective, like society?"—this "cry" justifies anthropology's invocation of a new unity, here the principle of symmetry, that the same causes assimilate and explain opposites, rather than treating differences as requiring separate explanations (91ff).

This plaint is itself, moreover, discursively threaded to an aesthetic embedding, a tendency for fusion.[20] Relying upon Shapin and Schaffer's work-up of the modern "divide" (later seventeenth century), established as a "constitution" which permitted the legitimization of the disastrous separations of the modern (for example, nature/culture, science/society, artifact/event), WHNB opts for the model of the Perfect Object, maximum fusion with a transcendence of oppositions:

> The beauty of Shapin and Shaffer's book stems from their success in unearthing Hobbes' scientific works . . . and in rescuing from oblivion Boyle's political theories . . . [they] outline a rather nice quadrant (16).

"Beauty," "success," and "nice quadrant," codes of symmetrical unification, or aestheticized epistemology, are appropriate because Shapin and Schaffer have shown that the Boyle-Hobbes "constitution" provides "the perfect fruit flies for the new anthropology" (17). The conclusion: "for the first time in science studies" there is a way out of modern knowledge and its vicious problematics. "First time" is of course a semantic marker of ecstasy, of "now is," an order-word.

The moderns create hybrids; examples might be talk shows as a new form of public humiliation recognition, endless books about the apocalypse of the working classes, voting patterns such that, in California, 16 percent of the electorate dictates public spending, all of these relations created as they are named, so that naming confers value on both object and the giver of the name, a definite positive goal of this new anthropology. Modernists refuse to fully acknowledge and hence integrate in some network these "monsters." The premoderns, on the other hand, conceived of hybrids and excluded "their proliferation." The moderns produce these hybrids without regard to consequences whereas the premoderns articulated a kind of antiproduction—things were more mixed there, but premoderns radically controlled their machines and affects.[21] The three-hundred year "crisis" of hybrid repression—an unacknowledged runaway production—requires an "enlightenment without modernity," and here WHNB affirms a semantic paralogism brought to bear against the modernist biases:

> We are going to have to slow down, reorient and regulate the proliferation of monsters [hybrids] by representing their existence officially . . . A democracy extended to things? (12)

Science studies, in refusing any epistemic separation, or allowing purification only in the name of mediation, will then operate the levers of a legitimation that will illuminate the "positions at the common locus where roles, actions and abilities are distributed." Aesthesis and politics are thoroughly blended here: In the name of control, science studies will make the integrative gestures of early psychoanalysis return, shifting repressed memory/neurosis into language and signifier, artifactuals. But this move is much stronger than simply opening the "black boxes" of societal production-repression; it involves the use of science studies as a device of cultural recognition. Consider these hybrids: the addition of forty to fifty thousand new words to the English language each year; the proliferation of property law carried onto every event; the extraordinary ease with which ubiquitous video cameras micrologize surveillance; or the sheer use of the name "network" in an array of scholarly disciplines; each of these hybrids requires mediation, translation, according to WHNB, but a mediation that gives them a certain propriety. The neoanthropological discourse of WHNB is recoding the dialectic of recognition, the politics of control by naming treated as legitimation.

Convinced of the social harm that issues from the repression of such hybrids, the language of WHNB avoids the blistering, nihilistic aspects of the modern—exploitation as routine, cultural dumbing-down, built-in cynicism—and embraces the enthusiasm of recognition-giving; it risks turning science studies and, ultimately, cultural studies into a defensive effort of professional writing groups who aim at sealing the monsters/hybrids in names and descriptions that, in doing so, legitimizes their future (including their disappearance via the pathway of obsolescence). In the name of liberation, critical evaluations will manifestly not run the risk of being labeled dissident.[22] That is to say, the language of WHNB veers toward a dubious premodernism in which the dominant social offense is nonacceptance or, positively put, the demand for more competition over claims of legitimacy defines cultural analysis.[23] Has the "iron cage" of modernity as conceived by Weber become a confirmation of reproduction itself, critical endeavors reduced to blessings?[24]

What Made the Modern "Modern"

The damning facet of modernity is its relentless asymmetry, which WHNB locates in the binarism of mediation or translation and purification or separation between humans and nonhumans; mediation/translation, disclosed in the conjunction between Boyle's eyewitness, experimental science and Hobbes's protection of collective authority, has regularly expanded and produced countless hybrids that the work of purification is unable to acknowledge. To be modern is to insist on the separation between well-constituted practices. As a result, once their nonseparation is acknowledged, "we immediately stop being wholly modern."

The "parajudicial metaphor" of Boyle's eyewitnessed experiment, which guaranteed the impersonality of scientific production, complementary with Hobbes's negation of "immaterial spirits" that incited forces beyond civil society, allowed for a "social bond [that] comes from objects fabricated in laboratories; ideas have been replaced by practices, apodeictic reasoning by a controlled *doxa,* and universal agreement by groups of colleagues." Boyle's creation of a political discourse within science, the repeatable eyewitness experiment, and Hobbes's exclusion of experiments from informing the rules of civil society—"they are inventing our modern world"—are figured here as a generative, categorical machine:

> They are like a pair of Founding Fathers, acting in concert to promote one and the same innovation in political theory: the representation of nonhumans belongs to science, but science is not allowed to appeal to politics; the representation of citizens belongs to politics, but politics is not allowed to have any relation to the nonhumans produced and mobilized by science and technology . . . the two resources that we continue to use unthinkingly . . ." (28).

Restated, the claim is simply that politics did not and has not been able to account for and integrate scientific production, and that this political failure itself is one of the guarantees of scientific practice. Nonetheless, it is a perplexing formulation: If one asks whether this is true, one falls back into the modern separation in which an epistemic question is already an agency of purification and not mediation. But if it is believed, perplexity ensues: exactly where is the lack of mediation to be found? It more than stretches credibility to be told that mediation has been neutralized. It seems more appropriate to ask when mediation did not happen. An answer to this is that WHNB so dislikes modernist mediations that it cannot see them as anything but negative separation and purification. The forms of modern economics—from straw companies to monetary instruments to modes of industrial spying—are these not hybrids and are they not themselves mediations? What else has the American legal system done but mediate every conceivable social relation? In making the hybrids the "secret of the modern world"—continuous with the "total separation between nature-culture"—WHNB categorically confuses the constitution which it believes is a causal actant and repression, so that science studies can be featured as an act of liberation (and isn't this a return of modernism?).

Nonetheless, the structure that WHNB isolates as the constitution was able to "lock in all the possibilities." Real, discursive, and effective, it allowed for nature and culture to be alternative forces so long as they were separated; God was allowed to "arbitrate" but only as a "literal ideal." The "conjoined production" of these pairs—nature and culture in alternation, their separation, religion nearly a private affair—demonstrates the reach of the constitution and

> renders the work of mediation that assembles hybrids invisible, unthinkable,
> unpresentable . . . and here the beauty of the mechanism comes to light . . .
> the modern constitution allows the expanded proliferation of the hybrids
> whose existence, whose very possibility, it denies. (34)

How things are done is "invisible," in the sense that few of us understand the ins and outs of, say, an urban doctor's routine over six months; we do not see the range of information in relation to temporal markers (for instance, in a crisis). But the second half of this citation says the products are "denied." This has to be "true" for WHNB's assertions about the reality of hybrid-repression, but, as before, the evidence is slim: From talk shows to the deepest laboratories, from phone sex to conferencing, there is the argument of a logic different than that of production/repression, where hybrids are the social, all powerful, their liberation proceeding via a resistance that is collusive and a repression that is simulatory.[25] This linguistic quagmire is just ignored; readers are to accept the ubiquity of hybrid-repression.

Indeed, to that now classically aged question, why did Western modernism succeed within and without, the answer provided by WHNB's version of science studies is that the critical resources of purification have an answer for everything; the logic of modernism is found in the circulation of evasion: "They hold all the sources of power . . . but . . . displace them from case to case with such rapidity that they can never be caught redhanded" (39). They "hold," "displace," and are "uncatchable": here we are far away from Braudel citing the West's "need" for the world, a famous, if ambiguous, motivation; for WHNB describes a system in which the physics of social participation "burn out" those without the resources to compete. This is a model of "soft violence" that makes it impossible to distinguish modernist prescription from obedience and interdiction from powerlessness. The descriptive terms neutralize the difficulties of participation. Here, too, the initial mention of imbroglios is recoded: Separately created, responsibility for hybrids is shifted as often as possible from one concentrated center to another; the "game of modernity" is nothing less than "making a move" in anticipation of becoming obsolete, unnetworked, which is to say avoiding being deprived of the chance to make moves. Social competence is nothing but the capacity to scramble. The moderns were "not liars and cheaters" but they were and are skilled at making what they "hold" appear socially necessary and attractive. But as emphasis falls on the self-permission of the West to be "daring" in its separations and displacements, "redhandedness" is replaced by "capitalization," which neutralizes a reader's inquiry as to "hold" and "caught."[26]

Instead of plunging into an account of how the modernizers got away "redhanded" with sometimes murderous games, WHNB sidetracks the negative onto the psychological plateau: the moderns suffered from an inability to think consequentially; unlike the wise premoderns, the moderns are adolescents who "insure themselves by not thinking at all about the consequences of their innovations for the social order" (41). But we need not worry—they are passing away in the face of their unacknowledged hybrids that today befuddle their categorizations:

> the moderns allowed the practice of mediation to recombine all possible monsters without letting them have any effect on the social fabric, or even any contact with it. Bizarre as these monsters may be, they posed no problem because they did not exist publicly and because their monstrous consequences remained untraceable (42).

Today, Monsters R Us. One might say that the writing of this is itself monstrous. WHNB adheres so closely to the order-words of a sanitized ethnography of new elites—networking, mediation, undoing of repression—that the writing constantly threatens to lapse into a celebration of "wise" premoderns who "knew" about consequences (no excess there) set against the modern's reliance on purification, or what I earlier called epistemic suffering. The writing is blind to actual mediations, ranging from endless studies of breakdown to modern critical art history, which has vigorously analyzed and mediated the emergence of leisure and urbanization.[27] Once again, it is a case in which WHNB modernistically negates the mediations it disapproves of and then asserts that mediation has not occurred. As an active force, incessant overmediation is arguably more pertinent than this historicity of repression.

Science Studies and Historiography

The critical agenda of modernism, our "exoticism" of the conceptual— our distinctions, definitions, contrasts, and pairs of opposition, our unnecessary "quartering" of existents and occurrences—belongs to the

> tragedy of modern man considering himself as absolutely and irremediably different from all other humanities and all other naturalities. In the middle . . . everything . . . at the extremes . . . nothing except purified agencies that serve as constitutional guarantees for the whole (123).

Those "historical" patterns of hope and decline associated with German Idealism, the catastrophes projected by antimoderns, and the "postmoderns, always perverse, [who] accept the idea that the situation is indeed catastrophic, but [who] maintain that it is to be acclaimed rather than bemoaned," and whose style is "inimitable," will be excluded from anthropologically informed science studies: each validates a modernism in which "history" (including antihistory as well as *posthistoire*) always confirms a (Western) distinction and difference instead of adding value to the great "middle."

Indeed, thanks to the "daring foray of science studies into history," all of the problems posed by modernist historiography are also resolved or put to rest as problems that never ought to have happened. The separate critical resources, the elements of the modernist quadrant—naturalization, sociologization, autonomization of language, and deconstruction—have resulted in paralysis, since each pursues its own trajectory, furthering an unnecessary divergence of knowledge and reality; to get them to work together, we should begin by "retracing our steps," and the way to do this is to set aside the cultural bias of conceiving historicity as a conceptual irreversibility (of whatever version) and instead deploy a "historicity without history" (my phrase), associated here with "intensity" instead of chronology, and with an anthropology that is called upon to "remind us" that "the passage of time can be interpreted in several ways—as a cycle or as decadence, as a fall or as instability, as a return or as a continuous presence" (68).

WHNB engages this reversible historicity in order to make the objection to the belief that time "passes as if it were really abolishing the past behind it." Nothing has been left "behind," which converges on the prosopopeias of Appleby and Derrida in chapter one. Against the modernist notion of time separation—rupture, break, revolution, the disappearance of the past—"the past remains, therefore, and even returns," and so anachronism and reconstitution of the past, of pasts, are reabsorbed into nonseparation. Once this is sensed, old Chronos itself negated and taken back "in," as it were, notions of revolution cease to belong to cultural and intellectual "disappointment," since revolution is itself a fantasy of Western separation "in time." The "daring foray" of science studies will make irrelevant every mode of historical irony since we will not want to project error and confusion into the past (they did not know what they were doing) or persist in the belief in the future as the production of new separations (71). If there is no problematics of the past, then the question is how to utilize temporality and not reconstitute modernist biases of time separation.

Progress and decadence, two of the more obvious historisemes (or conceptual nuclei of cultural *doxa*), which have figured as important time forms in various modernist practices, are removed by the new ethnographic science studies. The "impression" of a "time that passes" (the past as it was soaked up in outcomes) was but itself a "restraining imposed on entities which would pertain to all sorts of times and possess all sorts of ontological statuses without this harsh disciplining" (72). This suggests time multiplicities blocked by modernism. In addition, Shapin and Schaffer's history of Hobbes, Boyle and the vacuum pump does not give a clean break with epistemology or society; the gradual success of forgetting this—or monumentalizing it as a radical break—is itself a kind of cultural hybrid, the function of which one-sidedly served the divisions of purification: "A whole supplementary work of sorting out, cleaning up and dividing up is required to obtain the impression of a modernization that goes in step with time" (72). With this extremely acute insight—into what one could call fantasies of historiography, the latter is at once refigured and dissolved; we can now see that it was always a cultural mediation serving purification, the convergence of irreversibility and transcendence, objectified results of human practices considered to have added something that cannot be taken away, and thought of as unleashing consequences believed to be unwithdrawable. This conjunction is what gave (or gives) historicism its cultural force (now = necessity). But the moderns achieved this to the negative credit of their larger tragedy. Historical discourse purified claimants as to their good ancestry = future rights; but the purification of lines from past to future must give way to a contemporary "hotchpotch," "whirlpools and rapids," and dispossess itself of belief in a "laminary flow" of linear historicity. This is, to my mind, the most brilliant part of WHNB, its undoing of destructive historicity, that capacity of historicist discourse to stage models of rationalization of the negative (for example, that German history starts anew after Hitler), as well as generate entirely illusive comparisons (for instance, that the "new Russia" is really Weimar of 1919).

Modernist temporality "forces us to shelve the totality of the human and the nonhuman third worlds" (third worlds = hybrids). The Kantian a priori time forms of succession and telos must themselves be deracinated in favor of "connections among entities" that have "provisional" time "results." This is supported by an excursus on the present as a "mixing up of times," but since this must not be considered a postmodern "collage," the present becomes a dreamtime, everyone now becoming "premodern again" or at least no longer belonging to the straightjacket of the modern. Anthropological totality may then be said to replace historical totality, a position guaranteed to irritate what is left of classically modern historiography, with its "rise of" and "fall of" emphases. "Getting out of history" (*pace* Levi-Strauss) means that there is no mode of necessity whatsoever for taking up "history" in the first place. It has been stripped of its time-coding functions.

But despite these insights, the actantial grammar of WHNB encodes processes and hybrids in the metaphor of a bride rejecting the false suitor of any historicist epistemology and relentlessly aestheticizes. For once the hybrids are recognized as intrinsic to our anthropological matrix, they are reimmersed within a language of unitary generalizations: instead of classifying the hybrids on the basis of their linearity, we are free to treat them as we would any existent "file," which amounts to a conjunction of aesthetics (here, clarity and order) and the power of study:

> We have always actively sorted out elements belonging to different times. We can still sort. It is the sorting that makes the times, not the times that make the sorting (76).

This psychologically functionalist universal is an absorptive cultural "logic" of WHNB and this negation of modern time differences (or identity) is itself further contained by reintegrating the work of purification within time reconceived as a different identity than that of historicism: to exist is itself to sort, and to sort is to study. And to study is to bring into existence more hybrids, which, in turn, requires more sorting, which in turn. . . . [28]

The temporality of knowledge of this "Copernican counterrevolution" that now matters is that which produces ethnographers who will practice symmetrical "retying," since their criterion of competence will be to "compare the . . . balance sheets when using mediators or intermediaries" (80). Historiography will disappear once science studies grants recognition and "ontological status" to what has been unnecessarily separated. Instead of "history" ruling from afar yet immanent, as a restored "queen of the humanities," as E. P. Thompson put it, the new ethnography will "refill" the "urns" of society and nature, and this is encoded as the very modernist revolution previously scorned: "The serfs [hybrids] have become free citizens once more" (81). In giving "Being" to all the hybrids, science studies will then close the separation, cross the divide, and return the West to its inseparable "networks," thereby rendering a "gift," a "pragmatogony" "documenting the nth loop in the spiral," and the West's own disavowed "permanent renewal" that "has never stopped evolving" will return to an irresistible unity: "We have never left the anthropological matrix—we are still in the Dark Ages or, if you prefer, we are still in the world's infancy" (85). Here, indeed, is breathless *posthistoire*. In this version of a wacky super-historicism, the fact that "it's our turn" to renarrate, to rework, to network is established on (the myth of) Relationism: every "branching, every alignment, every connection . . . [that] can be documented" warrants study, for "Ariadne's thread"

> would allow us to pass with continuity from the local to the global, from the human to the nonhuman. It is the thread of networks and practices and instruments, of documents and translations (121).

Thus, "Ariadne's thread" must also be conceived as the most perfect aesthesis of relations, what historicism suppressed.

Indeed, WHNB is unable to recognize that its epistemological suspension is carried out as intellectual regression to an aestheticizing identitarianism. For if relationism ends historicist divisions, it accomplishes this by a language that closes and blinds—each assertion is "morphed" to an aggressive enthusiasm so as to deliver an anti-intellectual strike against a reader's possible objections.

So instead of historicist periodization, the more quasi-objects are able to proliferate, the less charges of anachronism, archaism, and futurism can be sustained against ethnography. While conceding that this notion of a temporal "whirlpool" owes much to "postmodern theory," Latour misses no opportunity to ensure that his own discourse is not contaminated by postmodern language:

> As always, however, postmodernism is a symptom, not a solution . . . they are wrong to retain the framework and to keep on believing in the requirement of continual novelty that modernism demanded. . . . It is a long way from a

provocative quotation extracted out of a truly finished past [modernism] to
a reprise, repetition or revisiting of a past that has never disappeared (74).

The rejection of "continuous novelty" is performed here by a coding
straight out of naturalism—that to be "provocative" is to be antinatural (or
nonsynthetic), a rejection of linguistic de-identification, for science studies
here wants to name, and the postmodern strategy of unwinding names
must not be allowed to interfere.

Why Is Anthropology
Hostile to Deconstruction?

The mechanisms of displacement, category switching, and repression
would seem to warrant a cultural studies in which deconstruction had an
integral function, since these (modernist) mechanisms are as much linguistic forces as not. But deconstruction is lumped with "critical indignation" and WHNB proposes to do to it what historians such as Francois
Furet did to the historiography of the French Revolution: the "particular
rabies" of criticism requires intellectuals who will terminate this persistent
"accusing one another," which necessitates that deconstructive criticism
be recast from that of "a resource . . . [and] become . . . a topic, one competence among others, the grammar of our indignations."[29] Dropped into
a sociomoral category of an underived need for scapegoating, deconstruction is thereby merely a symptom to be studied. And since WHNB
wants to establish mediation as the antithesis of this "critical indignation,"
a move that will terminate the "staleness" of denunciation, the preferred
categories are those of "triage and selection," "arrangement, combination,
combinazione, combine, but also negotiation or compromise . . . a supple
morality more exigent," which arises from the "whirlwind of the mediators" and which eliminates the need for cultural criticism altogether. In
short, deconstruction is unable to provide a requisite knowledge-base for
anthropological reconstitution. A conservative political idealist could not
have said it better.

Postmodernism, standing in for deconstruction, comes in for special
scorn, here a melange of left and right objections: it is "a symptom," it
"lives under the constitution" but does not believe in its "guarantees," it
can only "prolong" critique, and rejects "all empirical work" in favor of extreme purification; a single 1992 text by Baudrillard is cited for these judgments. Postmodernism is negatively symmetrical with the modernist
rejection of continuism—its suspension of imaginary, alternative futures,
utopia, confirms the "disconnected instants and groundless denunciations"
of the present. And those postmodernists just don't study enough: as soon

as we grasp in detail the production of hybrids, we can achieve a "retro-spective attitude" in which neither a projected new era nor a revolution-ary past matters at all, and which operates within the present to "deploy" instead of unveiling, which "adds instead of subtracting, fraternizes instead of denouncing, sorts out instead of debunking . . . nonmodern (or amod-ern)" (47). Postmodernism (deconstruction) hasn't a chance in the face of this ecstatic rhetoric.

In this culture-scape, deconstruction only signifies an excess spawned by the modern, a proclivity for unnecessary agonistics; in filling in the an-thropologic matrix, a better dramatics of study is counseled, one belong-ing to a new "canon of the savant":

> Seen as networks . . . the modern world . . . permits scarcely anything more than small extensions of practices, slight accelerations in the circulation of knowledge, a tiny extension of societies, minuscule increases in the number of actors, small modifications of old beliefs . . . no longer . . . saga . . . of rad-ical rupture, fatal destiny" (48).

Where the discourse of enthusiasm turns study into a kind of revivalist sal-vation, the persistent downgrading of violence in the name of these "tiny networks" and their "minuscule" differences involves the very repression WHNB claims to reject. One wonders what the forced diaspora of dozens of millions round the world since World War II could mean to this gram-mar of a flattened world. This downscaling of objectivist differences is matched by the overscaling of the new objectives of study—"nonmodern worlds . . . as vast as China"—where "vast" is equated with the described (a rather inept comparison, since "vast = China" is of a piece [woven?] with adolescent fantasies), and enables science studies to present an "ac-commodation" of hybrids, this to "give them a place, a name, a home, a philosophy, an ontology and I hope, a new constitution" (51). Deconstruction cannot enter:

> With the postmoderns, the abandonment of the modern project is con-summated. I have not found words ugly enough to designate this intellec-tual movement . . . this intellectual immobility through which humans and nonhumans are left to drift (61).

A lone but provocative citation from Lyotard brings this eliminative judgment, disabling these "hyper-incommensurists," and the charge is identical to the left-right sing-song in which deconstruction is con-ceived as a simple destruction of representational systems. Representa-tion is that kind of social bond that requires "tension," and no intellectual practice that removes the "tension" in favor of an extreme—as in the construct of a *differend*—has any place in the knowledge unities of the future. That these judgments against deconstruction repeat the form of a modernism (that never happened) rejected for its divisive exclusions confirms the discourse's adherence to *ressentiment*.

Indeed, when we finally get to see how language is treated in WHNB things become even more bizarre. Language is declared to be a mediation of purification, and not the other way around, hence any interest in the specific autonomy of semiotics and language turns discourse away from its service as a "transparent intermediary" producing "contact" between words and things. Deconstructionists give us an impasse of language instead of promoting "to pass." Because of the "inimitable" writings of the postmodernists, "language has become a law unto itself, a law governing itself and its own world," assertions that repeat the reactionary projections of conservative academics. "Everything becomes sign" is said to lessen the "connections" between discourse and the "referent," which inexorably leads to "the point of autodissolution" (64). Here WHNB crosses into the territory of *Telling the Truth About History* (Nietzschean "bestiality"), unable to notice that if language cannot be reduced to nature (signifiers always motivated) and cannot be conclusively analyzed (rationalized, socialized), then more reflection on language is suggested. But too much reflection on language's various performativities dissolves its capacity to serve as an intermediary. It must remain a "median space," an "excellent tool chest" so as to "stitch" nature, collectives, and discourse together (64); "if these domains are kept separate, we remain terrorized by disconnection." But what if disconnection is one of the positive values of language itself? Or a strategy of extra-political knowledge? WHNB is unable to think such thoughts, no doubt because they evoke a skepticism that science studies have already negated.

As before, it is the postmodern "prostration" in which language is rejected as a "delicate shuttle" that will be written out of science studies; rejection will allow for the restoration to texts of the "social bond" denied them. "Access to the real" must not be blocked, and there must be closure to the interminableness of the linguistic question: "Are you not fed up with language games, and with the eternal skepticism of the deconstruction of meaning?" (90) Unaware that the question telegraphs a terroristic pre-answer—"of course we are"—science studies provides exactly the proper prescriptive utterance in order to forestall the plunge into an agonistics of discourse, saving the aesthetics of weaving. Nothing should prevent us from passing from language to totality, a claim at once archaic and metaphysical. "Are you not fed up" precludes any "immanent" foregrounding of skepticism toward discourse.[30]

Finally, WHNB effectuates a kind of spell toward any textual-artistic practice of the marginal. Where antimoderns (reactionaries) are unable to abandon history conceived of as "fright" (for instance, decline), it follows for WHNB that this is just one species of maintaining the extremity of thought and judgment. Defense of any marginal social act is considered here "somewhat ridiculous": "It is fine to want to defend the claims of the suffering body," but since there is no denying the "universality . . . of suffering everywhere," the defense of margins is itself "grotesque" (124). Science studies liberates the repressed as it represses "margins," the latter an affront to networking as such.

The Status of Counterknowledge:
Aesthetic Blindness

To absorb all the divisions and ruptures of epistemology, this improved science studies puts forward a principle of symmetry; the generalization of this principle places the new anthropologist "at the median point where he can follow the attribution of both human and nonhuman properties" (96). The only quality that matters is what "the networks explicate" (104) in and of themselves, this "central mechanism of all collectives." The concept of the network is the contemporary version of that "perfect fruit fly" Shapin and Schaffer found conjoined in Boyle and Hobbes. The concept *overmediates* and may well suppress relations as to how "networks" force and compel certain behavior, for example, making descriptions within academic "networks" such that one loses "credit" if one's interpretations are judged aberrant. Conditions of possibility are not made explicable if the network model is transcendental.[31]

Collectives of every kind are moved into the "middle" and all of them, of no place and every place in particular, are "similar, except for their size." But this counterknowledge or extra epistemology is presented in a language that is more possessive of identifications than the worst sorts of naive writings WHNB associates with modern criticism. The reliance upon simile, for instance that collectives are "like the successive helixes of a single spiral," the "single" an obvious synecdoche for "whole," refigures "network" and "mediation" as practices totalizing and hypersymbolic, and stand as purifications (exclusion, division, separation) in their own right. To insist that this all-encompassing "spiral" makes new "turns," that it "translates" current forms of "impetus," a model without "mirrors" (that is, absolute epistemic certainty), one has to believe that there "are no differences in nature—still less in culture" (109). This assertion of identity dissolves the difference between aesthetics and epistemology. To write "no difference" means we can safely assume no inadequation between language and meaning, event and result, since "no difference" operates the levers of a thought which aims to be enveloping or, in de Man's phraseology, "particularly seductive."[32] Nothing is separate: and this is part of the new "canon of the savant" where "translation is the very soul of the process of relating" (113). The cultural fantasy of this prefigurative relationism is that it must "serve as an organon for planetary negotiations over the relative universals that we are groping to construct" (114). Show me your pass, based on your powers of advancing some network, and you can belong (network = work in the net); no pass = no play. Translation now is equivalent to delivering a difference to an identity ("planetary negotiations"). Or difference will be tolerated so long as it is canceled out in the concentration of identities that matter.

As one might expect from this identitarian, utopic, resolving, and translating nexus, there is no limit to the language of synthesis. If we should be "fed up" with deconstruction and similar movements, then networks and collectives let us avoid the "disenchantment of the world" with its many frothy psychological pseudodramas—"mechanized proletarians," "victims of reductionism," "rationalists" and "materialists," "technological determinism," the "cold breath of the sciences." All these are dissipated once we recognize ourselves as not "radically different" from other collectives and conceive ourselves as a paradox straightened out. Indeed, our "massive cognitive or psychological explanations" for "equally massive effects" prevents noticing "small causes for large effects." "Small" is a substitute for the lack of difference, and is meant to produce an ecstatic rationality: "reason today has more in common with a cable television network than with Platonic ideas." Why call either "reason"? Against epistemology, "branchings, subscriptions and decodings" will make it impossible to get "excited about virtues they [Monsters R Us] are incapable of possessing" (rationalization), and one will then presumably get very excited in studying the mediations: "the extremes, once isolated, are no longer anything at all."

At this level of metadiscourse, WHNB obscures a discussion of violence in favor of entering the spell of how existing networks are somehow the same:

> What, for example, is the size of IBM, or the Red Army, or the French Ministry of Education, or the world market? To be sure, these are all actors [mediators] of great size, since they mobilize hundreds of thousands or even millions of agents (120).

Identity goes further: as these different constructions "mobilize" (the masses, voters, students, homeless) science studies must as well: the new academic mode of writing should "mobilize a great number of objects for their description." All that is, is resource—for us. Is this nonmodernism or the very epitome of positivism's capacity to reduce everything to a discursively registered fact?

Capitalism, in this context, is a "skein of somewhat longer networks that rather inadequately embrace a world on the basis of points that become centers of profit and calculation" (121). The violence of extracting profit from unpaid labor is inconceivable via the focus placed on capital's "inadequately" formed "skein." The rule is that when violence is raised, it is downscaled. Alfred Chandler's narrative of American business is asserted as "not the Organization described by Kafka. It is a braid of networks materialized in order slips and flow charts, local procedures and special arrangements which permit it to spread to an entire continent." We know that Kafka was not a good "networker." Two hundred years of industrial deaths should not shake us out of the belief that capital is merely a network, prosaic and nonviolent.

Performatively considered, then, as propositions whose force "express a mode of existence" (Deleuze), this counterknowledge claims to remove the category of violence as such, so one should not be surprised if metaphor and comparison run amuck. We need not fear any longer "domination by machines" because "machines are full of human beings who find their salvation there." Blood-test workers are "saved" by tearing open the same sterile packages hundreds of times per week and finding a vein to poke. What if "boredom" is an artifact or hybrid of socially induced impossibilities? WHNB renders it inconceivable to think that "high tech," as manifested in self-poisoning (for instance, steroid consumption) or processed foods, or incessant dumbing-down through television or computer related illnesses might be practices attached to an extensively coded violent social system. The counterknowledge offered—"science studies can demonstrate the permanence of the old anthropological matrix"—promotes that one embrace "tinkering, reshuffling, crossbreeding, and sorting . . . the fragile heterogeneous networks" (126).

This too aestheticizes: that infamous cultural figure, the handyman, can only have a future in becoming the new scholar, "retying" everything in its own "saving aphasia."[33]

If the counterknowledge to epistemology is thus to be institutionalized, WHNB performs this by an idealization of a particular contemporary actant, that of the "delegation," those hybrid subjects who can "pass in the sense of this term as used in ball games." Epistemic separator's must leave the field, for the "ball game" model promises cultural validity against modernist deficiencies: "The world of meaning and the world of being are one and the same world, that of translation, substitution, delegation, passing" (129). As it is in "baseball" and reminiscent of such older historiographical models such as J. H. Hexter's famous comparison of historical discourse to "following a game," also intended for that generation's refutation of criticism, WHNB presents the "delegation" so as to knock out the evils of naturalism and socialism. The former reduces the hybrid to a state of nature; the latter denies hybrid production due to ideological sclerosis. Both overpurify, making the hybrids invisible. Against both, science studies declares itself done with purification by making this most modern of practices finally subservient to the work of mediation. The objective:

> To maintain all the advantages of the moderns' dualism without its disadvantages—the clandestineness of the quasi-objects. To keep all the advantages of the premoderns' monism without tolerating its limits—the restricting of size through the lasting confusion of knowledge and power (134).

Production without repression joined to monism; this mixture activates knowledge production or eliminates any barrier to study while it simply leaves the production of objectivities to the existing players. Can you start your own army? Can you. . . . Indeed, WHNB does not merely affirm the non-separability of mobile objects and subjects, humans and nonhumans, but calls on science studies to prevent interference by concepts, institutions or practices with "the continuous deployment of collectives and their experimentation with hybrids [an interference which] will be deemed dangerous, harmful and—we may as well say it—immoral" (140). Which is exactly what every powerful player always wants to say: Hands off, we're in charge. Does one then read WHNB as a proposal for cultural analysis or as a political determination that removes criticism from production?

A "freedom . . . redefined as a capacity to sort . . . hybrids" might strike some readers as a colossal begging of the question: why should most of the members of a society accept the passivity and reactivity of "sorting" instead of determining how and what gets made in the first place? It is this confirmation of the corporate determinations of production that makes WHNB a double of the language of producers cast in the language of a better "study." Science and cultural studies here serve "needs" overcoded by deadly modes of production that cannot be discussed.

"The mediators have the whole space to themselves." Instead of this meaning agreement in making the hybrids official, as WHNB desires, it more ominously suggests the disappearance of critical writing and its replacement with those who "will talk" (of ozone holes, chemistry, voters) and "what does it matter, so long as they are all talking about the same thing?" Writing can live only if it becomes merely a "patch" (a function not different from Freud's mystic writing-pad) underlining the "shared practices" of the mediators. Isn't this the full force of the network in relation to critical writing: the latter is tolerated only if it promises to not interfere with production? Thus science studies confirms one of the oldest of human terrors: "isolates" (Mary Douglas), or critics, watch out. And it confirms that language is saturated in violence, for it indexes de Man's larger argument that aesthetic significations are inherently violent, this because they often appeal to "clarity and control," operations that force language to submit to ideology.[34]

In WHNB's application of science studies, all the "theoretical enigmas" pertaining to language are directly suppressed; science studies are plunged into the discursivity of enthusiasm such that they aggressively preclude any "residue of indetermination" (de Man) that might intrinsically belong to knowledge production or cultural analysis. Despite many of its brilliant insights into modern historicism and other social formations, WHNB makes its text yet another project in the mimesis of demand, of order-words—here science studies—and renders a model in the desire for satisfaction (synthesis), a model that suppresses intellectual skepticism. De Man's notion, that epistemic suppression requires the violence of language directed against epistemology, delivered by aesthetic formations of grammar and logic, seems confirmed.

Language and Intellectual Dissidence

The texts read in this chapter might well be conceived of as a continuation of idealist antiepistemology, endemic to humanistic discourse: these texts invoke discursive "frames" in which order-words abound, based upon a continuum between language and reference, which is also continuum between order-words and historicizing culture. The maintenance of such ideals drives the text's respective elimination of deconstruction. To conclude this chapter and coil back on the end of chapter one, the deconstructive arguments rejected by these texts are again raised in the context of an "excessive" reader, an engagement with issues of language as productive of a certain kind of discrepancy. This coiling is a way of amplifying a Nietzschean strategem, to contest the passive nihilism of these writings by comparing their idealizations and aggressions to a sense of discourse treated as *initiative*. An alternative to order-words, and specifically not a negation of them, "initiative" evokes transformation of syntactic equivalencies, an act of discourse that does not claim, as WHNB does, to settle the question of language's place in the construction of knowledge by returning language to a mode of transmission ("shuttle"). "Initiatives" are more like instances in which language comes into its own as provocation of excess thought, thought in excess.

Paul de Man's essay "Resistance to Theory" deploys the phrase "at the very moment when"; *The Rhetoric of Romanticism* states that "from the moment the subject thus asks, it has already foreclosed any alternative" [to answers which are not really answers]; and from another essay, one reads: "From the moment the narrator appears in the guise of a witness and recounts the events as a faithful imitation, it takes another witness to vouchsafe for the reliability of the first and we are caught at once."[35] The phrases beginning with "at" and "from" open onto syntactic ruptures of time; they indicate the sheer impositionality of meaning and figure as a model of the discontinuity between language and meaning, *abruptions* of time in that they direct a reader to the discourse itself. Instead of assuming the smooth connection between writing and object, these "timings" are of the moments of sense they bring into existence. Discourse thought of as an abruption, or discrepancy, or initiative, allows one, de Man emphasized, to consider the asymmetry between language and meaning:

> By allowing for the necessity of a nonphenomenal linguistics, one frees the discourse on literature from naive oppositions between fiction and reality, which are themselves an offspring of an uncritically mimetic conception of art. . . . It is not a priori certain that language functions according to principles which are those, or which are *like* those, of the phenomenal world. It is therefore not a priori certain that literature is a reliable source of information about anything but its own language.[36]

What is said of literature holds for prose. The texts of Geyer and Latour cannot be said to have made any "initiative" concerning language in either their positive models or in their reductions of deconstruction. The writings show the assumption of the very relation de Man calls into question: the presumption of identity between language and phenomena.

In *Blindness and Insight* (1971), de Man argued that contemporary society was permeated by an intractable "intersubjective demystification," criticism producing as many new mystifications as it claimed to have "cured." It could not be further argued whether demystification was "progress," "decline," or something else in which, as one prose piece has it, if we cannot decide whether to use grammar and logic to decide between literal and figural meanings, then how might we decide any contested problem?[37] The hypothesis connected with this "intersubjective demystification" forestalls a recuperating, even negative, synthesis. It asks: what is cultural judgment in the first place, since the productive rigor of culture (for instance, a complicating text) suspends determinations of judgment, active cultural works being things that can only complicate cognitive, aesthetic, and moral terms. To Adorno's suggestion that contemporary (that is, post-Final Solution) intellectual endeavors had no option but to state "the inevitability of fragmentation in a mode that is itself fragmented, [and thereby] one restores the aesthetic unity of manner and substance," de Man persisted in emphasizing that the attractiveness (negative aesthetic unity) of this self-consuming negative identity was a "discursive elegance" ever more desperate in "matching" its own mythology of the world.[38] Demystification involved a social order that was now using myth-critique to ferret out contradictions (for example, Marxist theory), but notoriously not applying this critique to the language of criticism. The production of linguistic terminologies—think of Greimas and Courtes' monumental *Semiotics and Language*—may well have helped displace significations of consciousness (believed to be in charge of interpretation) but may also have had an even more consequential effect, that of installing linguistic models that underwrote a realism self-seduced by metaphoric privilege, a myopia of aestheticizing language taken to the point at which one is convinced that a few master terms can hold the vast interminglings of language and everything not-language. What would happen if WHNB had conducted a critique of its use of the term "network"? It could not because discursive systems such as neohistoricism are devoted to fear of language.

In the midst of this contagious profusion, *Blindness and Insight* maintained a heretical sense of language as discrepant:

> in the impossibility of making the actual expression coincide with what has to be expressed, of making the actual sign coincide with what it signifies. It is the distinctive privilege of language to be able to hide meaning behind a misleading sign, as when we hide rage or hatred behind a smile.[39] But it is the distinctive curse of all language, as soon as any kind of interpersonal relation is involved, that it is forced to act this way. The simplest of wishes cannot express itself without hiding behind a screen of language that constitutes a world of intricate intersubjective relationships, all of them potentially inauthentic . . . the other is always free to make what he wants differ from what he says he wants . . . a built in discrepancy within the intersubjective relationship.[40]

These words attempt to model something uncontrollable in language: the "at once" of privilege and curse, the satisfaction of having words mean something at the same instant they also mean something out of the grasp of speaker and listener. By claiming that language as such cannot coincide with what it is not, an idea that is also a reminder that language is not identical to logical, figural, and grammatical wordedness, an affirmation of the impossible emerges as well as an interesting concept: it is conceivable that the uncontrollable is not only constituted by language, but that language is saturated by uncontrollability, an asymmetrical proposition that at least accounts for the textual existence of discrepancies between syntax and meaning. The impossible, the uncontrollable, the discrepant, the sublime would figure instances of a war within representation.

Thus, the rhetoric of crisis in both Geyer and Latour, in which "now is" the time of obsolescence or "out of kilter," far from representing the phenomenal world, serves to obscure the sense in which their own writings follow commands whose being is nothing but the forgetting of language. Neither text allows for any gap between signs and meanings: neohistoricism renders synthesis and understanding in one stroke, intolerant of a sense of language as an asymmetrical system. Such asymmetrical thinking does not allow for shortening the distance between sign and meaning, but of working the "between" and asking after what is found. Lots of signs may signal "crisis," but all of them might well signal the crisis of the language that declares there to be a crisis. To be told there is a crisis is to motivate without many questions asked; a sense of crisis supposes a symmetrical identity between language and critique—and thereby flees from a sense of the uncontrollability of language meaning. To allow for the uncontrollability of meaning is to allow for the upending of all ideological readings because this allowance plunges one right back into having to choose—what to reveal and impose in any act of language.[41] Such experiences belong to "excessive" readers. In relation to the texts criticized above, perhaps there is no more mystifying sense of language than in their use of "historical schemes" that cannot be fully stated without falling apart: such texts "retreat behind a historical scheme which, apocalyptic as it may sound, is basically reassuring and bland."[42]

None of these implications about relations between the represented and discrepancy as a character of discourse manifests "stoical irony," as the introduction to one of the most widely distributed essays of de Man's insists.[43] Edward Said has it that "critics like de Man . . . direct their attention to the impossibility of political and social responsibility," the accusation of immorality; Said further claims that de Man makes literature "superior" in relation to "historical scholarship," counseling "powerlessness" and "originality" in the interests of a criticism that "accedes to the realm of acceptable form." A de Manian "corrosive irony" is the result.[44] These are serious charges because they are directed at a concept of criticism willfully disengaged from healing, restoration, and memory of death (or projection of hope), one that understands that dismemberment of activities (thinking, feeling, willing) has already taken place and that "memberment" never occurred, that signs (figures) cannot serve as the means of providing synthetic reintegration.[45] One could also respond to Said by pointing out that his argument reenacts an untenability built into "historical scholarship." Once "history" is construed as subject of our linear, irreversible, periodizations, a phenomenology of limitless redescription or revisionism, it is said to anchor "responsible" and "worldly" criticism, but what is there to criticize once you have said that "responsible thinking" returns to history? Said's model would never allow a conception of history to emerge that was asymmetrical, discrepant, incapable of accounting for its own initial impositions of meaning. We learn nothing about "history" if it is always *like* what we say—only if "history" and its meanings are like *unlikeness* is there any chance for some disruption of what we already know, or think we do. Representation, according to de Man, hovers

> between a state of knowing and not-knowing, like the symptom of a disease which recurs at the precise moment that one remembers its absence. What is forgotten is absent in the mode of a possible delusion, which is another way of saying that it does not fit within a symmetrical structure of presence and absence.[46]

This citation offers "possible delusion" as a chance within meaning ("at the moment when"); delusions about meaning are an ordinary effect of language. In this citation, the terror of language is not banished or exiled but affirmed as an event—delusion happens because language happens. In relentlessly suggesting connections between cognition, morality and aesthetics, or in de Man's terminology, the epistemic, grammatical, and rhetorical, in emphasizing that the movement of meaning "is a wandering, an *errance,* a kind of permanent exile if you wish, but it is not really an exile, for there is no homeland, nothing from which one has been exiled," discursive "initiatives" cannot emerge as a "correlative of the figural pattern"; raising the stakes in making cultural arguments is difficult to coordinate with giving orders to time.[47] In summarizing de Man as "symbolist," as "formalist," as leaving the world "behind forever," Said reduces perplexities of language and thought to a demand for conjunction between history and what he calls the "situated," so that the "worldly essay" form is best because it is the most "historically aware," and "historically aware" because it is "close to" concrete reality.[48] One is thus guaranteed to avoid having to think of language's nonidentity to what it then represents.

Instead of the neohistoricist worry about intellectual obsolescence and loss of function, or WHNB's concern for the transcendence of "network," it is left to critical readings to intensify that "residue of indetermination" that ordinary reading commonly eliminates because of the requirement that reading deliver the "timely." So considered, reading would not be contained by figurations of the law—the classic form of rendering a determinate judgment—and would be affirmed and denied in the production of more disputes, a position not dissimilar to Lyotard's theory of a *differend. Allegories of Reading's* exhortation "to come closer to being as rigorous a reader as the author had to be in order to write the sentence in the first place" is the very antithesis of the desire for synthetic paraphrase, of reading as another performance of the referendum; reading is (ambiguously) a "form of work" (Barthes), more deferral perhaps than referral and assuredly neither of these while it is something else.

Alice Kaplan's reduction of Fascism to a concept of desire, presented in the introduction, negatively joined romanticism and deconstruction; such reductions, in K. H. Bohrer's formulation, render a strong image of a "falsely objectified tradition," the kind of meaning that intellectuals give in the name of symmetry or aestheticized epistemology. Reduction works against the proliferation of semiosis, and the reverse is true as well. In this vein, Jean-Jacques Lecercle, in *Philosophy Through the Looking Glass,* suggests that texts are always caught up in perplexity: "signs are too few for the naming of reality, meanings are too numerous for the precise and un-equivocal expression of the speaker's 'own' ideas."[49] Meaning outstrips signs; we do not suffer from lack of meaning, for there is always proliferation. If so, then the sorts of writings I have called neohistoricist issue order-words as a denial of their incommensurability with excessive meanings, forcing language into functions of integration: both Geyer and Latour give us models of recognition (fear of the troglodyte, giving names to hybrids), a refusal to conceive the present as asymmetrical with the historical models we have inherited. If discrepancies, differends, and asymmetries are the starting point of "initiatives," then one has already imagined the element of terror when neohistoricization refuses names (for example, Geyer allows only two process terms, syncretism and creolization, one positive, one neg-ative) and prevents language from proliferation, even if coming on the scene to rename, as WHNB does. Neohistoricism wants to hear nothing of its own terror; it wants to maintain a hegemony of recoding, "the sign-function that reduces ambivalence and the symbolic."[50]

Chapter Three ◈

Neopsychoanalysis
and Cultural Nihilism

Psychoanalysis . . . produces and reproduces the unconscious as its institutional sub-
stance . . . the discourse of the unconscious becomes unfindable . . . the unconscious
programmed on demand . . . libidinal hyperrealism.

—Jean Baudrillard, *Simulations*

After Freud arrived in England, his collection of statues was given up to him by the Nazis, and he is said to have uttered a "Heil Hitler," in thanks for this restoration. Ironic, to be sure, but is there any moment in the history of psychoanalysis in which the negative was not turned into "capital"? Too harsh? This harshness is part of the heritage of psychoanalysis, what we could call its proximity to death. Freud showed his love of things perhaps only because of their immersion in death? It is by now a well-known story, this movement from instinct-death to language-death: from Freud to Lacan the line of continuation (succession) moves from naturalism, where the mental/linguistic apparatus is continuous with biology, to signification, which delivers the psyche to language, the latter figured forth as a mode of self-castration.

In this chapter, focus is directed to the order-words and cultural histo-riography of neopsychoanalysis in relation to the Lacanian repossession of the subject, today rendered as "in lack," "in failure," figures of the cultural politics of nihilism, affirmation of nothingness. After considering this model, the fusion of this negative idealism in curatorial discourse is taken up, examining why curators insist that an artist can culturally present the destructive aspects of what is called the "American Psyche." Following that analysis, Judith Butler's critique of neopsychoanalysis is read as a resistance to neopsychoanalysis, a resistance based on her use of the construct *re,* a reworking of an idealist cul-de-sac. The neopsychoanalytic modeling of "lack" as an ontological condition, "failure" as subjective destiny, and re-coding are brought together, as it were, in closing with Fredric Jameson's recent (1993) insistence that cultural studies as such cannot sever its deter-mination by religion. His essay ties psychoanalysis, cultural studies, and the theological in a conceptual nucleus of retreat from the promise of cultural politics, attempts to make a difference in the academic arrangement of knowledge, and that has now collapsed into academic squabbling and back-biting.

These readings are intended to bring out the incantations or word spells of language involved in this jumbling together of *re,* culture, language. If, in the previous chapters, focus was on historiography as willed order-words, here the emphasis is on neopsychoanalysis and cultural studies and models of subjectivity that have become automatic, or "intuitively true." A further line of analysis emphasizes that neopsychoanalysis seems to have an attraction for passive nihilistic culture; it accepts the disappearance of ac-tive culture, or ways in which groups generate what Greimas and Fontanille call "connotative taxonomies" that begin as practices, even de-vices, by which groups *realize* their existential simulacra of roles and norms,[1] such positive simulacra seen in the example in which Filipinas "take over" downtown Hong Kong on Sundays, impervious to Chinese "superiorism," and produce active memory, active resistance, active evalu-ations of themselves. In short, neopsychoanalysis is the way contemporary subjectivity is affirmed as nihilism—the disappearance of groups that make differences from nihilism.

The Lacanian Model

In his *Deconstructive Criticism* (1983), Leitch notes that contemporary psy-choanalysis has become structuralist and it was the writings of Lacan that "fathered a contemporary psychoanalysis, all the while seeming more and more to be a second Adam for semiology."[2] To place Lacan as the (neo) Fa-ther is mimetic and delirious, since this language uses the model of Oedi-pus to install Oedipus. What this "father" brings is the (old) iron law of terror given a semiotic gloss: to signify or articulate is "inserted" in castra-tion, and to speak as such presences a cutoff from ourselves, our experi-ences, the subject a subject of absence and lack. The castration fear is transmuted into saying that it is signification that castrates, a belief that in the very act of using language, one is ontologically separated from what is "real." To speak is to self-castrate. According to this model, we spend our life with language in trying to make it register what we have lost, which in the older idiom of Mauss and Freud evoked sacrifice and gift. In this appropriation of the universality of infant loss and subjection to castration, culture is turned into a place of pure symptoms, an Imaginary where psychoanalytic semiology closes back by invoking a religious or sacerdotal essence. For in this Imaginary there is only negative fulfillment, articulated by Zizek when it is insisted that

> . . . what appears in and to our experience . . . as the "otherness" of the object irreducible to the subject's notional framework, impenetrable to it, is always-already the fetishistic, "reified" (mis)perception of an inconsistency . . . the subject is that very "nothing," the purely formal void which is left over after the substantial content has wholly "passed over" into its predicates-determinations.[3]

Could one ask for a tighter series of "orders"? What appears to anyone, anytime, is already in the mode of fetish. To experience is to fetishize. This citation gives a little Derrida (the "always-ready" mantra), a little theology ("passed over"), a little existentialism of the Sartrean variety ("nothing"), a lot of Hegel—all across—and a negative synecdoche, the subject who is "left over," which makes the "subject" no threat to anything, a mere functionary for the display of fetishes. To see = to distort, to think = to fetishize, equations that are indistinguishable from theology (the identity of desire and evil) as such. How could such a model take cultural conflict seriously—that is, not "know in advance" that cultural work could not be anything more than a working-out of this "nothing," affirmed here as the "essence" of experience?

Now let us get closer to the conceptual glue of the Lacanian system, to its orders. In *The Subject of Semiotics,* Kaja Silverman gives a clear sense of what is involved in sustaining the Lacanian model. While semiotics goes back to Plato and Aristotle, it "achieved maturity only when it was consolidated with psychoanalysis . . . effected by Jacques Lacan."[4] How can this Whig interpretation of theory be supported? Silverman's objective is to modernize psychoanalysis, to save it from obsolescence. After acknowledging the difficulties involved (for example, the fact that Lacan's writings are contradictory, even oxymoronic), she goes ahead and presents "those parts of it which have proved assimilable to a broader psychoanalytic theory."[5] Lacanian theory has been established; therefore its value and importance are available. The being of the subject is the irreducible matter. Silverman insists that the subject "is dominated by the desire to recover its missing complement," a sense of wholeness universally longed for because lost, and, isomorphically, this "recovery" is powered by the initial sexual division that drives each of us into our biological determinants.

Taken together, loss, wholeness, and reduction can be made good, as it were, only by heterosexual success.[6] The first loss, what can be called its full presence (oxymoronic form), is identical with the act of birth: physiology imposes negation and lack, since the infant cannot be both male and female or feel whole, a lack that occurs "outside of signification"— that is, a universal event that is "real" regardless of how it becomes significant. The historical contentiousness surrounding the factors of nature and culture in making subjectivity are downcoded, since it is held that these categories presuppose the ontological significance of lack as the most fundamental category. It is important to stress, which Silverman does not, that a sense of loss or lack is attributed to the child just because biological division occurs. The model has an occult or phantasmic quality about it. Indeed, here is how Lacan puts it: After "lack" is discovered, we can assume that it "is real because it relates to something real, namely, that the living being, by being subject to sex, has fallen under the blow of individual death." One is/is not oneself in being "sexed," and sex and death are immediately joined—it is division, a death function, that accounts for severed lives, a disjunctive conjunction of the Platonic type, since the sexual dividing (male/female) is said to have no rival claimant in the production of subjectivity.

The "lack of wholeness" is complemented by a second lack, one that is directly cultural. This is conceived by the new theory as a territorialization of the infant's body, the "human omelette" becoming neatly partitioned as to its body parts, "the orchestration of the drives around sexual difference." Silverman calls this "culture's genital economy" and it determines the subject who, deprived of metamorphosis (what sexual identity *does*—the subject under the hammer of identity or lack thereof), enters the zone of the symbol. Here what matters are the series of "*petit objets a,*" or those objects "not clearly distinguished from the self and which are not fully grasped as other." These objects are already symbols continuous with a generalized "lack of being" (of the subject) and arise with subjects who have internalized themselves as this "lack." All of this is crystallized as an objective Imaginary, the subject giving itself an image of its identity because of a "hole" in its being, all such images being the procedure through which one misleads oneself, since internal self-recognition is based upon external appropriation of objects that are already narcissistically "chosen." The logic involved is of a piece with what Ernst Gellner once called the mixing of the "cozily human" (desire) and impersonal explanatory structures (theory of lack), a combination of behaviorism, humanism, and scientism.[7] Behaviorism adds the ingredient of an "internal" association, humanism the ingredient of self-recognition, and scientism the ingredient of "finding" an impersonal mechanism. Thomas Pavel has noted, incidentally, the intellectual heritage of this thinking, this "speculative Structuralism," in seventeenth-century pedantry.[8]

The subject gives itself a coherence that it lacks, an Ego-Ideal, and here too Lacan embeds this in negativity:

> This jubilant assumption of his specular image by the child at the *infans* stage, still sunk in his motor incapacity and nursling dependence . . . would have to be called the Ideal-I."[9]

The phrases "sunk in" and "incapacity" emphasize that all such "chosen" objects (*petit a*), especially those "reflecting" oneself as whole, are determined by an obsession with reducing an inchoative sense of the negative, achieving an attachment to something lost or lacking. Zizek gives exemplary nihilistic value to this Imaginary of ideals in a succinct and elegantly satisfying manner:

> These are the two basic fantasies: one is that the Other wants to steal from us our precious enjoyment. . . . The other idea . . . that the Other possesses some kind of excessive and strange enjoyment, which is in itself a threat to us.[10]

Zizek has it that this "fantasy background" explains the "real," but it can also be read as an encoding of *ressentiment,* here elevated to a metaphysics of cultural production: Envy and loathing are the "natural condition" of unnatural socialities. The Other is encoded in the discourse of metaphysical nihilism, the "logic" of the double negative: the Other threatens my enjoyment, I am threatening to the Other, hence I = Other, the Other = I, the doubling a tautology of the underlying identity.

When we turn to the category of the symbolic, which has been notoriously conceived as indifferent to the real but to which every subject submits (to speak = to die), things get strange. It is conceived of as a positive/negative reality so total that it constitutes "the share of his destiny . . . where the Word absolves his being or condemns it." To speak is to die in a way that allows one the illusion of having selected the means of dying (just as a subject's fetishes are a way of covering and masking, diverting yet repeating the being of "lack"). This separation of representation from the real, since linguistic signifiers only hold in culturally mediated systems, turns into its opposite: absolute representation. As Silverman writes, once the subject engages in symbolization, it has no contact with its feeling states or with the real, hence only with the symbolizations it is capable of providing to itself and to others (subject to their own imaginary fetishes). The symbolic Order is invoked as a "linguistic structure which does not in any way address its [subject's] being, but which determines its entire cultural existence."[11] The language one speaks does not connect with oneself, except as self is already competent to "hear" what the symbolic makes. The unconscious is already a full-blown colony of identifications, exclusions, and compressions of social language, in which the equations, identities, and disaffection of the social are reproduced as subjectivity. Is this a *metaphysical behaviorism?* Is this sense of self not a prison-house of language, in which the referential function always addresses what everyone shares as lack, lost, missing, absence? Cut off from need and drives, the subject falls under the power of an interpretation, like the allegory or story of the "fort/da" episode, a "signifying transaction," and once the self *speaks,* articulating itself on the identity of a separation—"Mommy is gone/I am here"—the act, as Silverman notes, ushers in "conceptual" and "signifying alliance[s]" such that the subject is subjected to endless substitutions of an unconscious type in which multiple "self-losses" are inscribed and reinscribed. This is a model of language/subject in which meaning enters with the loss of the real, all meanings assigned a value by reference to the symbolic (word to word). Desire as such is cut off from any physical or material source, dependent upon the symbolic (language) insofar as it is and would be significant. As Lacan puts it, "desire is the desire of the Other . . . produced as it is by an animal at the mercy of language."[12] What is unthinkable here is that this is a political interpretation turned into a metaphysics of the subject, that psychoanalysis might be a political demand (you are castrated!) and not an explanation of what ails subjectivity.

The Oedipal schema, which is just shorthand for universal subjective failure, satisfies the condition of serving as a mode of exchange and oversees the regulations of the signifier. As J. J. Goux emphasizes, signs are already meaningful translations according to the schema of an equivalence between the phallus and linguistic value. Signs can signify only if one signifier—the phallus—is their measure, serving as the general equivalent "for objects of drive." That is, the selections and choices made—energies spinning on ones *petit objets a*—are the "first substitutes." "The value of the lost object [for example, mother's breast] is expressed in the body of the object replacing it."[13] Language could only signify the second, the third, substitution for substitution, ad infinitum, rendered tolerable because what supports substitution—what we all seek to become—is the promise of the phallus, power and satisfaction. The phallus centralizes, concentrates, and distributes, but, as measure, cannot itself be said to ever actually appear. *The phallus is in no way different from language as such.* Language and phallus belong to same Platonic space, being then the conditions of representability.

The closed logic of neopsychoanalysis therefore rests on an immobilization of language, which can register only vicarious desires. The overall spell of language is to reconfirm the persistent failure of subjectivity to escape from the prison of the imaginary and symbolic axis. Universal nothingness lies at the "center" of meaning, for such emptiness, the missing, the lack, the absences are themselves "the" meaning of the human in struggle; language is turned into a purification so severe that any desymbolization is outlawed (you must have an image of what you negate; you must be ready to negate what is *indifferent* to your highly charged negations). Lacan insists that language is both the incessant destruction of any subject and the only means whereby any subject can be momentarily put together:

> The unconscious is that chapter of my history that is marked by a blank or occupied by a falsehood: it is the censored chapter. But the truth can be rediscovered; usually it has already been written down elsewhere. Namely— in monuments: this is my body . . . hysterical nucleus . . . symptom . . . reveals the structure of a language, and is deciphered like an inscription which, once recovered, can without serious loss be destroyed;—in archival documents: these are my childhood memories, just as impenetrable as are such documents when I do not know their provenance;—in semantic evolution: this corresponds to the stock of words and acceptations of my own particular vocabulary, as it does to my style of life and to my character;—in traditions, too, and even in the legends which, in a heroicized form, bear my history;—and, lastly, in the traces that are inevitably preserved by the distortions necessitated by the linking of the adulterated chapter to the chapters surrounding it, and whose meaning will be re-established by my exegesis.[14]

The body as monument, the archive-document, semantics, traditions, legends, and traces: every subject is stretched between language as symbolic castration and language as the only medium of restoration to the subject of this loss of autonomy. This passage provides for the *recovery* of loss, this because of an underlying identity of language with language as phallus: subjectivity is "already written down." Exegesis, a theologization of the negative, is the only "saving" moment in this system. Only from exegesis is there "meaning"—for lack is already nested in the symbolic domain, which gives the subject an irresistible *return* to itself as language. Why? Because the theory posits the subject as contradiction only in the absorbing dogma of repetition already affirmed. As one critic has noticed, this model makes phallicized language the norm of language on the model of money as the norm of all products.[15] Language is coded once as castration and once as recovery of castration, stabilizing the space between, the voided subject itself a zero-sum game with language. One can ask: does this model reflect neopsychoanalysis involved with a capitalism riddled by the contortions of debt management instead of a capitalism based on growth and expansion of "real production"? Or does the model suppose there is no growth at all, simply the permutations of the existing "stock" of capital (symbols, signs), where nothing is more "real" than the return of the "truth" of castration? Baudrillard has called this an ethnographic perfection, a "vengeance of the dead," for no one makes anything but what two terms—to lack, to symbolize—allow; given enough intertextual psychoanalytic descriptions, the spiral of censorship made, then lifted, then remade suggests an abstract plane that is subjectivity as recoding itself, another aspect of metaphysical behaviorism.

To summarize: The symbolic comprises those powers enjoyed by subjects who identify with and perpetuate what little "potency" accrues to the acceptances of "to lack." This too is convergent with a "vampiric" mode of capital (Deleuze), in which "feeding the lack" is judged to be publicly more important than out-producing it. Runaway phallicization has its cultural side in passive nihilism—the stock of negativity increases faster than the subject's creation of experimental decodings. The phrase "cultural genital economy" is just this ongoing perpetuation of the phallic in the guise of a constant recoding of the symbolic, so that the human Imaginary stays in bounds, especially within the twists of the "out of bounds." Interestingly, this represents a breakdown between the categories of economy and culture, since they "bleed" into the other at strategic points—a male subject "mortgages" his "real penis" for symbolic privileges (for example, in the imposed "politeness" of, say, academic inbreeding, where "politeness" operates as a break-point, and where "weak" discourse prevails in a general terror of "offending"). Alienated from reality and integrated via the symbol, the male subject (who is the model for any possible subject-position) is repressed and representative, whereas the female subject is allowed as censored and free floating. The symbolic privileges that depend upon the "mortgaged penis" are, in whatever twist of combination, simultaneously the actual power to castrate Others, inflicting repetitions of the infinity of to-castrate (reducible to: men = everyone = a prick, compressible to pure stereotype—"everyone is a prick," a recoding of religion's "everyone sins"). All social arrangements are assumed to follow the trajectory of impotency = need for the symbol = exegetical commands for comprehension. This certainly describes the *position* of the professional classes in terms of attraction and repulsion between subjectivity and maintenance of a "cool" image.

It is a critical notion of this model that language as discourse is discontinuous with the real, but the insistence that this break cannot be resisted without sliding into psychosis turns a discontinuity into an ontological separation. It remakes art, poetry, and criticism into discourses in which the "real" can be salvaged as privileged zones of exegetical restoration, which turns these practices back into souvenirs of failure.

Worse, once metaphysical lack invades language, speakers reiterate what will be acceptable by an Other, and no one can say anything not effected by the Others, which models intersubjectivity as conditioned by fear: to slip out of symbolizing language is to disclose what can be used against you, the very fetishes which make you "you." To speak is to fetishize, and to speak to this is suicidal—except as art. In this sense, the Lacanian model eliminates difference between language and the social, the law, the lack, the symbolic. Language is the "original prick" and must be phallic since it is made to cut—it castrates, it excludes, it eliminates.[16] Only one's acquiescence to the language of Others precludes one from going mad. Cultural ideals keep us from going mad as well. As Silverman notes, the "continuity of lack"—a genuine temporal oxymoron—rules the connections between being and meaning, imaginary and symbolic, self and other. "Continuity in lack" is pure order word. Cultural production is rendered secure: The slaves (everyone) recognize themselves in giving symbolic models of why failure is the common heritage of the subject. Again, the concept of the subject follows directly from the model of language: neopsychoanalytic discourse employs exclusive disjunctions (to speak = to cut) and cannot factor in "inclusive, nonrestrictive disjunctions" except as psychosis. The linguistic dice are loaded for a bad game when to speak comes to mean to segregate (desire from reality).[17] Neopsychoanalysis actively represses *public* as anything but doom.

Before moving on to how this model plays itself out in analysis of popular culture and art, it might be worth noting some of the objections Lyotard and Deleuze and Guattari have made to this model. Lyotard has drawn attention to the notion that dream-work is not comparable to "the operations of speech."[18] Dreams are not ruled by perceptual space, and metaphor and metonymy, as the basic figures of language, do not necessarily allow either the dream or an interpretation of one to be anchored in language. Language and dreaming are different materials, no matter how embedded they are in each other. It is an illusion to believe in the equation that the unconscious = language. Hence, Lacan's intervention in the Saussurian model, Lyotard notes, is archaic in extending the notion of analogical reasoning and systematically misleading about both language and the unconscious. In emphasizing, for example, metaphor as an authorized substitution and in that reestablishing nonconscious thought in its "truth" as substitution, metaphor is stripped of any critical element. In citing Victor Hugo's line, "His sheaf was neither miserly nor spiteful" as an instance of metaphor and "one word for another," Lacan restores the continuous desire of paternity, the "burgeoning of fecundity," metaphor installing what the symbolic order promises. The "sheaf" and "paternity" equivalence evokes a symbolic truth as it effaces Hugo's own description of the "sheaf," which "knows neither our reserve nor our rejections."[19] The example Lacan gives of metaphor is not a metaphor; Lacan makes a reduction of a surplus of the signifier, disarming poetic language. Lyotard reads Hugo's line as an instance of narrative predication, the "paternal" as a condition of subjectivity to be sure, but not a disclosure, as Lacan has it, of the "mystery of the father." As Lyotard comments, *"La nuit tome"* (night is falling) signifies (to the French), it has a certain transparency, various suggestions, but the turning of the phrase into a symbolic entity amounts to the imposition of a "good form." Is Lyotard correct in saying that the restoration of the symbolic establishes the theorist's *potency?* "When Lacan says: to love is to give what one has not, he means: to forget that one is castrated."[20] Lacan's model assumes subjects want to symbolize (mean) castration, that they want to turn partial objects and (dis)connections into something the Other identifies with. In making each subject a repetition of this "cut-off," the separation of language and desire ushers in self-symbolization (the split subject), the subject made equivalent to castration. The law of castration is the implicit presupposition of Lacan's reading, and it installs, with its demand to symbolize, a politics of the subject. In short, as Lyotard suggests, the Lacanian model has made a fatal error of mistaking language for castration, of assuming their ontological equivalence.

From another perspective, Deleuze and Guattari have a number of references and comments on this model. In the collection published as *politique et psychanalyse* (1977), they have this to say about their notion of desire and its difference from psychoanalysis:

> Desire is the system of asignifying signs across which one produces the unconscious flux in a social, historical field . . . Desire is revolutionary because it always wants more connections. . . . Desire expresses itself as an IT, the "it" of an event, the indefinite and infinitive proper name . . . it does not represent a subject, but diagrams an agency, not overcoded by enunciations.[21]

In these statements, Deleuze and Guattari emphasize that "desire" does not refer to sexuality or subjectivity but to agency, collective and social forces that create all sorts of devices and instruments so as to make immanent or inclusive connections. The famous "subject of enunciation" (who speaks) is a confirmation of oversocialization, "desire" merged with recognitions ("It was my problem"). Deleuze and Guattari ask us to consider symptoms and signifiers not as opening onto a theory of the subject's desire but to treat desire from the perspective of its effects, as produced, at work, a dissolution of our Apollonian and Dionysian constructs of desire. Desire is not about the symbolic apparatus, the world of appearances in which subjects know what things *look like;* desire, as concept now, makes sense only when the maximum number of differences are assembled so as to produce more stimulants to more productions, desire for Eternal Return. Faciality is perhaps so deeply embedded in visual and linguistic elements that it operates automatically in a symbolic way, but this symbolic system also can be said to *ruin* desire: To say that a woman has the face of an "angel" or the cunning of a "black widow" is a way of tying up that woman, returning her and ourselves to the satisfaction of a completing recognition. The Lacanian model forecloses initiatives of desire and, in that way, creates the territory of recognitions. As *A Thousand Plateaus* puts it, the equation of desire and unconscious, or subject and symbolic, is from the start a political program:

> The ultimate signified is therefore the signifier itself, in its redundancy. . . . The discovery of the psychoanalytic-priests . . . was that interpretation had to be subordinated to *signifiance,* to the point that the signifier would impart no signified without the signified reimparting signifier in its turn . . . this pure formal redundancy of the signifier . . . [has] its own substance of expression . . . *faciality* . . . the icon proper to the signifying regime, the reterritorialization internal to the system.[22]

In this sense, the Lacanian system delivers an ecstasy of passive nihilism. In charge of the symbolizing process, it repeats sacerdotalism's model of an internal world defeated by itself in advance, sinful to be sure, installing the concept of the subject as ever deciphering what other people think, overcoding recognitions (symbols, faces) of the symbolism of castration, the normal subject in terror.

Neopsychoanalytic Language and Popular Culture

Slavoj Zizek brings the "sublime theoretical motifs of J. Lacan together with exemplary cases of contemporary mass culture." The conjunction of "theoretical" writings and "mass culture," or mixing "high" and "low," promises to use the concept of montage as a model of analysis per se.[23] "Lacan with" further involves "reading" the established norms through their perversions, Kant by way of Sade, and then, in an aside, Zizek asserts that if "great authors," save Lacan, are mentioned, the reader can rest assured that "they are read strictly as kitsch authors." The writing has a smirk on its page. While the conjunction between Kant and Sade and "kitsch" is sure to chagrin purists, the syntax is what matters: It effectively seals Lacan off from being read as a "kitsch" author. Zizek gleefully enjoys what he calls this "introduction to Lacanian 'dogmatics'" as it "mercilessly exploits popular culture," an operation that will bypass the usual "straightforward academic look" at Lacanian writings. The moment of kitsch may establish a humor of *ressentiment* by professing "dogmatics" and of being "merciless" in exploiting popular culture, but why not turn this back on Lacan and read Lacan and the psychoanalytic enterprise that way? Kitsch is a welcoming of "insensibility, vicarious experience and faked sensations,"[24] and Lacanian theory is to be understood as the "truth" of "mass culture," "an excuse for indulging in the idiotic enjoyment of popular culture," where "Lacan himself is used to legitimize the delirious race from Hitchcock's *Vertigo* to King's *Pet Semetary.*"[25] The set-up of *Looking Awry* emphasizes the "inherent paradoxes" of cinema and subject, democracy and fetishes, of bringing together "high" and "low," shimmering in the ambience of kitsch. Art should be used to "read" art.

The impetus here is to bring the law of castration in the form of the Hegelian master/slave to bear on "popular culture." This theory comes to mass culture by way of paradox, the master/slave dialectic offered as the best way to present the theoretical stakes of popular culture. Theoretical discussion is set to the task of *staging* subjective attitudes, whereby "the very subjective position of enunciation undermines its 'enunciated,' its positive contents." If we "stage" the subject as the subject produces an effect of failure, of misguided knowledge, of errors cast in the mode of light, such self-contradictions should be considered the "truth" of the real: for the real is nothing but paradox. A citation from Hegel eternalizes paradox as the very form of the real and any subject in denial of paradox falls under parody, which includes any subject's mystified belief in an escape from paradox. Not-belief in paradox is fatal, and each and every of the subject's "hidden inconsistencies" must be made visible, every instance disclosed where there are gaps of subjectivity, since the subject is cunning even in its inadvertent parody. The "exhibition" of subjective undermining comes forward as surgery *on* desire's own excess (not-belief in paradox), a model of cleansing desire of reality, of making a new code of the slave mentality, here imagined as the analyst active in never letting any "evidence" go by. Everything symbolizes—there are no processes or events underway outside the law of paradox. Zizek tells us that subjective undermining (for instance, Kafka's devastating critique of Statism as he subjectively exercised his body into a "Jewish muscle") is always something "fecund," the organic or the continuousness of a "nature" in which something entirely unnatural, the subject's "enunciations," are embodied. The aggression of the analyst, figured here as surveillance of desire's excess or refusal of paradox, appropriates the "organic" in which it is natural that self-contradiction be the state of things, just as it is natural that subject's deny the truth of paradox. Sin drives the "logic" here.

This insistence on the "fecund" paradox, through naturalism and organicism, leads to all sorts of metaphysically imposed commands. J. Milner's argument that ancient writing is replete with literary modes of "dreaming," an uncontestable fact, is made to yield a highly dubious parallelism between dreaming, writing, and logical equivalence. The narration in which Hector cannot escape Achilles and Achilles cannot surpass Hector is transposed to the drama of the subject. Homer's story is said to have been written "as in a dream," which not only reduces literature to fantasy but also to an "organic" truism of the human: "What we have here is thus the relation of the subject to the object experienced by every one of us in a dream . . . the dream paradox . . . the inaccessibility of the object." [26] As it is in the literary manifestation of the dream, so it is in reality; the Homerian text registers that the subject Achilles = any subject, and his nemesis Hector = any object, which "proves" a metaphysical certainty: "the object-cause of its desire . . . can never be attained." How is this so? Because the notion of a "gap" between signifier and signified is assumed to be a law of all relations. Desire's failure to attain its object involves that initial gap within desire treated as signification, the latter reprojected as the schema of failure between subjects, which always "succeeds." Gap and void are not made—they just "are." "The object-cause is always missed; all we can do is encircle it." Notice that this expression of the paradox of subjectivity is not a paradox: it gives a "fact" ("always missed") and result (the repetition given by "all"). From a critical perspective, the "always" should be read as a cultural code, that of cognitive satisfaction—if we are left with the perpetuity of to "encircle," then the subject is given all that it can hope for: repetition of failure, the chance to repeat. The literary citation and the system of logic are fused in this cultural timing, which should be read as an order-word serving the despotic "god" of repetition. Or repetition has become God.

Another paradox, from *The Odyssey,* has the same counterforce: All demands from others signify that the "object in question functions as an index of a network of intersubjective relations. If the other complies . . . he thereby bears witness to a certain attitude toward us." If I ask you to close the door, the way you do it is a "confirmation" of your attitude; for the subject, everything is an object that tests our psychological equilibrium, test supposing not the testamentary, but aggressions of faciality—if you scowl when I ask you to close the door, the scowl, signifier of the relation, is moved to the position of the truth of the act.[27] Given the proliferation of signifiers, what matters is the disclosure of the "final purpose," here the involuntary nature of truth.

A third paradox shows us that the endeavors of Sisyphus "prove" the truth of such purposes, where "A goal, once reached, always retreats anew." This is reposed to mean that

> The goal is the final destination, while the aim is what we intend to do, i.e., the way itself. Lacan's point is that the real purpose of the drive is not its goal (full satisfaction) but its aim: the drive's ultimate aim is simply to reproduce itself as drive, to return to its circular path. . . . The real source of enjoyment is the repetitive movement of this closed circuit." [28]

The aim is the true goal—to keep filling the void, the hole, the lack; if Zizek is right, desire's "desire" is simply desire's self-reproduction, but notice that the argument has the structure confirming natural selection as its model-type. "To reproduce itself" is identical to survival; or could we say that the subject as gap, void, or lack is conceived as an effect of Nothingness, active nihilism in place of its passive cultural aspect? A close reading notices that the previous mention of "fecund" and the organic are synthesized by this Darwinist sense of "aim," with the twist that "desire" also always "knows" the failure that pursues it if it gets "too close" to its object—desire "knows" when to keep its distance, when to alternate between libidinal energy and withdrawal. But in this way, the model also collapses, for if subjects are aware that to get "too close" to objects is to ruin the game, then a kind of epistemology is introduced, so that desire is not desire but is already a kind of internal knowledge of the importance of reproduction (protecting the "fecund" and the organic). Here is the presupposition of a metaphysical behaviorism.

The three "paradoxes" which, it should be stressed, then "prove" Lacanian "dogmatics" are not instances of paradox at all. For they render orders of the truistic, statements always true, always in force, command utterances obscured by their focus on subjectivity, a concept whose fascination is exploited. After all, which kind of paradoxical formation yields (1) a rule of inaccessibility (unattainability of objects), (2) a rule of confirmation (desire is reproduction), and (3) a rule of circularity? Paradox is stripped of any event status—moved to the "timeless"—and functions as a transcendental a priori of the subject. In this sense, the invocation of paradox is a political move, of asserting that psychoanalysis is up to date in ridding itself of the charge that it projects nature onto culture. The price is that literature—culture—becomes absorbed by neopsychoanalytic theory.

In the competition of discourses over grasping the vicissitudes of subjectivity, it is philosophy that is said to exclude itself because it is incapable of "ascertain[ing] its nullity," meaning that philosophy inherently "lacks" the capacity to submit its work to the test of nothingness. Philosophy is blind to the nothing, it must always have a foundation, but psychoanalysis can reach the null and thus deserves the status of truth.

The affirmation of negation and self-confession of lack constitute a baseline of any subjectivity whatsoever. This is carried over to the concept of fantasy, said to

> designate the subject's "impossible" relation to *a,* to the object-cause of its desire . . . what the fantasy stages is not a scene in which our desire is fulfilled, fully satisfied, but on the contrary, a scene that realizes, stages, the desire as such. The fundamental point of psychoanalysis is that desire is not something given . . . but . . . constructed—and it is precisely the role of fantasy to give the coordinates of the subject's desire, to specify its object . . . *through fantasy we learn how to desire.*[29]

Fantasy produces desire. Fantasy has a performative function, giving "desire" "coordinates" and directions, supporting the repetition of aim. But since aim presupposes, is dependent upon, the syntax of failure, fantasy is subsumed by desire and "coincides with the reproduction of desire as such, with its circular movement." Desire must then *precode* fantasy, for surely the "aim" of desire (repetition) is the program of any specific instance of fantasy. The "this" of a fantasy may well focus on objects and states of things, fantasy as something we can manipulate and turn into a resource, but to fantasize has a nihilistic attribute, that of the subject undoing itself. Indeed, Zizek turns fantasy into another mode of negation by insisting that its opposite, anxiety, is caused not by lack of objects, but by "the danger of our getting too close to the object and thus losing the lack itself." In this sense, fantasy represents for a subject objects which will not cause undue anxiety; fantasy is a way in which the subject talks about itself, makes itself into a spoken subject and ensures that the "lack" will not be lost—will never be lost. Since the motions of lack are determinate, everyone's previous concatenations of *objet a* force repetition of the tautological movement of circularity; it as if the logic involved assumes that Nothing itself is what wants itself, and wants this extinction of everything but itself. To be saved from "losing lack" means the death instinct is desire. In reading *Looking Awry,* one has the definite sense that just as world-historical dimensions can be modeled as the proliferation of "lack" (extension of castrating social relations hence proliferation of gaps to be filled), the turn to popular culture—"Lacanian dogmatics" as it "exploits popular culture"—is of a highly political order. Avant-garde critical theory in the service of reactionary ends: the "popular" will not veer from its place.

Looking Awry mentions a number of films and stories, all of which instantiate a uniform product, that of the truth of a universal, negative, social imaginary, the nonplace of a "futile circular movement." Zizek writes that

The Maltese Falcon "shows" where the *petit objet a* is to be found, rendered in the narrative of a man's "break" from his previous life. From the point of view of social wisdom, which assumes there really is no such "break" with routine and order, the "break" is said not to be worth the trouble; but as an intensive break with "surplus, that elusive make believe that drove the man to change his existence," the break is worth it. "Make believe" or fantasy creates pathemic changes—until the reader is brought short, for the "break" performed in *The Maltese Falcon* is a function of an injunction-repetition. Popular culture shows that:

> We always find ourselves in the same position from which we tried to es-
> cape, which is why, instead of running after the impossible, we must learn to
> consent to our common lot and to find pleasure in the trivia of our every-
> day life.[30]

If to "learn to consent" is the order-word here, then fantasy is passive ni-hilism's engine: it posits object-relations, "make believe," in order to satisfy what can be called "desire's desire" for the identity of repetition. Popular cul-ture is brought under the model that introduces "desire" as a mode of coun-terproduction, for everything is marked by "this very distortion, of this surplus of confusion and perturbation introduced by desire." Again: "Desire takes off when something (its object cause) embodies, gives positive exis-tence to its 'nothing,' to its void."[31] Every object one might consider popu-lar is brought under the signifier of repetition, everything popular an object of distortion, distortion the truth of fantasy, as if the void were the sole mo-tivation of everything that passes for subjectivation and fantasy the sole mode of encounter with the real. Again, with Deleuze and Guattari as well as Ly-otard, this model of desire is a facsimile of the model of contemporary cap-ital, for it participates in an economy of futility in which the "goals are missing" (Nietzsche) but everyone is at war over the preservation and ex-tension of their means (aim/survival). Passive nihilism is expressed of a social system in which subjects demand the right to maximize their futile fan-tasies—which nonetheless keeps us going. The metaphysics of the subject cohere with the concepts of obsolescence and elimination of affirmations, functional negatives of capital founded on desire-as-lack. Just as capital cease-lessly transforms roles in an overall nontransformation of subjects (metaphor over metamorphosis), isn't desire, as repetition, a perpetual bad debt?

Neopsychoanalytic Art and Reactionary Language

Many contemporary artists feel pressure to blur category boundaries, to dissolve carefully constructed social identities, particularly those as over-invested as heterosexualities seem to be. Some of this work repeats the social process whereby yesterday's radicalism (criticism of identity) becomes today's reactionary dominance (a new solidarity of the sufferers, sufferers of the signifier). The blurring of the spaces between avant-garde and reactionary is definitely at stake in contemporary art. A recent show at the Museum of Contemporary Art in Los Angeles had for sale artifacts (shirts) of a San Diego based artist's collective mocking the Republican Party convention of 1996. The museum was selling mockeries made by artists. Obviously, such pressure necessitates an ambiguous relation with the very category of representation, since the latter must be challenged as "received" (wisdom, inertia, value) and must be produced as something "new" and differential. In this section, focus is on the institutional and academic valorization of the work of the Los Angeles-based artist Mike Kelley, as well as on some of his own writings. The purpose is to elicit how an artist's work and discourse, brimming with abjection, the excluded, the marginalized, works into "art" precisely the circuit of legitimizing the excluded. Kelley's work is continuous with neopsychoanalytic language: the "failed subject" of the model is transformed into objects that are said to confirm the theory. A preliminary framing of the question is this: What accounts today for the satisfactions given to the representation of the previously repressed?

Consider the cover of the Whitney Museum's catalogue of an exhibition of Kelley's work, the title of which is *Catholic Tastes.* It is a photograph of the artist dressed as a janitor, mop in hand, staring resolutely off-camera, a proletarian "Hawkeye" out of *The Last of the Mohicans.* Involuntarily, one thinks of the vicissitudes of the American working class, presented in the antiglow of a blue-purple "light," the face a ratcheting-down, as it were, of the combination of high style with low content, a staple figure, as Erich Auerbach noted in *Mimesis,* of the "desperately narrow" world of deadening labor. But *Catholic Tastes* is not tragedy expressed as the "personal, the domestic, the touching and the sentimental," as it was in middle-class tragedy,[32] but as "cesspools," "putrid substances," "refuse dumps," to be "examined" in "all its aspects."[33] The surrealist "mud" of the social and personal is assumed to be "the real" and the artist is now acting as a scientist, which is what "examined" means. The artist has become a scientist in the field mud, in the goop of culture. One would want to know what difference the artist makes regarding the scientist's examination. Clearly, though, it is not enough to manifest the "low," for what is required is that the artist make what has been negated pass into something which is for the consideration of visual experience.

In his introduction to *Catholic Tastes,* the director of the Whitney, David Ross, writes that Kelley's work has been selected for presentation because his art "continues to make demands of an art world often mired in false notions of category and at times overly concerned with issues of taste and propriety." Segments of this "art world" are in some sort of vague "denial" brought about by commitment to "taste and propriety." The intended audience of the work is not the public, even more vague, but insiders not completely "in" on their overcommitment to convention. Kelley's work belongs to the family—to the rivalries and claims made by institutions and artists themselves. The terms are set as propriety and its violation, one of the stock themes of modernism, more specifically the history of the poetic word and its production of transgression, of presenting matter believed to be inassimilable to reason (sex, madness, fanaticism). But this is immediately transformed by the language of the curatorial machine: why Kelley and not another of the thousands of competitors for the museum's attention? Because

> Kelley's art . . . stems from his honesty in dealing with his life as a working-class American . . . to explore issues of class and gender unprejudiced by conventional aesthetics . . . a profound understanding . . . of the folly and the greatness of our particular national culture . . . a feminist . . . a raging satirist . . . most significantly . . . grounded in the traditional conditions of art making.[34]

The articulation of the inventory is significant. The terms "honest," "unprejudiced," and "understanding" articulate the previous mention of "examine" and establish the work in the morality of an authentic scientism ("explore"), as a hermeneutics of political morality ("folly" and "greatness"). The working class has produced a "feminist" and "satirist" who is also informed as to art-history ("grounded"). The terms that install, as it were, the necessity of exhibiting the work link it to the institution by a synthesis: the work *historicizes the present, adding its corpus to the history of art,* carried out by application of the models of scientism and political morality; total complementarity obtains between the institution, under constant pressure to contemporize without jettisoning its traditional audiences, and the artist, who cannot reject an outlet which promises so much by way of acquiring sign-value.[35] But there is even more at stake for the artist and the institution:

> Kelley's concern with the sociopathology of everyday life is . . . his considered effort to construct an authentic representation of the American psyche.[36]

"Authentic representation" involves the museum's historicism, of the "history" of the failure to represent the dark side of that thing called "America"; that is what the other "insiders" have not considered in their adherence to "taste and propriety." The museum possesses this consciousness of "Art's transcendent aims," as the proper place for exhibiting the artist's plumbing of the American "psyche." The archaicism "American psyche" presupposes that there are relations between nation and psyche such that what resists presentation ("psyche") can now be "read." Better: the language of nineteenth-century discussions about "soul and destiny" have *re*-turned, prepared to be fitted in as contemporary classicism.[37] Institution and artist mesh because what is transcendent is the art of presenting the "psyche," a conjunction based on the historical failure of representing "America." Here we have an immanent cultural logic: avant-garde (artist, institution) presupposes failure (of representation) and will give us representation coded as reactionary, where "American psyche" operates as an "essence," the truth. We now must turn to sociopathology to provide what the novel, music, and film have been unable to accomplish. It certainly strains credulity to believe that now we arrive at the destination of American cultural criticism, but that is the very purpose of these order-words and cultural timings. We are in what Nietzsche called monumentalism or idealization of a rigid type.

Indeed, in her acknowledgements page to the volume *Catholic Tastes,* another curator, Elizabeth Sussman, notes that the authors selected to write essays for the catalogue "were also chosen for their personal knowledge of the artist or, rather, of the attitudes and obsessions that underlie all his work, performances and beyond."[38] The writings conserve a precious object, the artist's "obsessions." No writing will interfere with the institution's judgment since "obsession" runs from subject to object to "psyche," said to have begun in 1986 with the display of sculptured stuffed animals that were at once "pathetic, abject," and "raucous and ribald." They "exposed" a "psychological perversion [that] radiates through Kelley's work," compressed into what is said to be the "ridiculous foundations" of "social norms" (but not, obviously, the staging of curatorial systems). Hence this "deconstruction" of the "lofty" comes from what "is low, class-based, sophomoric, and apparently the locus of failure."[39] These are amazing order-words, aggressive toward any resistance to psychologization, obscurantist toward the social as such. In attributing "failure" to the "low," the writing saturates both in *ressentiment,* the qualifier "class based" dropping out of sight. What is "low" has no "class" and is presented as "closer" to "psyche." Institutional discourse uses this projected psychologization of the "low" to counter the "lofty," a game made by the "lofty." The stress on "obsession," finally, is historicized in this work as fulfillment of history, the present made "timely" as the curatorial discourse finally lets the artist's discourse loose: the present requires "mangling Conceptualism, of dragging it out of its dry theorizing into an open space of sheer theatrical rant," or the present returned to *ressentiment*.[40]

So it is Conceptualism that is "father" for both the new curators and the artist, set forth so as to be ruined by the truths of the "low." The operative contrary, "dry" concept versus "theatrical rant," privileges "rant," its own position, in the pure imposition of the equivalence. It is clear that Conceptualism can be overthrown only by showing it to be no longer capable of Oedipalizing, justified by "the facts of life" that it left unexamined. What Conceptualism could not say, what it of necessity "castrated," is to be made good in the discourse it repressed. This movement of affirmation through negation is an essential figure of passive nihilism, the return of the past made to speak what it was not, or absence insisted as the truth of what was.

As stated before, what attracts curators and artists is the opportunity to destroy categories by the "release" of a "deviation from the unconsciously normative."[41] While Kelley insists that his working method is based on "free-association," Sussman insists that "rich metaphor, lush descriptive passages, and lewd and bawdy modes of address"[42] are what matter, all of this in the service of providing a scientization of the negative, today's "pathetic," and giving a plus-value to the art:

> Ultimately, it is the note of the pathetic that differentiates Kelley's work from anything that came before it . . . the desire to move ever lower, debasing political attitudes and revealing states of mind and body considered unfit in more conventional, transcendent views of the function of art.[43]

But does this "move ever lower" change art as much as it makes art equivalent to all sorts of medical files, psychiatric reports, police records, sex-victim narratives? Howard Singerman, in his essay in the catalogue, writes that "Kelley, like Freud, links all knowledge to sexual knowledge; he too presumes that the source of the will to know is tied to and grows from the will to have that knowledge." Didn't Freud exempt knowledge from sex when he tried to establish that sex gives way to the Ego?[44] And why does this continuation of sex into knowledge involve the notion that "every explanation contains a certain degradation"? [45] Are there no exceptions?

If we read a while in some of Kelley's own writings, perhaps we can discern just what sorts of necessities are being made. An often referenced writing is "Plato's Cave, Rothko's Chapel, Lincoln's Profile" (1985), which one critic in the catalogue calls sublime, and which Kelley highlights as "the Dionysian force of a child who somehow missed the Oedipal stage and still loves to play with his own excrement."[46] Dionysus no longer dances. The reduction certainly "moves ever lower," but what Kelley has to say in "Plato's Cave" tells a different story than the one the curators have told. In noting his hatred for the South, one reads this amazing bit of rant that the curators find so endearing:

> Hillbillies have finally made it to Hillbilly Heaven: the goldmine of arma-
> ment factory work. Greaser, heathen, fuck your own sister. Drunkenly holler
> your "rebel yell" out of the back of a racing pickup truck. Listen to your de-
> graded form of music stolen from the very people you once fought to keep
> enslaved and laugh at the transcendent notes of a new music less coarse than
> that which is driven by alcohol. These are depicted in the mirror of society
> by a lineage stretching from incestuous idiot on one end to the "Southern
> gentleman," a decayed foppish limpwrist, on the other. It drawls and
> crawls.[47]

This is certainly rant, but it is scapegoating *ressentiment;* the earlier twenti-eth-century interest by "artists of the mud" (for example, surrealism) often thought they were working with the materials of a repressed system, up-ended here by unadulterated vengeance on the South, an easy target. Imagine an artist who made curator = "hillbilly." The "hillbillies" are syn-thesized and wiped out in a discourse that operates so as to confirm the very image of the "low" as trash. It is as if the ending of the film *Easy Rider* which has "hillbillies" destroying the smugness of urban low-lifers, was the template for this display of "it's your turn." It's not the "lofty" who are ridiculed but the "low" in their choices, their own vileness.

The artist even invokes an epistemology for this contemporary refash-ioning of "Plato's Cave." This epistemology turns the cave into something literal instead of a literary fiction, in which the image of the cave is the only truth: "the bottom of a pit and shrouded in darkness . . . no lies here." "In the richness of mud things cannot be changed for they are what they are. There is justice here—no mistaken identities, no wrong trips to the electric chair."[48] Completely symmetrical with the "heights" as "light," the "mud" is truth, exactly opposite the concept of truth invoked by an author such as Artaud for whom, in a memorable phrase, truth is a kind of "non-sense, [but] has teeth."[49] In the same way that Zizek's discourse celebrates the pure identity of desire-in-repetition, Kelley traces the certainty of the low-as-identity. This is exactly idealism: the "mud" resolves everything, the precise identity of the concept yields truth—the "low" cannot lie. How is the certainty here not conservative?

The category that is culturally affirmed appears in a discourse of com-plete obsession. This is the category of the adolescent. Another of Kel-ley's texts, "The Poltergeist," makes it plain that the contemporary artist has nearly run out of material and thus has to turn to the matter of what the media has made popular. This is the adolescent, thrown back at the art world with the qualities of a "specimen" from the masses, with "its" attributes:

> Bulging Eyes, Lolling Tongue, thousands of erect lumps all over the face—the embodiment of frustration—riding hot rods all over the house: no longer lovable—too obtuse to be tolerable—everything destroyed—sexual energy released . . . A Monkey-Like Phantom—A Rat Fink—a Poltergeist.[50]

Is this from the "mud" or from a cartoon transposed into language and called something "low"? In a statement for an exhibit at the Renaissance Society at the University of Chicago (1987), Kelley celebrates the materials of what were once "women's activities" (for example, sewing). He says that the exhibit's "outward form . . . is a joyous primitivism, a stylized adult misrepresentation of children's art." This is continuous with Zizek's claims for Lacan and film—adult perception is based on fetish and misrecognition. The extensive use of stuffed animals, here and elsewhere, is rationalized as bringing back the "adult's perfect model of a child—a neutered pet."[51] The artist's use of this material is intended say that the "stuffed animal," with dark connections to adult repressions and desires, has become the model by which children are repressed. This, in turn, is threaded to the artists capacity to "reinvest" sexuality and power in the child, in the name of a critique of the "false innocence" projected by adults onto children. The hypothesis is that in giving a gift to the child, adults are exactly instructing him or her in the rules of "repayment." We ruin children (fair enough). Yet in the name of attacking adult idealizations, the gap between what adults say and do, the writing posits a variation of the law of the father: because a child cannot return a gift other than its "love," it is a "perpetual indentured servant, forever unable to pay back its debt." The critical aspect is undone by this eternalization. This recodes the psychoanalytic notion of the (adult) subject as always castrating the child, now taken so far that the child (victim) is unable to close with making the passage into the symbolic; it confirms the theory of failure, the systematic "triumph" of the failure of complete Oedipalization.

The artist defiles any and all idealizations of the family, providing works that hold fast to "incompetence, subjugation, and filthiness."[52] But this defiling is threaded to the artist as providing, like the analyst, a function of representing access to what is believed to be inaccessible. Kelley insists that artists can "safely access, despite the usefulness or not, destructive forces." The artist as magician of the untamed is preserved; the role of the artist might be seen as being an agent of safety through representation. The dangers of human nature are represented so as to tamp our own fears and anxieties.[53] Bizarrely, this is linked to the activity of criminals: because John Wayne Gacy was a mass murderer of children, "we" examine his prison paintings because this "allows us to safely stare at the forbidden." Like the (sexual) criminal, the artist represents the "forbidden," and like the psychoanalyst, for whom the forbidden is that which is active yet foreclosed as ideation, the artist is a representational idealist. It is not asked whether our images of the forbidden might precisely figure forth self-satisfaction that we are playing with the Devil turned into safety, precisely what would undo the claims made by curatorial and artist's discourse. The forbidden yields to the artist as "examiner," which means it is suitable for representation, which can further be taken to involve the dominance of a scientistic encoding: The artist can believe that the forbidden tells the truth in artistic representations. Artists do not traffic in mere interpretations; they give us the real.

This conjunction of adolescence, negation, and idealization comes out very strongly in another of Kelley's writings. In asserting that "caricature" is dissolvable into "philistine images, which may provoke indifference or disgust in the educated art lover," "caricature" is drawn into the realm of a "negative reaction." Such a "reaction" is set off by caricature's ability to "disgust" and extends to "low intent masquerading in heroic garb." "Caricature" is most efficient when threaded to aggressiveness, where other modes, like joking, are bound to fail because of the persistence of repressive tolerance. As opposed to the "joke," low morality draws upon the resources of "controlled regression," "childhood pleasures," "magic beliefs," embodied in the "human persona . . . that can express itself in the grotesque and in caricature."[54] The lower we go, the more indifferent the matter involved becomes. The "logic" of the low descends to any "foul substance—any substance associated with taboo, and thus with repression." Each of these "any substances" is affirmed as "a literal enactment of . . . 'criminal' ornamentation." [55] The language tries to sustain the affirmed equivalencies between "philistine," "negative reaction," "low intent," "controlled regression," "magic beliefs," and "taboo." It breaks down, however, by means of a small transcendence. The equivalencies give way to the superiority of "taboo," which is the measure before which "any substance" receives the recognition that casts it as a signifier; but the instant in which "any substance" is affirmed is to eliminate every substance but the taboo—to make taboo into the "substance." What then is this "taboo"? It is created by the labor of sexual "disordering," a labor that brings about the social organization of the genitals, where this "erotic ornament" in turn indexes the archaic heritage of sexualization. The artist must regress to the "disordering" itself, this to bring back for visibility the founding "taboo" of adult sexuality.

Indeed, if sexuality presupposes taboo, both moments in the conjunctive logic of failure and repression, it is this failure which makes the present a bountiful garden of object-relations. Given the negative synecdoches of the discourse, the present is utterly stabilized: cultural artifacts like "splatter films" "continue the depiction of the body as grotesque." "As in the original Roman decorations, the body . . . an accumulation of pieces at odds . . . ," nonetheless achieves a transcendence: "Repressed into abstraction, they rise pleasurably back into consciousness in their new form."[56] Contemporary figurations of the body-as-part, which dovetails nicely with Zizek's assertion of the ubiquity of *petit objet a,* thus prove the collapse of figures in a return of the repressed. Minimalism's claim to authority and essentialism, for example, requires defamation and can be properly refigured only by female artists "who all pop the cherry of Minimalism to reinsert the body." Thus feminism is appropriated via the pathway of the body in revenge, the male "clear glass" defamed by a "petri dish of bacteria." When Kelley remonumentalizes art history as the history of defamations, the works are anchored in the project of negating the negations of adults and art history, like the parental "gift" of stuffed animals, this negating negation itself fused with a "shout of glee" at any and all images, enacted "like the children . . . when they see their parents and teachers covered in a disgusting mess."[57] The pre-Oedipal artist just hates Mommy and Daddy, the artist saying it all as ethnologist of adult perversion.

The artist speaks the unspeakable—that the symbolic order is shattered, but, again, this shattering of language is staged in the most integrative manner possible. The photographer Larry Clark, interviewed by Kelley, is still possessed by the desire for the "normal," a condition that Kelley, acting as analyst, quickly encodes:

MK: So the object of desire is to be the kids, not to have them.

LC: Right, it's to be them.

MK: You don't seem to be interested in "normal kids but rather in dysfunctional youth, kids involved in Satan teen murders and things like that.

LC: I think I'm just interested in anything a teenager does.

For the rest of the interview, Clark and Kelley wax eloquent in jogging each other's memories of juxtapositions of erections and various murders, for example, the "mental image of Lizzie Borden . . . used to get me hot" is compared to the ever-frustrated desire at fifteen for a teenage boy to "be fucking the beautiful twenty-two year old teacher. . . . This kid's got everything."[58] Is the unconscious, pre-Oedipal child in discourse here, or is the "truth" derived from *ressentiment,* as hatred toward the social that did not let our "adolescents" consume their internalization of adult images?

Resistance and Repetition: The Difficulty of *Re*

In *Bodies That Matter,* Judith Butler takes up what she calls the need for a "psychoanalytic rethinking" of subjectivization. Negatively, this is linked to a critique of those psychoanalytic "founding prohibitions and their het-erosexualizing injunctions . . . taken to be invariant." Positively, Butler urges a "retheorization" of "phantasmatic investment and expectation" such that "socially saturated domains of exclusion" can be "recast from their status as 'constitutive' to beings who might be said to matter."[59] "Re-think," "recast," and "retheorized"—these are the terms that might over-come the limits of the psychoanalytic model ("injunctions") where the "excluded" can be saved and affirmed as important. How can *re* do all this?

But even this *re*sistance to psychoanalytic "universals" is committed to a model of subject and discourse that gives so much to the language of negativity as to call into question what it does want: Butler accepts

> the subject is produced in language through an act of foreclosure (*Verwer-fung*). What is refused or repudiated in the formation of the subject contin-ues to determine that subject. What remains outside this subject, set outside by the act of foreclosure, which founds the subject, persists as a kind of defining negativity. [60]

The psychoanalytic model is founded on "exclusion" of what is not-heterosexual, fear of loss of identity, and as the citation above has it, Butler agrees with its linguistic derivation, that of the subject generated by "fore-closures" of signification. What one cannot discuss is what defines the self, at least in those experiences when self is risked. To this psychoanalytic ex-clusion, it is Hegel who is called forth to set before us a better "defining negativity," one that "haunts" such "exclusions," where the negative is not lost to subsequent linguistic expressions. First of all, why give so much to psychoanalysis or Hegel? Why grant, as an axiom of cultural critique, that "foreclosure" is defining? What makes one think one can work the nega-tive into the progressive? If the performance of language as symbolic ex-clusion produces the subject, a "ditto machine" of the negative, there will have to be a kind of word-magic of transformation that comes to elicit the positive. Butler offers the "historical" against an ahistorical psychoanalysis, or "cultural organizations of sexuality that exceed the structuring purview of that law," that is, of trauma (sexual division) and sexual antagonism. The event of "drag" gives such an excess. "Drag" signifies the suspension of "foreclosure," "drag" working both the negative and the positive aspects of sexual identity, upending the law of castration and those cultural "sexed-nesses" which might be said to "exceed" that law. But how can such an "excess" matter if it is real only on account of that law? What law creates, even by extreme negation, the law can repossess. Butler agrees with Zizek that political signifiers—for example, democracy and freedom—are "empty signs which come to bear phantasmatic investments," and then does not notice that she commits to the practice of also "overinvesting" in the power of a signifier. For if subjects make "investments" in signifiers that "can never be achieved," then to say that signifiers such as "women" are open to "new meanings and new possibilities" is both true and misleading in a way that is not considered. If, for every signifier, especially those as loaded as "women" and "democracy," we have to conceive foreclosure and exclusion as foundational, then how can any signifier not always promise and fail? The sort of suspension and argumentation *Bodies That Matter* wants concerning signification pits the blindnesses of prior "foreclosures" against the future consensus that might not ever occur, given the initial limitations.

On the one hand, Butler wants to loosen the psychoanalytic stranglehold on signification by lessening the "law of castration" or symbolic identity based on gendered negations (the overvaluation of any sexual "position"). The "cultural genital economy" of Lacanianism has to go. To do this, she opens signification to an "open ended and performative function . . . crucial to a radical democratic notion of futurity." Performative functions of discourse are the least buried in preexisting exclusions. On the other hand, if one keeps the signifier as that which receives a "final recognition that can never be achieved," the signifier is immediately a function of self-destruction if one makes any overinvestment in signification. Is such "balance" possible given "foreclosure" as the condition of discourse with others? To the repetitions that neopsychoanalysis brings, the "historical" (emergent) would have to break with signification, that is, openly come forward as simulacra released from participation in the false, because partial, identities of meaning and sense. Butler points to the performance of "drag" to negate sexed positions, but "drag" also confirms them. "Drag" is easily returnable to a difference become utterly normative, a balancing act, the restoration of equilibrium.

Butler's text is committed to the notion that subjects always want to become free through a linguistic process, what she calls "rearticulation." This *re* is intrinsic to the bringing forward of excluded voices and previously unrecognized "subject positions." But if "rearticulation" is accepted as also embedded in lack and negation, as Butler insists, then the claim that it is "more fundamental than any given social antagonism" is itself part of a fantasy. It becomes impossible to see how "radical democracy . . . constitutes within discourse the resistance to all essentialism and descriptivism," since lack and negation are precisely what is essential, that is, transcendental. If the "subject-position" of women does not coincide with the signifier "women"—that is, if one emphasizes the *gap* between name and entity—why should this gap be conceived, as Butler does, as an "instability in all discursive fixing" instead of what it manifestly is? Instability is affirmed as what is fixed, the form of another essentialism. In place of subject essentialism, Butler's argument comes down on the side of the logic of negation, affirmation of gap, the lack of the signifier, substitutions that fail to render ideological closure. Butler's particular query is well taken: how can "women" be spoken of or write themselves if psychoanalytic theory always writes them out by making the condition of to symbolize rest upon the desymbolization of women? Indeed, Butler carefully judges that Zizek's work is devoted to the oxymoronic defense of protecting the "threat of castration" from rival claims (for instance, Foucault, nonpsychoanalytic feminism, the very idea of castration as an instance of phallocentrism). His argument slides between designating the "real" as the law of castration that institutes "lack" and "lack" itself, that is, the "real" is both cause and effect of itself, which is plainly an impossible theorem unless we submit to a law of identity that can never be grasped. The system Butler criticizes has insisted that value laden relations (metaphor, displacement) are threaded to a primary belief that language promises precisely what it cannot bring: return of the subject to a point "before" the trauma of signification itself occurred.

But in her plainly courageous effort to dethread the screws of psychoanalytic theory, to move from a putative law of castration to the "softer" notion that what is foreclosed remains within "the symbolic order as a policing of the borders of intelligibility,"[61] so that no signifier is necessary and universal, especially that intractable phallus, Butler's argument is hinged to the idea that the category of the unsymbolizable is "real," that criticism itself is restricted by the practice of rearticulation. To rearticulate in the face of the "law" is to demonstrate that all such "laws" are social and historical, not preideological. *Bodies That Matter* insists that it is discourse that produces exclusions, and since exclusions are not equivalent—the ban on bisexuality is not equivalent to the male dread of homosexual abjection—neither the model of castration nor its concomitant notion, that charged signifiers are always unsatisfiable "promissory notes for the real," can be maintained.[62] We should drop the psychoanalytic notion that significant names—women, democracy, freedom, satisfaction—are "rigid designators" whose performative status is anchored so as to provide just enough neurosis to keep us from going psychotic in relation to our frustrations. Instead, Butler suggests, we might move to the notion that it is the "catachrestic use of speech that insists on using proper names improperly." That is, the way to enhance critical discourse is not to insist upon political signifiers as always refer-ring to a lost object of desire but rather to "open the term as a site for a more expansive rearticulation."[63]

Could it be clearer? Rearticulation is the action of democratic signifi-cation. To rearticulate is to suspend the investments made in signifiers in the name of opening them to contestation; but this positive moment is contained by the larger "defining negativity" of "foreclosure," as discussed above. Preserving that negativity, based on a default built into signification (to speak = to separate by foreclosure), was already granted a kind of "leg-islative" right—to depose the chains of association between language and patronymic discourse. All we can ever do is rework the articulations to en-sure that spurious identitites are not the last word, ruinous signification. As Butler says,

> the task is surely to make the signifier into a site for a set of rearticulations
> that cannot be predicted or controlled, and to provide for a future in which
> constituencies will form that have not yet had a site for such an articulation
> or which are not prior to the siting of such a site.[64]

Who could disagree with this idealism, since it precisely believes it knows what excluded subjects desire—a safe place for *rearticulation?* Because *re* is the saving signifier, it seems as if the Lacanian terms win out: how is the reiteration of rearticulation not what Zizek claims—a phantasmatic over-investment of a promise doomed to fail? In the citation above, "surely" for-tifies against insecurity and doubt, and the use of "site" three times in the passage indicates a desperate attempt to resist temporalization, or fear that the future cannot provide what is projected onto it. And doesn't this pas-sage exclude more drastic effects, for example, using the very name of fem-inism to produce, in the here and now, contentiousness that is "unpredictable" and not "controlled"?

Butler concludes her own critique of psychoanalysis by suggesting that if significatory identification always collapses—broken apart by realities—then it is incumbent upon those working for the future to politicize by creating effects of disidentification, "this uneasy sense of standing under a sign to which one does and does not belong."[65] "Uneasy sense" could be considered the minimum expenditure of reflection/alienation. We should, she continues, "affirm . . . slippage, that failure of identification . . . the point of departure for a more democratizing affirmation of internal differ-ence." But this hinging of affirmation to a prior negation is exactly what gives current Lacanian-based psychoanalysis its resonance, that it is making something out of nothing. It is the same logic, just turned once: To say that "prior negation" is the point of departure supposes that somewhere along the trails to the future, negation will just drop off, disappear below the threshold of difference. That is exactly suspicious: negation is too "sticky" for what will happen. Indeed, in calling for the political signifier to be "perpetually resignified," this *re* does not pass over into stronger senses of language; it assumes only the subjectivity of perpetual witnessing to changes of fortune affecting signification, a perpetual avant-garde of the signifier. To make criticism into, as she urges, a "reworking" of prior sedi-mentations built into signifiers, as "the production and promise of 'the new'," is precisely to want to repeat the divisions of thinking that already baffle, "reworking" suggesting endless correction of error concerning discourse. In moving toward "the force of citationality" as a way to dislodge overidealization of the signifier, why does one have to pass through "the compulsion to install an identity through repetition," and with that, to "disloyalty against identity" unless the aim—to produce a "hiatus in iter-ability"—is already embedded in playing the game better than the oppo-sition, a more intense idealism?[66] For Butler, the failure of description is what we academics have to teach, yet the wisdom proffered is thin: "to learn how to live the contingency of the political signifier in a culture of democratic contestation." What is this but an admonition that we had bet-ter get over our past idealizations, like Geyer's "troglodytes" mentioned in chapter two, and that for us there is nothing but *re* treated as the last ideal?

Psychoanalysis and Culture:
The Reactionary Threshold

The neopsychoanalytic model of the subject as "lack" (in place of Freud's notion of drive) and negation culminates in a moralized and aestheti-cized model: it equates the law of castration (symbolic universal) with language, eliminating the possibility of meanings that are not symptoms and indices of failure. This discourse moves to the popular, whether in the writings of Zizek or a contemporary artist, carried out in such a way as to confirm the metaphysics of nothingness, exemplified in Kelley's lan-guage in which art, in its impropriety, provides a new safety to represen-tations of the "mud." Finally, language is metaphysicalized, in being made into an equivalent of the death instinct, since language is itself modeled as void and lack. These notions are resisted by writers such as Butler, based on the fiction of *re:* by forgetting that the concept of performance offered as a positive choice would have to decisively break with lan-guage, which is precisely what it refuses to do. Now these notions are brought to a reading of Fredric Jameson's essay "On Cultural Studies" in such a way as to indicate the reactionary politics at stake. The order-word model his text gives is that of a criticism that must accept the negations, lacks and voids of a religious type, rejection of cultural studies unless it "knows" what it already "is."[67]

"On Cultural Studies" was published in *Social Text* (1993) and brings forward Jameson's attempt to control the boundaries and significance of such "studies." Jameson defines the concept of culture as a "weaker" form of religion, although the latter is not defined other than as the psychological; in keeping with modernist notions that every important cultural conjunction, including negations, resolves into elementary relations (for example, a semiotic rectangle), culture is stripped of any substance and is not to be construed as "a phenomenon in its own right." First identification: culture is religion. Culture is an "objective mirage," a "nimbus . . . perceived by one group when it comes into contact with and observes another one."[68] This is a restatement of one of Jean-Paul Sartre's obsessions, that to perceive is to negate. Although this statement is Manichean in its primary formation, Jameson immediately raises it to a psychological transcendental: to perceive an Other is to objectify "everything alien and strange about the contact group . . . the ensemble of stigmata one group bears in the eyes of the other group." Second identification: To perceive is to mark and negate and separate, rhetoricized here by means of figures that dissolve into the natural. Contact = stigmatization. So when we do speak of "our own" culture it is to be understood as

> now . . . identified as the recuperation of the Other's view of us; of that objective mirage whereby the Other has formed a picture of us as "having" a culture (33).

To think "our own" culture is to confront the pictures we imagine as to what we are not, as the Other is imagined as possessing or having something that we lack; the Lacanian foundation is intact, allowing for an enthymeme or misleading conclusion to be cast:

> [a culture] is the ensemble of stigmata one group bears in the eyes of the other group (and vice versa) . . . projected into the "alien mind" in the form of that thought-of-the-other we call belief and elaborate as religion (33).

Lack and negativity are thus the conditions of culture, carried over from the mystery of religion (Lacan's "mystery of the Father").

Hegel and Lacan meet, as they always do, in denial of any affirmation that comes without envy and loathing; the Danzon of Veracruz, where every class and age "cut and mix" (*pace* Hebdige) and the gathering of Filipinas in downtown Hong Kong on Sunday afternoons where there is exquisite sharing of language and food are events stigmatized by this model. But perhaps it is only ourselves who require this emptying-out of culture?

Affirmations cannot intrude on this Lacanian and Hegelian eternalization of cultural misstep, our bad dance. Culture simply "perpetuates the optical illusions and the false objectivism of this complex historical relationship." Envy and loathing, the binding categories (third identification) of and between any defined social groups, suture continuity between religion and culture:

> an attempt to appropriate the culture of the other group . . . is a tribute and a form of group recognition, the expression of collective envy, the acknowledgment of the prestige of the other group (34).

That envy and loathing over prestige is "primordial" is attested to in the nearly universal tribute one group more powerful than another pays to the lesser group's cohesion and solidarity; what we desire from the other group is its solidarity or capacity to negate one's own internal sense of dissolution, where a powerful group "unconsciously regrets its tendential dissolution as a group as such" (35). Next to that identification, a universal envy of what we lack, group loathing, whose principal form of conflict is over "purity and danger," a negative copy of prestige, aims to defend its boundaries and is the negative imagination in an "abusive fashion" (for instance, in racism). The primordiality of envy and loathing is cemented in place, and its categories mark out the history of cultural transformations tied to an unyielding negative identity—and can be dislodged only by the impossible, by Utopia ushered in as that nonplace or suspension of conflict in which "external stereotypes . . . never arose in the first place" (35). The *religious* trajectory is absolute. Naturalism and essentialism are joined.

Astonishingly, a digression takes us to the idea that contemporary liberalism has worked out a solution for the "envy and loathing" out of which it too is constituted. Scholarly cultures have worked out a rule by which our own stereotypes (current images of Others) are a *least negative,* a *pretense* within liberalism: "fortunately we carry on as though it were [a fact] for most of the time" that is, we cannot do without pretense.

Jameson valorizes those papers in "On Cultural Studies" that move to this negative imaginary. An essay by Crimp is affirmed because it raises the dyad of envy and loathing to the status of representation. He offers a critique of photographic work on AIDS, focusing on the destructiveness of the victim genre. "Phobic images, images of the terror at imagining the person with AIDS as still sexual," opens onto, Jameson asserts, the omission of the imagination "of the sick person as a sexual being." The American public's negation of homosexuality, omission, will in turn be negated, by insisting that sexuality is at the basis of the human: Jameson seems not to notice the conspiracy theory at work in Crimp's argument, that the imaginary of sickness always overwhelms (homo)sexuality, nor does Jameson notice that it is legitimate to question how sexuality can be presented if you photograph ill people. Neither Crimp nor Jameson is able to offer a really positive judgment: Why not photograph very ill people engaged in sexual pleasure, which would at once alienate the power of sickness imagery and affirm the ubiquity of sexuality? Those essays that pursue the agenda of envy/loathing are selected as more valuable than those that do not. Indeed: Hook's essay, on the black fear (loathing) of white is judged important because it raises the stakes in reconvening the Hegelian/Lacanian topic of subject positions: this "whole new field" "restores to culture its hidden inner meaning as the space of the symbolic moves of groups in agonistic relation to each other" (38). But we already know that this is an old "field": religious to the core, unyielding, and unchanging. For what else does religion assert? This rigid conservatism, because negation and lack provide the regular sing-song of political reactionaries (that history professor, Newt Gingrich, now speaker of the House of Representatives, is an expert in describing what we lack—prayer in schools, work rewards and punishments), is bolted into place by Jameson's treatment of those essays in "On Cultural Studies" that dare to suggest a change in the "subject positions" of intellectuals. Simon Frith is taken to task for his "uncharitable bluntness" for declaring that popular music is in and of itself a "solution" to intellectual work, insofar as popular music provides a medium of non-separation of the requisite social distancing. Immediation suspends envy and loathing.

Here we cross to what absolutely matters. Frith's "uncharitable bluntness" concerning the positioning of intellectual work and "cultural studies" threatens to unravel the conjunction or negative identity between intellectual work and critical distance: Jameson retreats to the "great sociologists," all of whom shared "the tragic sense of life" that allowed them to produce "disabused knowledge" and that perforce "excludes any activist participation in the social" (39). Knowledge and activism make up a nice binary couple but only because knowledge is given a privilege denied to activism: the social is knowable "on pain of losing the very insights, the very power of demystification, paid for by just this epistemological separation from the human" (39). This fear of loss reinstalls the equivalence between knowledge and loathing: the spell of negation is at the basis of knowledge—not joy, not pleasure, not magic or mimesis (extreme suggestibility). The "very real truth . . . of the intellectual as observer . . . that status . . . that intervenes between the object of knowledge and the act of knowledge" must not be disrupted (39). (One notes the redundancy of "very" and "real"). For the "passion for seeing through the ideologies and the alibis that accompany the class and group struggles" necessitates

> that such lucidity as to the real mechanisms of social relationship demands the price of *a single white lie,* a strategic blind spot in the area of the intellectual, the occupation of everything that is social about our own observer's viewpoint itself, the renunciation of social commitment, the attempt to surrender social knowledge from action in the world, indeed the very pessimism about the possibility of action in the world in the first place, will come to seem an act of atonement for this particular (structural) sin. For the intellectual is necessarily and constitutively at a distance. (40)

All of these identifications culminate in Jameson's discussion of university and society. In taking on the institutional dimension of university writing, he makes this astonishing statement: "no one [in the volume *Cultural Studies*] seems particularly enthusiastic about the prospect of undertaking an ethnology of their culture, fearing perhaps rightly the anxieties and the dreariness of such self knowledge" (40). The "white lie" that allows us to perform also prohibits self-analysis; the place from which we write cannot itself be written. If culture is anchored in religion and, as we saw above, self-reflection is itself embedded in apprehending our own "envy and loathing," then "dreariness" might indeed be one of the elementary categories of self-knowledge and not something eliminated, as it is here. Shouldn't we "know" this? "Perhaps rightly" repeats the rhetoric of "fortunately," but instead of the least negative of racism, it installs defeat in advance of any ethnography of university culture. The affirmed "tragedy" and "original sin" that subtends our collective and individual (critical, university-based) labor lets us all off the hook of having to account for the organization, distribution and evaluation(s) of knowledge production. The aforementioned "wrenching self-consciousness" may then be reinterpreted as the negative put to work so as to ensure that postreligious questions are not raised. The limits of knowledge are set in the inability of transcending religion—distance is absolute.

Jameson acknowledges the necessity of oppressed groups to avail themselves of the image, to "go toward the light" of the "new reunification by the image." The image, the visual correlate or double of the verbal quote reduced to sound bite, is affirmed so as to forestall immediacy: those critiques that emphasize the body and power literally lose sight (cf. the example of Martin Jay in the Introduction, p. 10) of the "multinational corporations" and "corporate culture" that are the worthy objects of serious study. Indeed, only the *study* of this (supposed) new formation is capable of preventing the worst of critical sins, "cultural studies" focus on power (actuality), which brings with it "a repudiation of economic analysis . . . a forthright anarchistic stance on the thing itself, the unholy marriage between the heroism of dissidence and the "realism" of 'talking to the institutions'" (45). If Utopia is the holy union of the symbol and history, dissidence is the unholy; critiques of the body and of power are to be set aside—ordered out of study— by another absolute, that of fatalism: You cannot "talk to the institution" (a bank, a church, a state) and such moves are judged "anti-Marxist" insofar as they obviate the study of the mode of production.

Once power and actuality are treated as mere "remainders" of culture, itself reduced to religious superstructure, you can hardly avoid stigmatizing each and every performance of critical immediacy. Thus a complete spell: turn away from the analysis of the institutions of study, for its "dreariness" will mark you as unable to have a "good marriage," one blessed by Utopia and Tragedy (Utopia negates dissidence and Tragedy negates analysis, which implicates the institutions of writing).

This version of the scholar, like Derrida's, accepts that "social autonomy [is] no longer available for anyone" (47–48), so long as we note that "anyone" does not include the subset of the tragic intellectual previously invested with a positive "original sin." Issues of articulation fall away: nationalism is to be seen as a "kind of nostalgia" for this unavailable autonomy, a toxic symptom. Writings that are too immediate are to give way to a new "relational discourse on these global and spatial matters," a "superposition of incommensurable dimensions" in which local, regional, national, and international frames of action and experience only allow for an *agenda* to restore a "symbolic process" to writing. *Critique* is pointless next to this agenda, which alone enables one to move from the dialectics of envy and loathing or conflicts marked by intra-intellectual disputes to a group transcoding, in which intellectual differences are superseded by a geographical analysis that will provide a "crucial seme or atom, which binds the codes together momentarily by way of its own polysemousness." The unity of part-whole is reconfirmed: from dialectics and symbolics to transcoding demands a higher symbolism, here attached to a "third dimension" where the figure of the world corporation is to be treated, an analysis "for which we have as yet no particularly adequate language." This demand is set forth as a "new requirement of geographic reflexivity or geopolitical self-consciousness, and to demand the validation of some account of the 'national' situation from within whose standpoint the analysis has been made" (50). But since the national situation of the United States is presented as synonymous with global capitalism (an absolutely wild fantasy) this new "reflexivity" or research program "demands" commodity analysis, a return to the negativity of consumption. Beyond all this "lies Utopia" insisted as "secretly at work everywhere in these pages."

Thus, the only analysis that receives the valency of affirmation by "On Cultural Studies" is the most impossible kind: massive research programs that can be performed only by the most connected and networked of investigators. For everyone else: get out of the way of University Corporation, which is here, I would say, the "secret" symbolic model or identification that gives Jameson's essay its obvious identity with capitalism. Along with Big Global Capital, there will be Big Research.

Conclusion

Instead of utopia "everywhere," as Jameson insists, the texts analyzed thus far issue many orders. Neopsychoanalization of the subject brings a cultural regimen that installs passive nihilism as the very stuff of subjects-in-language. The subject is congealed in word pictures giving entry to the inner world in which everyone is characterized by voids, absences, and lacks, but this is no existential world. The subject is worth, in the constructs of neopsychoanalysis, as much as failure. Capitalists of the symbol can embrace this model of the subject (in endless debt). Philosophically, neopsychoanalysis reworks modern intellectual history as a submergence of epistemology and pleasure, washed out in the bath of the transcendental negative, a defining characteristic of reactive culture. Its model projects language thought of as a participation in limitation, the subject placed within a metaphysical fate, instead of trying to produce events and thoughts that could unfold an *amor fati,* or affirmations of a more interesting type. In different ways, the writings of Silverman, Zizek, Kelley, Butler and Jameson exemplify widely shared beliefs and show attentive readers nihilistic mixtures, or idealistic ones, for a society in which nihilism has been normalized. Passive nihilism (Zizek's insistence that we can only "submit"), aggressive passive nihilism (Kelley's appropriation and use of the category "adolescent" and the curatorial idealization that accompanies this embracing of the "mud"), explicit nihilism (the reduction of culture to religion), hope against nihilism (Butler), are but some of the modalities implied by the overall embrace of nihilism, which comes as soon as language is reduced to symptom and its cultural leash, that of *re* projected as alternative. These writers, artists and curators, precisely because their "work" is so visible, thus index something like a state of cultural replenishment, outfitting the attractiveness and satisfactions of cultural despair. There is no necessary limit at all as to how far, collectively speaking, we can "go" in this antiproject of turning every possible cultural relation into instances of affirming negation and the negation of affirmation. In this sense, nihilism means the neutralization of will and difference, a "body which despaired of the body—which groped about the last walls with the fingers of a maddened mind" and now stays with us to terrorize.[69]

Chapter Four ⬣

Historiography, Scholarship, and Mastery

History is the most dangerous product evolved from the chemistry of the intellect. . . . It causes dreams, it intoxicates whole peoples, gives them false memories, quickens their reflexes, keeps their old wounds open. . . . History will justify anything. It teaches precisely nothing, for it contains everything . . .

—Paul Valery

K ant speculated that one might treat historical knowledge as a self-justifying "insatiable desire to possess and to rule" without which "humanity would forever sleep."[1] Knowledge of history was a function of "desire for mastery." Mastery and history are linked by desire, and nature made us in such a way that history is the history of "masteries," "mastering," the overturning of "mastery," without end. Historiography discloses the written and visual recording of the conjugations of this sensibility ("desire"), its "highest" distortions and "lowest" equations. Knowledge of "history" is useful to "master," since it claims to show the history of those knowledges that are continuous with "desire." We do not like to "hear" from "history" that, say, the fairy tale has been used in the subjugation of children; we prefer to believe in artifacts whose articulation mediates an overarching continuity between culture and history, even if such continuisms are prosopopeias turned into positive narrative subjects.

But we "know," or claim that we do, that models of "desire" guiding cultural knowledges are coded, that is, they are language- and value-based, so that historiography cannot have a "natural" basis, whether in storytelling, structures of promise and forgetting, or commemoration for the dead because desire (need, interest, goal, aim, project) is worked up in ways that return us not to nature, but to "training," "discipline," and norms. These and all similar practices are cultural operations before they are "historical" or natural in their formation and outcomes, it being historiography that turns every social coding of time (and decoding) into retrospective "truths" found in "the study of history," including those pertaining to "desire."

Sharply put, "desire" belongs to a historiography based upon philosophical naturalism, yet historiography, as writing, is antinaturalist, made by writing elites, and so is always coded. Can desire and code be synthesized?[2] Does the "desire to historicize" not register its epistemic ideal—to make present, to punctuate a continuum, to introduce difference—as an understandable function of cultural warfare, the ranking and sorting of claimants, a mastery of claims to mastery?

The above topics will be taken up in a close reading of some of Carlo Ginzburg's historiographic writings. Why Ginzburg's texts? It will be argued they are historicist and naturalist, manifested as a scholarship that incessantly "prunes" false claimants from the "throne" of historiography. Ginzburg's texts claim to be able to resolve a legendary binary of historiography, that it is both art and science (desire and code), and that among other works, Hayden White's *Metahistory* stressed was an irresolvable tension given the tropological basis of prose narrative (the writing of history represents models of interpretations, not the possession of things). A reading of Ginzburg's work and some commentary on it indicate that it claims to be able to resolve the difference between the writing of history and representing the real. This is frequently set in the register of a historiography coded as "falling in love," as a "lightning enthusiasm" for the past, motivated by one's "lack of awareness" of the past, of being possessed by a "euphoria of ignorance." These and other figures were noted as merging the epistemic and desire, including a mixture of aggressions (dismissal of deconstruction) and servility (the historian coded as in surrender to past witnesses), its scholarship both cutting and passive, insisting upon divination and reception of the "spirits" of time past.[3] At the same time, Ginzburg has contended that there is a transcendence of historical writing:

> Neither the past and future developments of the language we speak, nor the existence of other languages, affect our commitment to the language we speak or its grip over reality, [4]

in which "grip over reality" stands in for the generalized desire of historians to use language and not to have it come back as something that is uncontrollable and uses them. Enough textual evidence was gleaned so as to enact the role of a lowly, proletarian reader who is not unaware of the time immemorial "theft" of the lower orders by those who claim to represent them.

Historiography and the Word *Fascism*

The recent discussion by W. V. Harris of two posthumous books by Arnaldo Momigliano painfully notes that Momigliano was a member of the Italian Fascist party from the late 1920's until he was expelled in 1938 for the crime of being a Jew. His association with the Fascists was voluntary, and the sole reason given for this is that "anyone who desired a university chair in Fascist Italy had to conform." That one of the leading historians of this century was a Fascist whose influence was unparalleled in postwar America and England is immediately joined to the de Man "file": "This is not another Paul de Man case, for Momigliano wrote nothing criminal on behalf of the regime."[5] De Man's *writing* was something criminal while a scholar's voluntarist politics of acquiring position and opportunity with a criminal regime is severed from that name. Apart from the fact that it is not settled how writing can ever be criminal in and of itself, the acceptance by Harris of such "conformity" has a certain resonance within historiography. One is immediately reminded of an historian's rule—writing must conform to facts, a fact always given as the refutation of a concept, an interpretation.

Fascist is a hard word in a profession in which reputation is everything. At the UCLA conference (1991) on "Probing the Limits of Representation," Carlo Ginzburg used the word *Squadristi* in referring to Hayden White's "genealogy," said to include Gentile, Barthes, and, categorically, modernist writing. [6] No less a scholar than Arnold Davidson, editor of *Critical Inquiry,* echoes the *Squadristi* charge by accusing White of practicing the "epistemologically vicious," of "brutely" forcing truth and effectivity together. [7] Relying upon assertions that there is a "regulative ideal of truth" that is not up to us to decide whether it is real and operative in historical writing, Davidson brings into focus the name Fascist and the politics of historical writing. Insisting that there are no "formalizable set of rules" by which "historical evidence" can be deciphered, Davidson insists that Ginzburg's writings are "groundbreaking" in reading the evidence and so must themselves embody the authority of a "regulative ideal of truth." Ginzburg's writings are not just strong interpretations but carry a regulative ideal into the practice of historiography.

Ginzburg's practice is thus of a piece with the antifascism of Momigliano. Ginzburg's own judgments as to Momigliano's unprecedented significance and White's "negative genealogy" are given credence by Davidson because he thinks Ginzburg's writings stem from the incarnation of an ideal. [8] But that the editor of *Critical Inquiry* arguably crosses into hagiography in validating Ginzburg's work, who in turn has promoted Momigliano as a vital model of regulative truth within historiography, each on record as to the deleterious effect of White's text-based arguments, suggests a genealogy that might well start with Ginzburg's "regulative ideal of the historian." What is undertaken here is complex—to examine the construction of this "regulative ideal" by closely reading Ginzburg's texts, said to embody exactly that truth-ideal. Historians have always accused one another of political nonconformity, abandoning ideals, pursuing whims, but historians rarely discuss, as has happened with Davidson and Ginzburg on White, charges that connect ideals and fascism.

In the essay "Nietzsche, Genealogy, History" (1971), Foucault, after Nietzsche, asked: Who is the type called "historian"? What enables the historian to straddle nature and culture, continuity and discontinuity? How can narrative description signify knowledge when made out of word fabrications, composed by political beings whose scholarship may be exceptional and overcode an "eternal will in the object of study," that is, "truth as a regulative ideal," and that then provides "cover" for scholarly politics, the politics of rhetoric? Foucault asked his readers to consider the historian as part of a genealogy in which the human moves from "domination to domination," the "complex mechanism" and temporal processes of systems of control written as the substitution of the name "history" for the actual workings of modes of control. History is much more reassuring than "control." The "regulative ideal of truth" and "regulative sense of the historian" are entwined, and genealogy also inquires as to the functions and operations of "to regulate." In this regard, Ginzburg's controversy with Hayden White will serve as an initial focus, followed by reading a number of Ginzburg's texts so as to specify the point at which the discourse of truth gives enough textual solidity with meanings which are intellectual and political, where truth acquires significations other than the "regulative." Some of these textual solidities are of a type that reflects on Momigliano's conformity and Ginzburg's historiography of the connoisseur.

Controversy with Hayden White

Ginzburg's dispute with Hayden White received a forceful presentation in the essay "Just One Witness," Ginzburg's contribution to a 1991 conference at UCLA on the Final Solution. Saul Friedlander, organizer of the conference, introduced the papers by insisting that the Final Solution was the "most radical form of genocide encountered in history," hence a singular, without comparison. Its singularity prevents comparison, but this raises some questions: is the Final Solution singular because of its three year span, as an instance of industrialized mass murder, or the rising to the surface of a peculiar German Christianity? Embedded in singularity, the destruction of the Jews is not more dramatic than, say, the destruction of the American Indian—it is truer.

Moreover, Friedlander asserted "some claim to 'truth'" is required for any historical inquiry; otherwise, relativism, of the type in which truth and effectivity are joined, becomes unpreventable. True interpretations must be severed from the effects of an interpretation, from their effectivity in the here and now. White's historiographic arguments are reduced to the belief that "specific emplotments, explicative models, and ideological stances" eliminate "outside criterion to establish that one particular interpretation is more true than another."[9] The connection between "outside criterion" and "more true" is murky; presumably, the historians have such "outside criterion," different from White's plot, explanation, and ideologies mixed in any particular interpretation. How can "outside criterion" be separated from the language used to transmit it? Friedlander's discourse goes silent at that point.

The real objective in raising "outside criteria" is to sever historiography's "outside" from that of the "sublime," which is not of the order of truth, sublime meanings being far more unstable than truths. White argued that "one must face the fact that when it comes to apprehending the historical record, there are no grounds to be found in the historical record itself for preferring one way of construing its meaning over another." White says nothing about "truth" here, focusing on the difference between criterion of truth and criterion of meaning, the latter, for him, always connected to the ineluctable question of judgments of taste, discontinuous with the putative "facts" decoded and narrated. Once a perspective is narrated, there is nothing relative whatsoever about that narration. But Friedlander returns to what can be called the stock figure of an idealist condition of historiography: "For most historians a precise description of the unfolding of events is meant to carry its own interpretation."[10] That statement makes historical-writing one with true-description, *ekphrasis* and *enargeia* (description and vividness), joined in such a way that the true description is not to be further interpreted: the "ground zero" of historiography is found in those linguistic acts that manage to do away with the exposure of the linguistic apparatus. This is another version of antitextualism, writing not to be too closely read.

Now Ginzburg's essay "Just One Witness" opens with a story, a fragment of a Jewish survivor, the sole survivor, of a massacre in La Baume, 1348, one Dayas Quinoni, who "left a painful memory of the episode in a few lines inscribed in a Torah." Was "painful memory" Quinoni's?

The authorial use of this fragment does not specify who spoke "painful memory," source or historian. When is a "painful memory" not dramatic even if true in some way? This massacre followed upon earlier killings of Jews and lepers, chronicled by an anonymous monk whose tale told of Jewish mass suicide, that sole survivor killed by the townspeople after breaking his pact to join in the suicide; this chronicle, in turn, shows textual affinities with passages from Flavius Josephus's *Jewish War,* especially the historiographic *topos* that there can be "just one witness." The legalistic criterion of truth—two witnesses—is not the last word on historical truth.

Ginzburg argues that in both the Jewish and Latin legal traditions there was the "well-known rejection of a single witness in court."[11] Dayas Quinoni and Flavius Josephus, however, refer to their respective massacres through only one witness, a truth unacceptable to the legal traditions. But for historiography: "No sensible historian would dismiss this evidence as intrinsically unacceptable." Even if the chronicler of the massacre at La Baume was "echoing"[12] Flavius Josephus's older account, "the account itself would still give us a valuable piece of evidence about the reception of Josephus's work . . . in early fourteenth-century Ile-de-France." Here it is the phenomenological coding of description and truth that matters: The historian must accept that everything from the past is evidence of something, this something is more important than formalisms and legalisms about interpretation. There is, Ginzburg insists, something "before" discourse, an "irreducible . . . reality." Drawing upon remarks by the distinguished historian Vidal-Naquet about certainty, it is insisted that the historian comes after reality.[13]

At this juncture, Ginzburg moves to the genealogy of White's supposed equation between truth and effectivity, repeating Friedlander's introductory comments, already cited. Beginning with White's changing views of Croce's thinking about history—White had once labeled Croce's "youthful essay" on history-as-art "revolutionary"—the story is brought up to *Metahistory* (1973), in which White's "appreciation" of Croce had become "colder." This because Croce's notion of art was a representational notion, White separating historiography-as-art from recent nonrepresentational "advances" in art making. For White, the limit of Croce's viewpoint was that Crocean aesthetics was decidedly restricted by its inability to incorporate experimental artworks: no *Finnegan's Wake* of historiography could appear on the basis of Crocean aesthetics. Ginzburg then separates Croce's views from Gentile, who had been Croce's "closest intellectual associate" between 1897 and 1900, Croce opting for inclusion of philosophy within "methodology of history," Gentile moving toward an idealism in which he claimed it absurd that "historical writing presupposes historical fact."[14]

White's own development parallels the process by which Croce and Gentile's argumentation dissolved into a "bitter political and personal feud." That is to say, as soon as White was to affirm that rhetorical discourse "constructs the objects," Croce's position was negated and Gentile's affirmed. Ginzburg then makes the following conjunction: White's argument is a "subjectivist . . . discourse creating its own objects . . . an imaginary combination of Croce and Gentile." There can be no affirmation that "historiography creates history," so that Gentile's philosophical discourse is merged with the more recent critiques by Barthes and White of historical representation. The common ancestry is said to be that of nihilism toward the facts.

Where Gentile had idealized Marxism through the rule "spirit creates reality" and had supported futurism as "revolutionary," his antihistoricism is set against Crocean "antifascism," a liberal-conservative "perspective." In other words, White's support of a historiography "written in a modernist key" (nonrealism) is evidence of an "extreme subjectivism . . . a definitely radical flavor," an analogue of Fascism. Like the Fascists, the line from Gentile to Barthes to White is the elevation of desire over truth, the historian's language judged political and representation put in doubt. White is our contemporary Gentile and Ginzburg our Croce, the analogy culminating in this astonishing denunciation: "if one regarded *desire* as a left-wing slogan, then *reality* (including the emphasis on 'real facts') would have looked definitely right-wing . . . attitudes implying a basic flight from reality are certainly not restricted today to some factions of the left."

The analogy results in an equivalence: Real historians do not construct so their narratives are not the result of desire; when historians desire, they are constructing. And in a bizarre topic jumping, this equation is identified with today's "extraordinary appeal of skeptical ideologies."[15] A final equivalence: to construct = acceptance of skepticism. Such thoughts are very similar to the hostility analyzed in chapter one concerning Appleby et al. and deconstruction, a staple of contemporary historians, more than content in their "enclosure" and "discipline" (new semantic markers for ambiguous practices).[16]

Even White's explicit argument that skepticism can entail tolerance, utterly incompatible with Gentile's monism (which resolves skepticism into pure ideality) is shunted aside in order to make an equation between Gentile's embrace of the Italian *Squadristi's* blackjack and White's "moral dilemma"; for White has dared to suggest that fascist attitudes toward history cannot be rejected on purely "historical" grounds. Why? Because fascist antihumanism may not be the Other of the West as much as it is a Western inherence. Because he refuses to demonize fascism, White must therefore be tolerant and desire an equivalence between constructed narratives (desire) and the imaginary (fascism).[17] Because White makes a skeptical evaluation of the distinction between "positive historical inquiry" (evidence) and narrative, insisting that distinctions between lies, errors, and mistakes are difficult to draw, his argument converges with Gentile's "transcendental subjectivism." For Ginzburg, "the positive terrain of history" must never be separated from a concept of truth that negates the effective: "if Faurisson's narrative [denial of the Holocaust] were ever to prove effective, it would be regarded by White as true."[18] In other words, because constructivism does not negate effectivism, Ginzburg inverts this as saying that the non-negation of effectivism is the same as the affirmation of it as a criterion of historical truth. Repeated by Davidson in his article referred to above, an either/or (truth versus construct, ideal versus the effective) is made the only choice, nonaffirmation of the positivized side made identical, through the logic of the syntax, with negation. The syntax seems to be of the type *hypophora,* the staging of a trial.

In textual fact, this rhetoric of execution continues onto White's skepticism toward "factism," said to be a mode of intolerance. Quoting Voltaire, Ginzburg insists that only those with "strong theoretical and moral convictions" can be tolerant because "absolute skepticism" (which White never argues for) must logically contradict tolerance. White is entombed even deeper as our contemporary Gentile, philosophy of history gone haywire. Unless truth subtends moral and political differences "there is nothing to tolerate."[19] With Rhetoric in agreement, Ginzburg hurls the ax: White's arguments "connecting truth and effectiveness inevitably reminds us not of tolerance but of its opposite—Gentile's evaluation of a blackjack as a moral force."[20] That Davidson and Ginzburg, two very powerful academic players, can work such notions into "ordinary discourse" suggests politics has already eaten into any notion of scholarly discourse as "truth."

"Just One Witness" closes by bemoaning the "skeptical attitudes" of the 1960s. This bemoaning sadly recalls the name of Renato Serra, whose essays from eighty years ago "reflect the complex personality of a man who, besides being the best Italian critic of his generation, was a person of erudition." Serra had to choose between a "real event" and "historical accounts," which are always based on fragmentary evidence. Serra chose Tolstoy over Croce, for "Serra, ironically defining himself as a 'slave of the thing itself'," affirmed that "every testimony is only a testimony of itself . . . that's all." Because reality came first, because he did not oppose narratives to the "stuff they are made of," Serra's reflections offer us, Ginzburg asserts, proof that while narratives may have a "highly problematic relationship with reality . . . reality ['the things in themselves'] exists."Writing is secondary: what matters is the positivism "of itself." Indeed, so *gnomic* are these assertions that the writing finally transforms itself into the very affirmation it demands:

> . . . a different reading of the available evidence immediately affects the resulting narrative. A similar although usually less visible relationship can be assumed on a general level. An unlimited skepticism toward historical narratives is therefore groundless.

Because there are different "readings" absolute skepticism is unwarranted: but isn't "different reading"White's constructionism? Finally, invoking a citation from Primo Levi that survivors have a "need" to tell their story, "to make the rest participate in it," this demand is accepted on the dubious philology that witness means survivor; the witness is continuous with historians. But in lines not quoted from the same author made to say witness = survivor, witness and survivor are also "truth . . . in the fact of 'divining' what one has not been present at," and "*superstes* . . . the gift of second sight which enables a person to know the past as if he or she had been present,"[21] notions that make the continuity between witness/survivor and historian highly evocative of belief in magical presencing. This is something *vicarious,* a spiritualization such that historical narrations are witnesses to the lives of the dead. In the end, what is opposed to desire and deconstruction, falsely linked, is a sense of prosopopeia considered as an act of thought *natural* to the historian, a genealogy of the historian that also supports "regulative" notions of truth. In short, the historian is *unquestionably* purifed of a dubious genealogy, or a genealogy of the dubious. "Just One Witness" models the rhetorical elimination of deconstruction, here called "constructionism," on the basis of the rhetoric of presence.

Two Readings

Drawing upon Roger Chartier's argument that Ginzburg's well-known *The Cheese and the Worms* is significant because it brought analytic techniques of "reception" or reader response to remote/past anonymous actors who were also readers, that it opened a "direction in which historical research should go," Dominick LaCapra believes something is nonetheless amiss with Chartier's rendering. LaCapra notes that Menocchio the miller's discursive responses to the Inquisition are turned into indices of the persistence of an autonomous peasant culture, rendered by Ginzburg as a "foundational" myth, evidenced in "archeological, arboreal and ocular metaphors." These metaphors have an uneasy relationship with the "repressed" that Menocchio is said to signify. LaCapra is suspicious of the symmetry between Menocchio and the "popular," the "popular" and the historical repressed. This long suppressed oral culture is figured by Ginzburg as "almost an extension of the body," while the tortuous discourse of the Inquisitors was "a thing of the mind," the "abstract over the empirical." [22] For LaCapra all this overly antithesizes, providing readers of *The Cheese and the Worms* with the satisfaction of two cultures, yet one in their identity with the other. The documents that allow this mindscape to occur in the reader's consciousness are then monuments and condensations, representations and illustrations, expressions and determinations giving access to the long negated past. LaCapra's questions intensely ask: How is it possible for documents to say so much?

LaCapra goes on to point out how the writing in *The Cheese and the Worms* plays off highly coded figures of reversal (Menocchio was more rational than the rationalist Inquisitors) and uses anecdotal examples (the telling picture) presented in fragments (that mime the destruction of peasant culture), even obsession (Menocchio's supposed defiance of authority becomes Ginzburg's insistence that ideas do not stem from high society). For LaCapra, this comes together in Ginzburg's unthought-out transference: *The Cheese and the Worms*

> relies on a structural concept (or fixation) of the unconscious as a grid or filter that unifies experience. It thereby represses the more challenging and disconcerting "notion" of the unconscious as a paradoxical name for processes of repression, displacement, and condensation—processes that bring to the fore the significance of the problem of the historian's own transferential relation to the past. . . . [23]

Similarly, LaCapra believes Ginzburg erects a "misleading linear reduction . . . at times . . . close to the inquisitorial logic that he explicitly rejects," that Ginzburg uses the ideas of the Russian linguistic and cultural theorist Bakhtin for conservative purposes. None of the values imputed to Menocchio and to the popular culture he supposedly represents qualify as Bakhtinian "carnival," because Ginzburg eliminates the "joking" attitudes of peasant societies.[24] Further, the documents or Inquisition registers "do not simply represent but also supplement the realities to which they refer."[25] Texts, for LaCapra, are not quarries but, rather more with Derrida, events that must always have a tenuous relation to our modes of encoding. LaCapra makes two judgments:

> it is often impossible to address critically the question of what is coming from Menocchio and what is being projected by Ginzburg [26]

and, in a warning,

> there is a significant relation between intellectual and institutional mat-
> ters. . . . If a certain level of culture represents primordial reality [Menoc-
> chio, orality, peasantry], then it is a very short step to the assumption that
> those who study it are the "real" historians, those who focus on the most
> important things. . . . The result is a bizarre and vicious paradox whereby a
> vicarious relation to the oppressed of the past serves as a pretext for con-
> temporary pretensions to dominate.[27]

Arnold Davidson's essay on Ginzburg's work asserts that Ginzburg's historiographical considerations "ought to inform how our histories . . . are
constructed and written."[28] That is a claim contrary to yet neatly symmetrical with LaCapra's skepticism. Davidson insists that Ginzburg has revived
the ancient concept of *enargeia* or "living narratives," historical truth rendered as an "illusion of reality." Truth requires illusion, but illusion is controlled by a "regulative ideal of truth" that subtends rhetoric itself;
rhetorical effects are acceptable in a given narrative because a truth-ideal
is operative. Here is how Davidson puts it:

> Both judges and historians invoke the notions of evidence and proof, but
> their respective regulative ideals of justice and truth decisively contribute to
> the understanding of what is to count as a piece of evidence . . . What is ev-
> idence for some purposes may be beside the point for others. Obviously
> enough, the *concepts of justice and truth* are compatible with a diversity of con-
> flicting *conceptions* . . . substantive disagreements . . . [do] not imply . . . that
> a historian's reconstructions can ignore the demands of truth. [29]

All this restates the transcendence of an ideal concept over conception,
idealism over semiotics: truth is not semiotic, for no other sign *signs* it but
the assertive and imperative "this is truth."[30] What are these "demands of
truth"? Nothing more is offered than "whether someone possesses the
concept of truth is not up to us to so decide." [31] As LaCapra wondered
after the volatile mixture of vicarious writing and "real historians," Davidson's "regulative ideals of truth" are beyond language, subject only to some
special faculty of the historian.

These gnomic pronouncements indicate the strong presence of political presuppositions. Even more, when Davidson does specify the issue of
truth, the latter is given moral exemplary status, not epistemic force.
Ginzburg's project has provided historiography with a new obligation:

> an adequate historiography must attend to the heterogeneous procedures
> by which we encode evidence . . . Codes that seemed impenetrable can

eventually be deciphered, and new evidence, encoded in new ways, can shed light on old evidence. . . . *There is no formalizable set of rules that tells us how to decipher historical evidence . . .* [the power of] *truly great historical works . . . partly resides in the ability of a historian to read the evidence, to show us how to enter into the codes of evidence in order to see what the evidence is.*[32]

"New evidence" or evidence recently *recognized* and "new ways" of encoding could be interpreted not as truth but as *fashion presented as order-words*. "To read," "to show," "to enter," and "to see" are names of processes not of truth, but of rhetoric outfitted with an aestheticism of cognition and vicariousness, focused on the equation of to read and to enter; it is the rhetoric of *understanding as ideal* that is the determinate concept here. A strong interpretation is equated with truth, exactly what White was accused of doing in his historiographic practice. Davidson insists on "truth" as his writing affirms conceptual possession. When he does turn to *The Cheese and the Worms,* a "truly great work," we encounter this:

Ginzburg's . . . extraordinary ability to read the codes . . . gives us a *more accurate* characterization of the *benandanti* [witch sabbaths] . . . a cultural reality that is no longer inaccessible to us.[33]

All the sense here pivots on "more accurate." What kind of phrase is this? How is a better encoding "more accurate" and not, say, entirely differential, perspectival? That "more accurate" renders "access" supplies readers with the presence of a past, a vanished peasant culture. But syntactically, this must mean that to "read the codes" of past evidence is the truth of that evidence, and should truth come up at all rather than the concept of interpretation? Is this because historians are not interpreters?

(Return to) *The Cheese and the Worms*

In the preface to the English edition of *The Cheese and the Worms,* Ginzburg notes that this "episode" drawn from the preindustrial peasantry is actually an "extraordinary fragment of a reality, half obliterated, which implicitly poses a series of questions for our own culture and for us."[34] This fragment is the "three or four pages" of the inquisitorial trial of the miller Menocchio, continuous with a reality which belonged to the preindustrial, prereformation, peasantry, which once upon a time had a "culture of their own." "Three or four pages" and entry to this "world," a "culture produced by the popular classes," based on the "carnival . . . myth and ritual . . . celebration of fertility and abundance, the jesting inversion of all values . . . cosmic sense of . . . the passing of time."[35] But already this description eliminates key features of carnivalesque discourse, crucial for Bakhtin, cited as the authority for this model of the peasantry. It eliminates that sense of primordial struggle internal to any social group, particularly with peasant discourse that, for Bakhtin, was a discourse always on the *border:*

> ... ancient struggle ... on the boundary line between cultures and lan-
> guages ... two of these factors prove to be of decisive importance: one of
> these is *laughter,* the other *polyglossia.* The most ancient forms for represent-
> ing language were organized by laughter ... the ridiculing of another's lan-
> guage and another's direct discourse ... [36]

Hence, for Bakhtin, there is no such thing as a "culture of their own," but only culture internally and externally in conflict without repose, without singular identity. *The Cheese and the Worms* truncates this sense of conflict in order to give us a peasantry which belongs to a different ancestry, stripped of Bakhtin's suggestive and radical notion about ridicule and laughter.

There are approximately forty descriptions through which *The Cheese and the Worms* installs its writing of the presence or the return by "decoding" of "oral culture."[37] Menocchio's "incalculable significance" and presumed resistance to High Power is hinged to sememes with a pull to symbolic incarnation, that Menocchio was, "in his own person," a "peasant Heraclitus" and so dangerous to the authorities. "In his own person" involves the presupposition that the past is present, a marker of continuism, language here of the cultural-theological type, since the writing emphasizes the nonrhetorical presence of the literal.[38]

The sememic weight of the forty or so qualities attributed to the historical significance of Menocchio cluster in six overlapping categories: metaphysics (1), peasant beliefs (10), political values (3), science/cognition (8), cultural modernity (8), and explicit symbols (5), or bridging figures. To say, for example, that Menocchio was an "inspired reader" is to locate him as part of sixteenth-century cultural modernity, their interest in reading and writing, but this overlaps with science/cognition (Menocchio "mulled" things over, was possessed of an "imperturbable reason"), which is not necessarily antithetical to peasant life, and may be complementary with politics (Menocchio as "heretic"). To Menocchio's peasantness, for example, belongs "utopia," a "store of aspirations," "desire for renewal," belief in "millenarian cycles," the "feast," and "oral and mumbled" culture.[39] While Ginzburg's text writes of the return of the past, one's reading picks up the installation of Menocchio as a good natural scholar. For most valued are those markers which place Menocchio in the tradition of an erudite cultural modernism, specifically descriptions where Menocchio was an "inspired reader," disbelieved in a "hereafter," was antidogmatic, echoed Dante, was intellectually curious and "open-minded," and served as a "translator" for his illiterate townspeople.[40]

If we combine these tags with those pertaining to scientific modernism, that Menocchio "mulled" over "exalted things," was productive of analogies, antimetaphysical, possessed of a materialist value system, and was a "relativist" toward questions of religious foundation, the verbal order slides away from the presence of Menocchio's pastness in favor of symbolic terms: here is a "rational" religion of the "heart," someone who believed in a practical literalism of morality, hardly a "peasant Heraclitus." The qualities which pertain to entering this ancient/obscure "peasant mythology" are those of Menocchio's demand for "prosperity," his "exaltation," "heretical" attitudes, stress on "equality," insistence upon a "new-world," the belief that Christ was "a man like us," the synthesis of utopia and feast[41] and acceptance of a "primordial chaos." But such tags are continuous with the Christian tradition of *renasci* or "spiritual rebirth, with connotations which could range all the way from vegetative to cosmological renewal."[42] In addition, the ancient millennarian idea of "absolute or total perfection" was not distinctly of peasant origin, having as much "play" in the ideas of Jewish syncretistic speculations as in pagan sources. Many of these ideas did originate within sacerdotal wars.[43] Furthermore, as to Menocchio's affirmation of a "primordial chaos" as bound to an "instinctive peasant materialism," where "instinctive" is the way idealists have always set forth the peasantry, the chaos = primordial fusion was a philosophic commonplace; Lucretius, among many ancient writers, used it. That Menocchio believed the world had its "origin in putrefaction" may testify to the power of the paralytic function of myths, about which Lucretius again had something to say, just as much as it may refer to extraordinarily widespread mystery cults absorbed by Christianity.[44] Empedocles mentions putrefaction as part of the belief in the mysteries of Aphrodite, ancient but hardly of the subordinate class (see his *On Nature,* for the presentation of Orphism, which was extremely widespread).

Instead of "access" to a sixteenth-century incarnation of the continuous, yet repressed, what dominates these descriptions is the unacknowledged interpretation that Menocchio bodies forth the *humanism* of the repressed. His critique of "irrationality," insistence on practical religion, his repeated "asking himself" as to foundational questions, his belief that there is no hereafter, his toleration, his genius at producing analogies, his intellectual curiosity, his open-mindedness, his imperturbable reason, his function as translator for illiterate fellow villagers, and his argument as to the relativism of values—all of this identifies Menocchio the miller as an ancestor of the scholar from the subordinate class. But when Ginzburg asserts that "in his own person" Menocchio gives us the "incalculable significance" of the "gesticulated, mumbled, shouted speech of oral culture," the reader is given an interpretation at odds with its own significations. The peasantry is, first, frozen ("mumbled") and then idealized when it resisted authority by engaging the inquisitors with the discourse of a proto-scholar. There is plenty of material here for LaCapra's Derridian psychoanalysis.[45]

Finally, the writing of *The Cheese and the Worms* has at least fifteen significant uses of the term "echo," for example, Menocchio's "analogy between the coagulation of cheese and . . . the terrestrial globe . . . unknowingly echoed ancient and distant myths." "Echo" is one of the constructs that renders continuity in the mode of return, the triumph of what was never lost, or restoration in the form of the return of the repressed.[46] "Echo" functions epistemically in that it offers connection but is at once spiritual in that it asserts the never lost of the archaic and is aesthetic in that it delivers to the reader the way culture works—we of the present are not cut off and some of us, of the present, can commune with the dead. Menocchio is a hieratic symbol of the peasant/scholar, allegory at its most self-flattering.

Idealism and the Good
Doctor of Historiography

Some time later Ginzburg wrote the intellectual ancestry of the historian who could write of a Menocchio. In his introduction to *Clues, Myths and the Historical Method* (1989), Ginzburg says that his interest in "apparently negligible phenomena . . . witch trials" required a new historiographic method, since the "persistence of forms" (oral, peasant culture) irreducible to their "original" context was as much a fact as is definite evidence bound to a precise context. "Demonstrating the significance of seemingly negligible phenomena" required "instruments of observation and scales of research different from the usual," for it involves treating an "immense sweep of time" and "details" from "close-up" as well as connecting "resemblances" between "historical links" and "typological relationships"; these syntagms of historical research are brought to a halt by a startling disclosure: "I have permitted myself to be guided by chance and curiosity, not by a conscious strategy."[47]

To connect different contexts to identical forms or to show forms irreducible to context is one of the great problems of historiography. And making some aspect of a past once again "visible" through reconstructing apparently unrelated historical forms has a genuinely radical potential: It pressures chronology, especially since formal identities might show repetitions and production of an achronicity that would devastate the names and dates of history. Achronicity might make history, with a capital "H" float in the atemporality of forms, so that we could really mean such phrases as a "Cleopatra effect," a "slave effect," an "X effect," all eternal. If a demonstration could render the forms of history as eternal and immediate, immediately eternal and eternally immediate, then the infamous problem of part-whole is conceivably resolvable. This seems to be heavily indebted to the historiography of Ranke, the master of synthesis, and a flirtation with Derridian "specters," Ginzburg inadvertently attached to a deconstruction he insists elsewhere is "cheap."[48] But *Clues* has it that morphology and details connect through "myths and beliefs" that "go back to a much older past," "older" standing in for the originary, the truly before yet a never past "past" presented as a "mythical nucleus that retained its vitality fully intact for centuries—perhaps for millennia," although this "continuity . . . cannot be generically credited to a tendency in the human spirit." Does this mean that continuity is not also "spirit"? Strange sentence.

Clues opts to narrate a history of the scholar as type, to give historians a continuity based in considerations of form, a morphological model. The story of the historian parallels the narrative of Menocchio; as he was rescued, now the historian is to be rendered immune from criticism. For there is something "incalculable" about historians, about which even most of them are blind. *Clues* sets out from the idea that the humanities possess an epistemic model or paradigm that is not to be equated with what is today called "theory," nor identified with what is written, since writing can never be removed from art. Set in the context of the "fruitless" opposition between rationality and irrationality, the humanities might be able to break out of the binary as such, if a formal model can be offered for narrations that combine evidence, truth, and fiction.

Here is what *Clues* textually enacts.

The art historian Morelli found that the best way to make correct attributions of a painting was through the "most trivial details" ("earlobes, fingernails, shapes of fingers"), a task Ginzburg takes pain to separate from Romanticism and its supposed interest in fragments and aesthetics. Morelli was working within a "philological order," employing the same method as Sherlock Holmes, which Ginzburg calls the presumptive method, where the art connoisseur "resembles the detective who discovers the perpetrator of a crime." Both, in turn, are readers of "evidence that is imperceptible to most people."[49] Morelli and Holmes are then joined with Freud, where all share the belief that the "inadvertent little gestures" of our "character" are worth more than "formal gestures." We could say that they share a gift for the trace, this continuous with the earlier mentioned "falling in love" with the past. That is to say, Freud himself cites the story of Morelli, making the latter's efforts favorably comparable with psychoanalysis, of "divine secret[s] and concealed things from unconsidered or unnoticed details." Freud is given the authority to pronounce the model appropriate:

> Freud himself tells us: it was the idea of a method of interpretation based on discarded information, on marginal data, considered in some way signifi- cant . . . details . . . [that] provided the key for approaching higher aspects of the human spirit.[50]

Such "details" are then a historiographic *spell:* Freud and Morelli and Sher- lock Holmes commune in a context that is pure fiction,[51] the power of connecting part/whole, synthesized in this way:

> In each case, infinitesimal traces permit the comprehension of a deeper, oth- erwise unattainable reality: traces—more precisely, symptoms (in the case of Freud), clues (in the case of Sherlock Holmes), pictorial marks (in the case of Morelli).[52]

These connections elicit the truth of the fiction of continuity, close to Freud's notion of the uncanny.[53] Clue, symptom, and trace are encoded as continuum, where the presupposition of identity has been placed in the object (recoding the earlier reality comes "before"). The invocation of achieving "deep" understanding through the "discarded" not only attrib- utes a power of condensation and representation to traces, an altogether magical invocation, but is speculation of the type rhetoric has called *exem- plum* (and symmetrical with Menocchio's "in his own person"). If it is the trace that "permits" (our knowledge) and not the interpreter performing an interpretation, then present fragments must already be part of a special meaning.[54] Indeed, in the passage cited above, from the mention of traces on, there is a systrophe or collection that fails to define (negative proof of speculation), while the first part of the citation is a canonical instance of *aggressio,* from the family of the enthymemic, where "comprehension," a knowledge-ideal, is installed by fiat, by "suppression of a proposition whose reality seems incontestable and which is, for this reason, simply 'kept in mind'." The suppressed proposition is that of continuism, conveyed by analogy, and that involves belief in an involuntary repetition.[55] This kind of syntactic operation is also entirely *aestheticist:*

> The enthymeme has the pleasures of a progress: one sets out from a point which has no need to be proved and from there one proceeds toward another point which does need to be proved . . . the pleasure of the enthymeme is

assigned less to a creative autonomy on the part of the listener than to an excellence of *concision,* triumphantly given as the sign of a *surplus* of thought over language." [56]

In other words, clues, symptoms, and traces are embedded in an order-word operating at the level of *imputing* objectivity to the relation between subject/object, signifiers made continuous with the signified; the act of interpretation is made continuous with the "deeper," and "trace" is asserted as connection instead of a sign or event requiring thought about language's ability to cast the spell of identity.

As we go further "inside" *Clues* we are told:

> In each of these cases the model of medical semiotics is evident: that discipline which permits the diagnosis of symptoms sometimes thought to be irrelevant in the eyes of the layman. [57]

The "irrelevant" is joined to the "discarded," merging in the disappearance of the "layman" from any serious scene of observation or participation. Notice that clues and pictorial marks have been neutralized by the integrative force belonging to symptoms: The psychological symptom is directly productive of character, the clue and mark having stronger cognitive relays to issues of reading, to absences; character involves present tense, clue and mark more a sense of past. In a few strokes, medical semiotics is idealized, medical and legal forensic fused in the literary persona of Holmes-Watson, whose literary life results, Ginzburg believes, from "the splitting of a single real person, one of the young Conan Doyle's professors, renowned for his extraordinary diagnostic abilities."[58] The text affirms absolute continuity: from different traces to one model, from one model to one social type—the professor. A noble ancestry, the good doctor, the humane doctor, an angel of interpretation, for or before whom nothing significant can remain hidden or neglected. Such ancestral or genealogical significance is bolstered by the use of panegyric or eulogy, for "renowned" is to locate our doctor model in the genre of praise. As Louis Marin put it, one can think Ginzburg's "conjecture" as aesthetic and moral enunciative act, installing the beauty of an object.[59]

Once Morelli, Freud, and Holmes are fused, prepared by the rhetoric of eulogy, the writing delivers what one might call desire for the morphological:

> Man has been a hunter for thousands of years . . . he learned to reconstruct . . . invisible prey from tracks . . . to sniff out, record, interpret and classify such infinitesimal traces as trails of spittle. . . . This rich storehouse of

knowledge has been passed down by hunters over the generations . . . folk-lore . . . transmits an echo, though dim and distorted, of the knowledge ac-cumulated by those remote hunters.[60]

This list of generics, narratively moving from man to hunter to learned to storehouse to folklore to knowledge, renders an ancestry of scholarship grafted to an equational/analogical "logic" (hunter = scholar), a meta-physics of continuism, the latter a presupposition of an identity between nature and culture. Is this a Cratylism of the historian? The good doctor is linked with the autonomy of scholarship, the humane sciences' "presump-tive paradigm" of 1870–1880, close, like the hunter, to traces, someone who can relentlessly cultivate the "impersonality" and "self-forgetfulness" necessary for a successful "hunt." The desire to join narrative and mor-phology presumes an adventure narrative, one in which scholarship and cold-bloodedness are released from the blood-letting of the hunt, replaced by the pain of humanity as the scholar's particular laboratory, the study of the shattering of history.[61] It plunges its reader into the "ghostly bones" of spirit, downcoded, for our times, to a "blind ecstasy . . . of reconciliation."[62] The "echo" of *The Cheese and the Worms* is synecdochic: "echo" straddles origin or engendering and inscription or later readings;[63] "Echo" is the Return of the Same and hence origin, and the recollection of this Return of the Same as the "spirit" of the historian. It is Hegel and Plato at once, or change and return are really one. "Echo" is exactly the kind of ideal that historical synthesis requires, a name of the never-discontinuous (like "spirit"), which the "history" of idealism variously recodes as presence (of the past, of the subject, of structures). "Echo" privileges what is believed impervious to time; it is language in maximum assertion against skeptical implications. Criticizing an "echo" is futility itself.

That "man," apart from its questionable implications, does not fit into this rigid model of the hunter or has also been many other things "for thousands of years" is just relegated to the margins. Torture, for example, as Page duBois notes, is part of Western practices from the start: inquisitors are just as good models as are hunters.[64] "The rich storehouse of knowl-edge" is soaked in suffering, including that delivered by Ginzburg's hunter, who mysteriously does not hunt to kill. As this hunter extends into liter-ary folklore, as "echo," it is so basic as to be pure myth, set out as "the abil-ity to construct from apparently insignificant experimental data a complex reality that could not be experienced directly." The hunter's contribution to civilization was in making conjectures. Conjecture here means narrat-able knowledge dissociated from "charms, exorcisms or invocation," rest-ing on "venatic deduction" bringing together part/whole, effect/cause, and metonymy "with the rigorous exclusion of metaphor."[65] Writing is equated with metaphor and metonymy with hunting/thinking, a separation that is also part of idealism, since venaticism has to be construed as prelinguistic and so not subject to distortion (metaphor). The idea that metonymy is predistortive is slightly mad. Or, since metonymy is privileged by means of metaphor, the delirium involved takes an imaginary subjectivity of a hunter as a model for an actuality, prosopopeia serving as construction of purity.

The nature of hunting is then incarnated as the origin of narrative knowledge, the transmission of sequential signs:

> The hunter would have been the first "to tell a story" because he alone was able to read, in the silent, nearly imperceptible tracks left by his prey, a coherent sequence of events.[66]

This cinematic encoding of an image ("silent," "alone") is another recoding of the continuum nature/culture, for "to read . . . silent . . . tracks" identifies hunter *as* storyteller and may well be derived from an aristocratic ethos, the social content of "alone . . . able to read." Who is this hunter without speech, who could yet read? But this fairy-tale undoes itself: who could know whether the hunter did or did not produce dull stories, as narrators often do, or stories narrated in the name of coherence, a logical property, or for an aesthetic sake, or whether the hunter is not continuous with older, less flattering, modes of thought? Exactly why wouldn't some generic model of thievery account for the existence of "coherence/sequence," since thieves have to make up stories all the time? Hunting and coherence: but so is drawing water from a river "reading"; so is walking in and of itself, taking care not to slip. Ginzburg absolutizes this continuum of hunter/coherence by referring to an utterance from an imaginary observer, a model hunter, who could have said "Someone passed this way," and which can be read as the protogram of remembrance. The phrase is a projection of an originary scene that would contain the event of memory, a verbal symbol, which says "there is before." Hunting installs "before." The issue is of course at the limits of idealist repression, since it has no theory at all as to the necessity of forgetting, nor of the impurity of memory. "Someone passed this way" says there is before and it is recuperable.[67]

If "Someone passed this way" is at once a myth of memory, a moral demand, it has an astonishing climax, a *metalepsis* that separates the affirmative strands of divination from the one adversary left, as it were, in the archaic past; this adversary—"divination by inspiration . . . an ecstatic type"[68]—was destined for obsolescence because positive divination, physiognomics, law, and medicine share an interest in "specific cases," in "concrete examples," in "diagnostic and prognostic" disclosures, and

> behind this presumptive or divinatory paradigm we perceive what may be
> the oldest act in the intellectual history of the human race: the hunter squat-
> ting on the ground, studying the tracks of his quarry.[69]

The hunter into narrator severs the origin of historiography from politics and social ranking which often provided a substitute for the epic, as
Herbert Butterfield noted. The persistent image of an isolated hunter por-
ing over traces seems a filmic appropriation from Goethe's *Faust*. Historiography is removed as a discursively contentious area of human conflict.
Butterfield emphasized that ancient historiography was nearly obsessed
with "the attempt to range the deities in proper order and to establish the
relations of heroes both with gods and with families still living in the
world,"[70] hence devoted to a "self-rectifying" use of analogies to support
political command over time, along with the familiar scientemes (for example, Hecataeus used the court-model to scoff at poetics).

From here, *Clues* passes to the social dimension of narrative knowledge.
Thus, in Greece, the "constellation" of "disciplines" for the "deciphering of
signs" matured in becoming autonomous; called philology and historiography, they allowed for "the body, language and human history for the first
time [to be] exposed to objective examination."[71] "For the first time"
means the hunter was domesticated with and by these "disciplines," and
those mindful of the hunter are "heirs of this decisive turning-point in the
culture of the *polis*." Present-day scholars are connected to a continuous
historicity of study. Analytic divination triumphed in the Hippocratic
study of symptoms, a "conjectural paradigm" that was sanctioned "in the
denial that reality is transparent." Can such an epistemic claim, based on
negation, be sufficient to support the claims for ancestry? Or to put this
differently, once positivized and set beyond criticism, conjecture is itself
"proof" that certainty can be disclosed by "study," and *Clues* insists that the
combination of evidence and conjecture marks out a resistance to science
as we know it, a resistance to quantification and repetition. The humane
sciences concern individual "cases, situations, and documents, precisely because they are individual."[72]

The history of historiography has, therefore, of necessity an antiquarian dimension, mostly suppressed until the seventeenth century, when its
"conjectural" aspect flourished. (Antiquarianism is another continuum).
Throughout, the "original feature" of historiography is ever present: "a social science *sui generis,* forever tied to the concrete."[73] *Sui generis* means
peculiar, continuous with "indirect, presumptive, conjectural." This is, in
some ways, convergent with R. G. Collingwood's idea that historical
knowledge results from the historian's reenactment of past thoughts,
where all "knowledge of mind is historical" precisely because it grapples

with "the inner side of the event," a "reasoned knowledge of what is transient and concrete."[74]

What matters is for the historian to engage "material data" that alone justifies the "hazard" of "diagnoses." Thus Mancini, physician of Urban VIII, made "the first attempt to establish connoisseurship . . . lightning diagnoses . . . [and] could divine." His application of the knowledge of connoisseurship to painting was a "methodology . . . identifying fakes, distinguishing originals from copies, and so on."[75] The antiquarian Mancini recoded the hunter/prey couple as the rule of "sniffing out" the invisible, now become the original, for in a society ruled by contracts and signs, the hunter becomes a reader in the mode of a verbal *thoroughbred,* taking this term nearly literally and exercising judgments of pure quality. Indeed, *Clues* sets out to expand qualitative judgments, while acknowledging them as "the principal pitfall of the humane sciences." Mancini, so as to date paintings, entered into the study of handwriting, and this culminated in a near obsession with the "master's hand," in which "the parts of a painting executed most rapidly, and thus potentially freed from the representation of reality (tangles of hair, cloth)" offered the best chances for hypotheses as to origin. *The best objects to study are those from connoisseurs themselves,* those whose "boldness, strokes and flourishes" showed such self-mastery and hence afford luxury to later readers. The modern historical narrative in which facts seem to "tell themselves" is not defended by this model.

This narrative of the professor as connoisseur makes the "moment" of the connoisseur's own *originality* into one of those founding moments of our humane knowledges, even if subsumed by the triumph of the anatomist and Galilean generalizers, whose embrace of the "suprasensorial eye of mathematics" left only "sight" to the humanists. "Sight" recodes the hunter's "alone was able to read," joined to "scientific knowledge of the individual," while holding fast to the "emotional distance of the observer." The antiquarian-connoisseur preserved what the hunter provided: the power to substitute a justified "intuition" for the documents, artifacts, evidence from times past, such hunter functions being the knowledges of the "living voice, from gestures and glances . . . subtleties impossible to formalize . . . the patrimony . . . from all social classes . . . concrete experience." Conjecture has suffered from "the inability to make use of the power and terrible weapon of abstraction."[76] As the human sciences became subject to modernization, the hunter-connoisseur was "victimized," subject to modes of thought without "taste."

The signifiers of continuity and discontinuity in this narrative of the scholar hold the connoisseur aloof from the "bourgeois" appropriation of every kind of knowledge that had resulted from "acculturation begun earlier . . . by the Counter-Reformation."[77] *Before* this counterreformation "the flexible and rigorous insight of a lover or a horse trader or a card shark," while *after* it the "novel . . . a substitute for and reformulation of initiation rites—that is, for access to experience in general."[78] The idealism ladled over "horse-trader" recodes hunter-connoisseur, just as the "printed page" must be of a lesser value, since it is vicarious by comparison to "rigorous insight" or direct sight. The before of "initiation rites" is asymmetrically coded with "novel," but the latter is not so much negativized as it is made supplemental: As a "literature of imagination," the modern novel earns the right to historical significance because, as an endnote has it, that aspect of the novel that is a "true descendent of the fairy tale" is "serendipity." Serendipity, legitimized by Walpole, has an ecstatic genealogy like the hunter. An Oriental fable (from Ceylon), transmitted by the scholar Sercambi, from which it traveled to Venice in the mid sixteenth-century, receiving eight translations and passing through Voltaire's *Zadig,* coalesced in "the embryo of the mystery novel." The scholarly ancestor's mentioned in *Clues* are all cases of serendipity, hence "proving" the model. The "mystery" novel, with its clever detectives, before whom truth is revealed, supports historiography, since the latter is under the sign of being "guided by chance and curiosity." "Embryo" precisely naturalizes these aspects of the ancestry of historiography, giving it an origin in venatic actions, but always present (the meaning of *sui generis*) when the right combination happens, for instance, Cuvier cites *Zadig* to support paleontology's use of conjecture, the "cloven hoof" allowing for the guess that the animal was a "ruminator." "When causes cannot be produced, there is nothing to do but to deduce them from their effects."[79] But to go from "cloven hoof" to "ruminator" so quickly destroys the very possibility of conjecture, for if in deduction one makes equivalencies between the seen and the known so that one directly substitutes for another, as in Cuvier's example, then "ruminator" is obviously destructive of the abductive model Ginzburg has in mind as the ideal act of historical thinking. "Ruminator" is an interpretant, not a quality of the thing itself.

All of this, in turn, is telescoped in the figure of a carpet, the humane sciences in a "tight homogeneous weave," continuous with a "common epistemological model" that in the nineteenth century separates from natural scientific deduction and its rival, the anatomical model promulgated by Marx. The humane sciences not under the spell of quantification become the domain in which more weaves are added to the "carpet," the latter a synecdoche for the totality of human knowledge. The "carpet" symbolizes conjecture as something pertaining to the acculturated, the familiar domestic object that has something mysterious about it. Continuous with what is found in well-to-do families, the "carpet" is both natural/continuous and cultural/artifact, connected to absolute and absent causes that can be assessed. This figure, claimed as model and as trace, is essentially a literary device, the "carpet" a signifier of success, of successful interpretations ("carpets" also unravel, and are often made by twelve-year olds, unnoticed here).

So this machinery of "like by like," of recall by analogy, of connection by resemblance, carries over even to the "criminalization of the class struggle," the nineteenth-century obsession with recidivists.[80] Bertillon's combination of photograph and verbal description of the ears of criminals "cannot help but recall the illustrations in Morelli's own works appearing at this time" (1879). The emergence of fingerprinting, though put to use in the name of criminalization, owed its origin to Prukyne, who in 1823 devised a way of classifying nine papillary lines, this descendant of Leibniz individualizing such "infinitesimal characteristics" that palmistry was dropped into the void of "hasty conjectures" (bad divination). Purkyne writes in Latin and is not read until fifty years or so after his discovery, another good doctor long suppressed. Meanwhile, Bengalese, Chinese, and Japanese "soothsayers" responded to the challenge of the imperceptible and remained in touch, as it were, with "divinatory" powers. The Bengalese, who invented their own mode of fingerprinting, were fingerprinted by their English masters, the efficiency of English bureaucracy having "appropriated the conjectural knowledge of the Bengalese and turned it against them."[81]

The originality of venturing conjectures is much more difficult to sustain in an industrialized social system, as the example of fingerprinting makes clear. Here *Clues* becomes extremely compressed and partly unintelligible; for if, as is asserted, *true* conjecture is part of the "same . . . paradigm employed to develop [negative] . . . capillary forms of control," it

> can become a device to dissolve the ideological clouds which increasingly obscure such a complex social structure as fully developed capitalism. Though pretensions to systematic knowledge may appear more and more farfetched, the idea of totality does not necessarily need to be abandoned.[82]

Conjecture belongs to the "penetration" of and connection with "totality," while its destructive application belongs to "system": The very distinction presupposes a "divination" of the entanglements of positive and negative. "Totality" is asserted as "deeply rooted" (continuum), where the opaqueness of reality has "privileged zones—signs, clues—which allow us to penetrate it." Hence "penetration" of the opaque and connection to "totality," quite apart from its erotic charge, is an idealist prejudice: synecdoche, or integration of part and whole, in which "privileged zones" must already be part of a "totality." How such "zones" got started is, of course, a dilemma for any rational analysis. The writing of *Clues* is here extremely projective, virtually a demand-wish: "slender clues" render access to "the world view of a social class, a single writer, or an entire society,"[83] the grammar of which reinstalls holism against modern quantification.

As the narrative of positive divination reaches the present, the writing begins to implode: psychoanalysis is sanctified, as is the aphorism, where, from Hippocrates to Nietzsche, it is said to be the very genre of divination. This ignores the fact that aphoristic statements are great dangers to thought, as the case of Nietzsche should have made clear. Indeed, even Proust's *Recherche du Temps Perdus* is thrown into the hopper of identity, here insisted as a "clue" of the modern crisis of connoisseurship, a misreading, since it ignores that Proustian writing affirmed nonidentity, the violence of signs "which forces us into the search, which robs us of peace," giving the possibility of more betrayal by signs, instead of signs giving us beautiful lies.[84]

This apologia for "divination" returns to the choices facing historical writing: a "lax" use of science might give noteworthy results, whereas a tight scientization gives "results of scant significance." *Clues* rejects such choices for something altogether more elementary. This purified genealogy presents itself as a model bridging that famous "gap" between history as art and history as science. The choice is for the "vivid" over the "exact." This is because the historian is after

> forms of knowledge most linked to daily experience—or, more precisely, to all those situations in which the unique and indispensable nature of the data is decisive to the persons involved,[85]

anchored in a very precise concept of the human—

> It was once said that falling in love is the act of overvaluing the marginal differences which exist between one woman and another (or between one man and another). But this can also be said about works of art or about horses. In such situations the flexible rigor (pardon the oxymoron) of the conjectural paradigm seems impossible to suppress.[86]

The telling of this model thus returns to legitimizing its own morphology. Let's unpack this, taking as our focus the phrase "flexible rigor," which is the only phrase repeated in *Clues,* a recoding of the earlier mentioned "flexible and rigorous lover." The irony is drenching: "falling in love" = overvaluing; works of art = horses = women, all thoroughbreds, that are thoroughly bred. "Can also be said about" enables our good doctor to affirm the identity of women, art, and horses, objects of taste for the connoisseur's "power" of "divination." The structure of this is precious and tautologic: The historian is always at the hunt, ready to discern those objects that testify to their own divinatory value, those built up themselves as the result of conjectures ("in his own person," Menocchio was "incalculably significant"); and to say conjecture is "impossible to suppress" is to confuse premise-making, which Collingwood noted was a mode of justification, with intuition; if one believes that there is a "totality" or that knowing is "like" "falling in love," one thereby merely authorizes oneself and others to believe "who wishes to do so."[87]

Further, to say that conjecture is not suppressible is to assert it as a "natural" act; the text says even more, laying down that conjecture may itself not allow for formalization or to be spoken: conjecture is "mute," where "no one learns to be a connoisseur or diagnostician by restricting himself to practicing only preexistent rules," since "instinct, insight and intuition" are presupposed when conjecture is activated as historical *thinking*. And here the text makes its last Platonic move: the reader is provided with a saving division so as to separate connoisseurship from the "ecstatic" divination the ancients themselves supposedly broke with; for if we speak of intuition, we must separate intuition into its low and high forms:

> Ancient Arabic . . . *firasa* . . . the ability to pass . . . to the unknown . . . from . . . *sufi* and designated mystical intuitions as well as forms of discernment and wisdom. . . . This "low intuition" is based on the senses (though it skirts them) and as such has nothing to do with the suprasensible intuition of the various nineteenth and twentieth century irrationalisms. . . . It is . . . Bengalese . . . of hunters; of sailors; of women. It binds the human animal closely to other animal species.[88]

Intuition separates into a "bad" suprasense and a "good" discernment/wisdom. "Good" intuition is empirical but "skirts" the senses, "skirts" meaning that it moves around the mystical yet avoiding the "supersensible," where the intellect intuits the transcendental. The "good" intuitive is the subject itself, making conjectures. On account of all this, a reader can now assume that the specific intellectual activities of what is rolled into the actant of the historian are natural, that the historian does not make mere interpretations but divines the connection between trace and whole. The entire project may be said to be aestheticist, packed in the signifiers of erudition, a historiography returned to *naturalism*. One order-word controls the textual system: the historian has an unquestionable genealogy, the hunter outfitted for judgments of taste.

Extreme Idealism—Symbol, Context, Rhetoric

Clues thus antithesizes the value of a good doctor set in opposition to both the wrong kind of divination (ecstasy) and ordinary science (reduction and quantification, repetition). The subterms that support the good doctor are the hunter, medical semiotics, studying, philology, antiquarianism, self-rectification, fairy-tales, the image of the "carpet," and intellectual "penetration" of mysteries; supported by assertion, eulogy, and apology, or dogmatism and emotional pleas, by the poetics of "echo," the force of the language of *Clues* aims at undercutting the act of interpretation in favor of sanctifying intuition. Connoisseurship should not have any rivals.

Because Menocchio's world was reconstructed through the documents left by his accusers and his own "hesitations and silences" were apparent, "the hypotheses, the doubts, the uncertainties became part of the narration," a narration one with Tolstoy's *War and Peace* in its assertion that "a historical phenomenon can become comprehensible only by reconstructing the activities of all the persons who participated in it." This is Davidson's "regulative ideal of truth" recoded as phenomenological totality. But *The Cheese and the Worms* removes its own possessive reading of Menocchio from interpretation, as its writing tried to install only one sense of Menocchio, his vivid importance as a concrete subject of scholarly continuity with the repressed underclass.[89]

As microhistory is articulated in subsequent essays, it involves, as with *Clues,* reliance upon the rhetoric of synecdoche, increasingly cast as an ideal of research, the search for exceptional and esoteric data embedded in "wholes" accessed only by connoisseurship. One essay, citing an Altdorfer painting from 1529, leads its reader to the conclusion that historical events are "invisible" until "an abstract diagram or a visionary imagination such as Altdorfer's can convey a global image," Altdorfer turned into a connoisseur of an event. Drawing upon Siegfried Kracauer's work, the model of narration best suited for microhistory is said to be a "cinematographic close-up," continuous with Warburg's dictum that "God is in the details" as well as with the practices of Tolstoy and Namier. In recent essays, the rhetoric more and more embraces phenomenological juxtaposition between close-ups and extreme long shots, so as to bring "back into discussion the comprehensive vision of the historical process through apparent exceptions and cases of brief duration . . . reality is fundamentally discontinuous and heterogeneous."[90] This citation insists that conjecture is validated by exceptions which prove there is some totality, that *vision* is not a literary or philosophical trope but the connection between continuity and discontinuity. Microhistory is severed from the postmodern "fragment," because the latter is unable to rely on the careful

"insistence on context." The fragment is like the novel of *Clues,* its infe-
riority embedded in its lack of context. "Context" is one of the great esoteric words of historiography, an order-word in and of itself. A simple
Nietzschean response: context for whom? Ginzburg notes that a topic
may be selected for historiography "because it is typical . . . or repetitive,"
but "Italian microhistory has confronted the question . . . through the
anomalous."[91] Why? Because microhistory "hypothesizes the more improbable sort of documentation as being potentially richer," research driven by rarity, the unexpected, improbable events, what science/aesthetics
have in common. Microhistory makes claims as to unifying the divide between art and science. But what is offered as proof of the "anomalous" or
the exceptional is a flashy rhetorical "quip": there is such a thing as the
"exceptional 'normal'" case and evidence, this euphuism of connection
and balance, the apparent paradox of the "exceptional 'normal'" said to
bring an object under descriptive control. The anomalous is threaded to
what is lost and invisible, an ideal that does not multiply problematics of
interpretation, but which instead demands closure: "Any social structure
is the result of interaction and of numerous individual strategies, a fabric
that can only be reconstituted from close observation." "Context and
"fabric": hence the figure of the carpet allows for contextual divination,
quite different from saying that context is itself the result of "visions," radical and incommensurable interpretations, all of which might make the
"exceptional 'normal'" hardly a credible model.

In a recent piece published in both *New Left Review* and *Critical Inquiry*
(1994), with the creaky title "Killing a Chinese Mandarin: The Moral Implications of Distance," the immediate topic is present day world civilization's "feeble" sense of a "moral imagination." Starting from Aristotle's
concerns over natural law and particular law, the problematic concerns the
"contradictory implications" of feeling for others: "If extreme distance
leads to indifference, extreme closeness can lead either to pity or to destructive rivalry."[92] Balance and perspective, indistinguishable from a "feel"
for context, must matter. The further one is in time and/or space from others the greater the possibility of moral indifference; the closer, the greater
the chance for identification, others as a danger. Perspective, or sight, as
Clues had it, is everything.

The essay leaps 2,000 years to negate a text by Diderot, whose work,
written in a "broken, abrupt style," with an "ill-woven digression" (a "bad
carpet," as it were), entertains the possibility that "remorse springs . . . from
fear of others" instead of from "horror of oneself," what Aristotle taught.
Diderot's position led "to an extreme." Diderot's writing is part of the discredited "ecstatic divination," extreme views because they are unnatural or,
better, evoke nature as irrelevant to what humans are capable of doing to

each other, including self-deception. Extremes destroy the unity of the subject. Where Aristotle noticed that men can lack pity because of distance, Diderot argued for the "lack of remorse of the murderer . . . a split self," which threatens to unravel natural law. Natural law is thus a cultural analogue of the hunter-model, both rendered as positive solutions to moral relativism, to improper distance or the not-proper of the wrong type of divination (for example, Diderot's speculation about ratios of moral distance). Indeed, what is disturbing for Ginzburg is that Diderot even contemplates a "moral experiment" at all, that such thinking could obliterate natural law. Diderot's hypothesis that the killing of a Chinese mandarin is made acceptable by sheer distance is analogous to his belief that the deprivation of the blind leads to their "lack of humanity and compassion." Diderot practices the wrong form of analogy, one based on *contextuality:* "According to Diderot, morality is the result of specific circumstances and constraints, physical as well as historical," and this is related to the way Diderot thinks—"through a sudden twist, typical of Diderot's way of reasoning."[93] This is an extreme statement: Elimination of the contextual in the name of the eternally true. Diderot's "reasoning" culminates in Sade "arguing the legitimacy of murder." Diderot and Sade, in short, produce an erroneous mode of "divination," the "ecstatic type" that the hunter-connoisseur rejects as a foundation for the humane sciences. Chateaubriand picks up the "thread" of the story of the killing of a Chinese mandarin, modified by Balzac's *Modeste Mignon,* which replays Aristotle versus Diderot: modern "backwardness" and imperialism have enabled "moral indifference . . . [to imply] a form of complicity." Nonetheless, Aristotle has been proven correct by negative example: "Airplanes and missiles have proved the truth of Diderot's conjecture," culminating in the mass murder of the Jews—

> The sharp distinction between *us and them* that was at the core of the Nazi racist legislation was related, on a theoretical level, to an implicit rejection of the idea of natural law.[94]

But there is a saving *cultural norm,* the "general" itself in the form of natural law not completely effaced, for the Nuremburg trials showed that

> the juridical notion of crimes against humanity . . . can be regarded as a belated victory for Antigone . . . in Aristotle's view . . . the supremacy of general laws over particular laws.[95]

As if this extraordinary use of analogy was not enough, it becomes pretext for what Ginzburg actually wants to connect with: historicity is now in danger, a loss so incalculable that the traces of the past are threatened with extinction. Now it is Walter Benjamin who is pulled into the breach:

> The impulse to rescue the past from an incumbent menace has never been so poignantly articulated as in the "Theses on the Philosophy of History" written by Walter Benjamin.

And what is this "impulse" to rescue the past? Is it the same "impulse" as *Specters of Marx?* It is a combination of morality (*must, should*) and ecstasy: The dead are waiting for us to save them, we have a responsibility to do so. Not Nietzsche's question—what is selected here?—but continuity justified in the name of continuity. The historian embodies this responsibility insofar as a "feel" for the past—"exceptional normal"—legitimizes giving propriety to what the past is said to want to tell us. More: Benjamin is soon replaced by a quotation from the late-nineteenth century philosopher Lotze, neglected, according to Ginzburg, but who formulated what we need, an "echo of Aristotle," an attitude of "freedom from envy which the present displays toward the future," for only by means of this attitude can we rekindle our sense of historical messianism toward the past. In other words, we are threatened today with the conception of a future that is nightmarish; only by saving the past from oblivion do we have the chance to "speak the future." But to say that the past has a claim even on our "weak messianic power" is to use the past as an alibi for our interests; indeed, Benjamin's statement that there is "a secret agreement between past generations and the present one," is a proposition worthy of critique, not repetition and adulation, for what exactly is this agreement known to scholars? Is it an excuse-structure for our fiddlings with the present-future, discreditings and legitimations for changes in fashion, in which interpretations replace one another according to criteria that no one in the past could have recognized?

Earlier it was stated that one of the edges of Ginzburg's work was its non-defense of narrative presentation. Description matters more than narration. This concerns the topic of *enargeia* "to convey a vivid representation of characters and situations" and whose sources are ancient.[96] The ideal historian offers convincing descriptions, just as the hunter provides effective facts. While "in the last twenty five years words like *proof,* or even *truth* . . . have acquired in the social sciences an unfashionable ring, evoking positivist implications,"[97] both the positivism of documents as an "open window" and the antipositivism of skeptics who treat documents as a "wall," blocking "access to reality," are rejected. These assumptions are "wrong . . . and unfruitful." Why? If evidence is neither window nor wall, there is an alternative: "a specific interpretive framework is needed . . . related . . . to the specific code according to which the evidence has been constructed." We must assume that the evidence first be read for its distortions, as in Menocchio's trial; but this can also mean that there is no evidence, for if signs, of whatever type, are constituted by our interests, to say that the evidence is "coded" does not mean that we can decrypt it—decoding cannot be set forth as decryptology, because written data may be coded and *undecidable,* there being no unitary codes in written documents.[98] Furthermore, L. Canfora has suggested that vividness was also inseparable from analogy and ancient notions of superiority, never withdrawn to a purified sense of descriptive facility.[99] What is this rhetoric of the vivid that makes it more important than questions of proof; exactly why is description more important than argument?

The essay from 1988, *"Montrer et citer,"* protests that criticisms of historiography only analyze "typical sentences" of historians and ignore "what kind of empirical research was behind them."[100] What "research" is we do not know. From the other direction, any overemphasis upon the literariness of historical writing ignores "the interaction between 'historical imagination' and historical evidence, between history as a literary artifact and history as a research activity."[101] Reaching again for the timeless ancestry of Aristotle, it is insisted that the mode of presenting historical research is irrelevant so long as the historian makes "statements about reality, which claimed to be true." Is every sentence under truth? Is rhetoric under truth? Research is clearly the salvation of historiography, a positivist claim, and decisively impossible to affirm the instant a reader pays close attention to the writing of research. Brushing aside all other issues, "Montrer et citer" insists that today philosophers, literary critics, and symbolic anthropologists teach the same thing—the referential fallacy. Neoskepticism abounds, and "I have no sympathy with it."[102] Ginzburg grants that historical and fictional texts share "some elements," but he wants to explore "why we perceive as real the facts related by a historical text." Is the reality effect due to truth or to language of truth, epistemology or rhetoric? As formulated here, the argument is that reader's perceive as "real" written significations, descriptions. But this raises to the status of truth written descriptions, it makes the referential illusion intrinsic to historiography, that description = the real. Can a reader perceive the written as real or do readers, at best, think about the real through the writing of it? Ginzburg's argument is very close to that of Ankersmit's, discussed in the first chapter; only here, instead of formal resemblance between text and picture, it will be language that renders the connection sought for.

Polybius, quoted by Strabo, said that the aim of history is truth, and what Polybius wrote, Ginzburg insists, aimed at vividness (*enargeia*), not to please or astonish. *Enargeia* "is not a live word anymore," having been replaced by *energheia* or "energy" (for example a 900-page biography of X that gives no new perspective). As supposedly descended from Homer, what the historian renders is "clear," "palpable," "a sphere of direct experience." This installation of *enargeia* supposes straightening out all the distortions of evidence, "vividness . . . regarded as a guarantee of historical truth."[103] Once again, we can note here that this idealized sense of *enargeia* assumes, on the basis of a few classical authors, an agreement and authoritative role that was extremely contestable, especially for ancient writers. Ginzburg gives us ancient models stripped of their verbal/social conflicts. D. L. Clark, in his *Rhetoric in Greco-Roman Tradition,* notes that *enargeia* was the figure of a "word picture" so as to display "particulars to the eyes of the mind," yet also a figure that "forces itself on the notice."[104] Vivid descriptions are often violent, like any absolute. An exercise for boys and so highly charged for maintenance of the security and propriety of public life, the linkages between vividness, public life, and force are eliminated by Ginzburg's ancestry of the concept.

Unbothered by such issues, our historian cites Quintilian and Cicero to stress the revival of the "palpable, the obtruded," which will permit us "to behave as if we could have been physically present to those events." Rhetoric gives "presences" continuous with reality. That Cicero's notion of *historia magistra vitae* was also about "lending immortality to a history that was instructive of life, of rendering perennial its store of experience" is unmentioned.[105] This rhetorical "core" is aestheticized, made a "nearly magical gesture of the orator pointing at some inexistent object, made visible," affirmed "by the nearly magical power of his words" and "putting an invisible reality under their eyes." Historical writing passed into autopsia, "direct view," the illusion of a reading that has no risk of vicarious interpretation (for instance, misreading), and so unable to think within its own territory the idea of the postmortem, what we call autopsy.

Favorably quoting Demetrius, for whom *enargeia* meant "nothing is omitted," transmitted to Greek historians as the claim to have recorded "all the events," Duris and Philarkos produced a historiography "inspired by tragic poets and centered on mimetic effects."[106] But even here, the old sources conveyed the contrary. Plutarch confirms that vivid writing was necessary, this for the "desire to make the reader a spectator." What Ginzburg has selected from the past confirms the bias: a deproblematized mode of writing was issued, which is given as the equation "historical narrative—description—vividness—truth." A single quotation from Quintilian is offered: truth is based upon the "appearance of palpability for the facts which he [historian] narrates," severing this apology for the vivid from its didacticism, which Polybius synthesized as "learning how to bear the vicissitudes of fortune," that is, moral embalming.[107] Only with the seventeenth-century resistance of antiquarians to skeptics did their conservation of classical historiography's rescue of nonliterary evidence mesh with the annalists of the sixteenth century, resulting in the emergence of the *quotation mark* as the "effect of truth." Here too there is the amazing dissociation of the quotation mark from its functions in disqualification, as rhetorical treatises have noticed.[108] Joined to vividness and not to dissociation, to narration and not to skepticism, the quotation mark indexed the separation from the fictitious orations common in historical narratives, historians such as Baronius insisting that their citation of authorities "will be found in the margin . . . I am not writing . . . learned fables."[109] And in a final idealism, this one attending to the triumph of research over writing, it is asserted that

> Quotation (either direct or indirect) has superseded *enargeia*—a fateful victory . . . the victory of a dialogic over a monologic attitude.[110]

It is a kind of madness to say that to quote is automatically a "dialogue" with the thoughts of the past; once again, a Bakhtinian term is severed from any dynamic, active, disruptive context.

Conclusion: Historiographic Vicariousness and a Question of Writing

Momigliano once wrote that Vico was a "great thinker" but not a very "exact scholar."[111] The best historians, like Grote, combined "passionate moral and political interests, vast learning, and respect for the evidence," but many modern historians have given their writings over to "idle and misleading speculation."[112] "We must not allow people to get away with doubtful pieces of evidence."[113] He concluded his famous essay "A Hundred Years After Ranke" by calling for "improvement" because "too much historical research is being done by people who do not know why they are doing it and without regard to the limits imposed by the evidence."[114] These are severe judgments from an acknowledged master-scholar and connoisseur. Yet as late as 1982, as G. W. Bowersock reports, Momigliano could write that his essay from 1936, his Turin inaugural, "is to be published only with an indication of the personal and political situation of one who spoke as a Jew and nonfascist."[115] As said at the start of this chapter, one can assume that political membership in the party was not judged by Momigliano as a political act. Being an historian overwrote all other codings.

Ginzburg's extraordinary textualization of the connoisseur as the ideal historian, continuous with primeval hunting, medical semiotics, detective stories, ecstasy and divination, and rigid insistence that all of these modes connect with "evidence," indicates that he believes he has access to a "special power," the one that goes by the name *vicarious,* very close to prosopopeia. What is "true" is "invisible" but there is a "way" to it. That is to say, the persistent recoding of the historian as someone who connects with the spirit and body of the past results from the judgment that the connoisseur's description is removed from ordinary judgment—the connoisseur is in possession of an intuitive schema that is beyond language. Ginzburg's writings, collectively, are conversant with Ankersmit's claim that historians are intuitively based and yet not excluded from the strange cultural historiographic zone worked by Derrida in *Specters of Marx.* To put this another way: is it ironic that the author of *The Cheese and the Worms* cited Bakhtin in order to access the past, when it is Bakhtin who reminds us that vicarious writing was associated not only with priestcraft but also with that *presencing of absences* whereby writing institutionalized itself as the "straightforward, serious word"?[116] Is this sacerdotalism? As Umberto Eco suggests, prosaic writings that traffic in the vicarious often resort to the textual strategy of citing "a preceding *auctoritas*" that has "already established the appropriate contextual selections," this in order to give signs of proof—here the signifiers of ancestry that subtend Ginzburg's historiographic texts.[117]

The *OED* defines the "vicarious" as what (1) "takes or supplies the place of another thing or person; substituted instead of the proper thing or person." It also means (2) something "endured or suffered by one person in place of another," as, for example, in the Passion. And finally it means (3) power "exercised by one person, or body of persons, as the representative or deputy of another." (1) is offered as a universal process, where "substituted" is installed as proper, where one for another has the sense of the proper for the proper; (2) is also a substitution, involving the complex notion that the proper cannot itself appear, be here, and it does not say whether or not only something proper must be substituted for what is already proper; (3) is a political-economic construct. *Vicarious* must then, as a figure at once deeply grammatical (role) and rhetorical, play off and be playable off the likely interminability of what makes substitutive play thinkable. The vicarious is infinitely thinkable, or as representation it can never end, because the vicarious is attached to what Derrida once named *economimesis,* where representing the unrepresentable reproduces the very "source" that we cannot live without (for example, Mother Nature, Father Time, the Great Gift, specters) and that we cannot know.[118] But if interpretations are vicarious, when are they proper?[119]

Now, if we follow Eco for a moment historically, the vicariousness of interpretation was connected to the medieval formation of allegory (retelling), an attending morality (conversion to grace), and mysticism ("sanctified spirit," "eternal glory"), which prevented the charge of vicariousness from setting off disputes. The sense that an interpretation is in any way forced was (temporarily) halted in the medieval systematics by a kind of "theological epistemology," with controls on "aberrant" thought. The charge of vicariousness was equivalent to saying that one had made an aberrant presencing of absences, a forced allegory. To accuse an interpretation of vicariousness was already to begin to ridicule it.[120] As Reinhart Koselleck pointed out, when the vicarious dualism between Hellene and barbarian proved semantically inapplicable due to population shifts and political loyalties, it was recast as an allegory of education, the Hellene someone who could speak Greek, even if a barbarian.[121] Substitution and the vicarious come to associated with truism, likelihood and probability, severed from the vicarious by exegetes, authorities on the authorities, who render aberrant interpretations unacceptable. Rhetoric must itself be used to suppress figural "colors" in the very act of using them.[122]

The historiographic texts of Ginzburg involves, I have suggested, a high degree of vicariousness, in the sense of writings that operate in the mode of a denial of interpretation, and this because the writings are finally dogmatic. The insistence that the meaning of Menocchio the miller is bound to "peasant materialism" is written in a discourse that transforms Menocchio into the "natural scholar" ("in his own person"); the spiritualization of the past ("impulse") transforms writing into theology; the use of "echo" threaded to incessant continuisms turns on the symbolism of the never-lost; the denunciation of the "Diderot effect" gives us the alibi of puritanism; and the idealism of "vividness," this persistent attempt to return historiography to a place it has never been—pure research and unobtrusive—indicates the concentrated intellectual toxicity of the vicarious. Most disturbing of all are the modes of order-words, particularly the idealization of "vividness" as the way the vicariousness of language is itself suppressed. These texts bring the furious struggle between the historian and language, the historian and conformity to the surface: it may be that if Momigliano's self transcendence of politics led him to view fascism as tolerable, this is of the same logical order as Ginzburg's overestimation of the connoisseur as transcending and sustaining historiography. In that case, the discussion of Momigliano and White at the opening of this chapter now suggests that attacks on "constructionism" in historiography (read: rejections of deconstruction) by attaching it to *Squadristi* indicate a desperation and terror threaded to the very idea of "doing history." Historiographic ideals may well be the form of *ressentiment* directed toward those who would read historical texts *too closely*.

Chapter Five ▨

Three Existential Simulacra of Language: Thinking the *Amor Fati* of Language

> *We call* order-words, *not a particular category of explicit statements . . . but the relation of every word or every statement to implicit presuppositions, in other words, to speech acts that are, and can only be, accomplished in the statement . . . a "social obligation."*
>
> —Deleuze and Guattari, *A Thousand Plateaus*

> *If objects are perishable and no longer exist, how can we know what term ought to refer to them? From this point of view the name Julius Caesar has all the referential objecthood of Peter Wimsey or Squire Allgood.*
>
> —Stephen Tyler, *The Said and the Unsaid*

> *. . . as if the distinctive feature of our civilization were the suspension of choice and the tendency to* understand *everything without* doing *anything.*
>
> —Tzvetan Todorov, *Symbolism and Interpretation*

In Vincent Descombes' amusing yet chilling story, when someone addresses a question or demand to an entity such as God, State, or Nation by deploying "you," as in "God, you must . . . , " one has already stepped over to an exquisite sense of a delirium intrinsic to grammar, its own connection to imaginary objects, fictions in the mode of certainty, certainty in the mode of wish, waking thought in dream. At such moments belief in the referent, on the basis of extending grammar to the invisible, induces language-madness, the certainty of one's own order-words, one's own connections to obligations of all sorts. The "American psyche" is such a piece of madness: It offers everything and is hence so incorporative as to be immediately unreal. Such madnesses are diffused throughout every level of language, because grammar and hallucination—prosopopeia—are not antithetical to the other. Reflection on grammar leads to a sense of grammar's impurities, mixtures of imaginary objects and logical syntaxes, themselves mixed with figures. These ideas, hardly uncontentious, were stated at the beginning of this book by specifying the nonseparability of what is socially and discursively always separated by scholarship: rhetoric from credibility, ideals from rhetoric. Scholarly writing may well signify relations of separation/nonseparation that are so perplexing that their relations and implications must be brought under that "single white lie," as our politically correct writers have it.

The effects of such self-deception are not amusing, however, for they make up a considerable portion of the order-words that run through everyday life. Derrida's *Specters of Marx,* for example, leads us to believe that "ghosts" can be addressed—they address us—and for some who want this to be so, one's not believing in the address stamps one for disqualification from the ranks of the "new scholar." That his own model of language recodes the functions of the rebus is kept from sight.[1] Instead of introducing dissension into the concept of the "new scholar," this name effects modes of exclusion: the "new scholar" is authorized to give names to other entities, name giving become the profession of giving names. As argued in the previous chapters, a significant aspect of discourses which claim to make necessary orders, give names (for instance, Latour's use of *hybrid*), is their activation of writing as war, for what else does Ginzburg's model of the historian as connoisseur give to mean if not the elimination of the connoisseur's rivals? The grammatical "misadventures of the understanding" (Descombes) open onto every aspect, every conflict of language, scholarship, and politics.

Descombes goes on to suggest an interesting enigma: "it is by remaining with language that we will resist its seduction; it is by no longer transcending it that we will finally transcend it." [2] Proximity resists seduction, seduction in language as satisfying discourse (subsumption of epistemic issues under political-moral ones), and the abandonment of desiring to overcome language points to a concept of work: Work language as hard as possible and its seductions dissipate, releasing an unknown factor into writing. Descombes' enigmatic proposition is stimulatory, especially as it intersects, by difference, with the modes of ordering analyzed in previous chapters, for his proposition implies that order-words, co-extensive with language, are nonetheless only a coding. They are not language "itself." Descombes' enigma implies that if order-words seduce and we stay with them long enough, they cease to "read good" as much as they indicate that within these orders there are other places—what Descombes' "remaining with language" looks toward. In this chapter, which might be read as an alternative to discourses based on commands, notions of language are suggested that do not so much give orders as imply alternatives for thinking about language, historical cultures and critical work.

Wittgenstein's Theory of Open Paradox

Some of Wittgenstein's hypotheses about language have become widespread, ranging from Feyerabend's work in the theory of science to Lyotard's application of language games to notions of Western justice. Noticeable exceptions are areas like historiography or cultural studies. Cultural studies, at least in the United States, are often hostile to any strong version of linguistic questions, even as some of its writers lay claim to every cultural problem in sight.[3] Is it the austerity of Wittgenstein's texts that makes the sectors of the humanities concerned with history and culture so nervous? Or is it that the *Tractatus* and *Philosophical Investigations* argue for a *suspension* of the very clear-cut reasons that enable humanistic scholarship to make necessary judgments, upending the autonomy of descriptive language ("as it is")?

More than one context supports readings of Wittgenstein's main works, but a proposal can be made that the difficulty some sectors of academe have in using his works is that these texts presuppose twists in modern life that make language more than problematic. We seem to have no strong appreciation that both of Wittgenstein's key texts were suffused with notions of war—especially real ones. Both texts can be said to *incorporate* the modern world's structures of limit and suppression, as well as the release of ambiguities between limit and norm; for what remains of language conventions in a world of extremes, for example, World Wars, a Holocaust (more than one), capitalist decoding, the sense of cultural "reckoning" in a Darwinist social system? The methodical pace of the propositions of the *Tractatus* carves out not just the limits of philosophy but also multiple disruptions of language as such. Some of the writing in the *Tractatus,* its pacing, rhythm and deliberation, suspends order-words, and sets reading and thinking in conflict with minds given over to intuition, instead of to analysis of our rules of projection, our thinking. When Wittgenstein argues that pictures are not identifications of things, when, for instance, "we cannot compare any process with the 'passage of time'—there is no such thing—but only with another process (say, with the movement of the chronometer)," this sense of gap between picture and thing indicates new questions about language, asking as to what kind of pictures (interpretations, models) could make *necessities of representation?*

The notion of language game, for example, can be interpreted as offering a sense of language in which no identity or homogeneity can be considered as capable of modeling language. "Ordinary speech," Stephen Pinker has recently insisted, "is a paradigm of engineering excellence, a technology," but this model, which idealizes the "effortlessness of conversation" as to what language *is like,* also belongs to the game of repressing contradictions internal to language's functions.[4] No usage of language (that is, theory or interpretation) necessarily transfers to the significance of what is said by another language game. And picturing and language games are disruptive, as both notions affirm maximum nonidentity, or conflict, about our rules of projection and what language uses such rules depend upon. Written signifiers enact continuity between themselves and objects of every sort, but since any such continuity is perspectival, the question is always how any one perspective comes to stand as a model more than perspectival. To make pictures (propositions, models, maps, diagrams, etc.) supposes the extraordinary narrowness of each game as it expands to the limits of its *exclusiveness.*[5] The "innumerable others" that are language games one can neither evade nor control, like bullets in wars, create "moves" that contain their own pressures and forces and affirm that "we do the most various things with our sentences," disallowing a "game" of "games," for instance, where naming provides for our mastery of language.[6] There is a notion of active flux that the *Philosophical Investigations* added to the bright desert of the *Tractatus,* and in both cases, metalanguage (order-words) is judged as a power move, not an intellectual necessity outside of the coding that requires language to give mastery over things.

Order-words make picturable equations, like Ginzburg's hunter squatting and reading spit, so that as hunters have good eyes, historians are good connoisseurs (positive divination). This proposition should be thought of as opposed to the picture of the hunter as "thief." The *Tractatus* and *Philosophical Investigations* argue for incommensurability between the incommensurables of every human relation, since there is no such thing as a language move, game, or form that is capable of resolving different perspectives. For example, the critic Zygmunt Bauman writes that postmodernism requires a shift in intellectual work, from providing concepts of intellectual legislation (modernist ideas of autonomy) to that of rendering interpretations for the self-assembly of diverse audiences and groups aiming for consensus (for example, engineers taking a stand on ecology). The older "legal" model of intellectual work gives way to that of "dialogue," but the latter does not synthesize the former as much as it must come up against what it cannot say: its forfeiture of intellectual work as legislation, becoming a "listening post" for the contradictions our engineers get themselves in.[7] The concept of a language game would then serve as a marker for the expression of language in conflict: pictures and language games are destroyed by other pictures and language games.[8] Language, which we cannot know, has a lot to do with war, a continuation of Nietzsche's theory.

"The totality of propositions is the language" says a proposition from the *Tractatus,* and this allows that pictures are propositions as well.[9] Totality can have no picture, however, for the proposition that addresses totality is not the totality that it addresses. Picture does not mean something photographic or imagistic, something objective or subjective (these terms have a meaning but cannot be said to have a reference that we can understand in a univocal manner). There are elementary propositions, like "the red chair," which corresponds to elements that are objects "in states of affairs," and while some states of affairs, cases, are "like" this, most are more complex. Is a proposition conceived as a picture to be compared to a diagram (of an accident, for example) or a map? Wittgenstein emphasized the nontemporal aspect of pictures or their logical character, which is their capacity to activate reflection. Paradoxically, a picture is not visual but formal or structural. The *Tractatus* asks what are the "rules of projection" such that we can adjust language to effects, to hypothesis and to belief, since one cannot take for granted there is an isomorphism between proposition and world; there may be isomorphism between the "pictured" and its rules, but that isomorphism does not allow us to transfer this to another picture. What matters is to specify what the "picturing function" is itself all about, what the "picturing form" activates. "The proposition shows how things stand, if it is true. And it says, that they do so stand." [10] The forms of standing—true, false, tautology, and senselessness—may not be final, but picturing is "how" we make statements stand for. While language is not itself paradoxical, it always supposes a genuine paradox—the sayable is what we can express at any given moment, subject to rules of compossibility or syntax; what cannot be expressed are those rules in action. We cannot enter any hermeneutic circle concerning language, for language is always exterior to our conceptions of it. Language "lets us" project but all projections about language are bound to fail to encapsulate our attempts to possess language. Logical form or the form of picturing as such cannot be expressed by language—it expresses itself as the "how" of any particular linguistic modeling. We cannot express in a sentence what allows us to express it. Once we do, we regress to having to then say what it is we have just expressed. Above all, no supposed function of language—to communicate, to express, to define, verisimilitude, nonidentity—can be said to "be" language.

The *Tractatus* rejected the classical notion of meaning as reflected in grammatical forms. The effect of grammar, as in agreement between predicates, is not a reliable "picture" of anything other than its own effect. Wittgenstein shifts the emphasis to questions of logical form. To say that "Caesar conquered Gaul" and that "Gaul was conquered by Caesar" is to use different grammatical forms that do not have the same conceptual content: Concepts cannot be reduced to their grammatical presentation. In the above example, the logical predicate, "to conquer," and Caesar, the argument, are both different from the function "conquered Gaul"; we can draw inferences from the logical functions regardless of how we figure out the dominant subject. On logical grounds, the statement "Seven is a man" has a sense, but its reference is false. There are cases when we can pass from meaning to reference, saying "It is raining" while it "is raining" (or is it "pouring" or "inundating"?), but despite all these distinctions, propositions can only show, not say, their form.

The forms of arrangement that any given picture presupposes are not themselves directly expressible. The rules themselves are inexpressible, but we cannot say anything without them. Think of quotation marks and various contexts; if I say to my wife "I love you" in direct discourse, there are no quotation marks; I am saying that in the context in which it occurs, threaded to everything else active in that scene; but I have reported saying that "I love you" in the context of the sentence-example "If I say to my wife 'I love you.'" Every change in level of signification involves rules for the projection of that particular proposition, no exceptions being conceivable. Consequently, anything we say about language in the medium of language is held in suspense by the inexpressibility of the rules making that particular projection. Even if we conclude language is made in such a way as to generate pictures and propositions, any proposition or picture of language involves rules of projecting *that,* and so all we have are the pictures and our extractions of how they model. There is a definite "existential" tone to this embedding of language in choices and paradox, a Nietzschean strain of that "pathos of distance" in which reflection on the dynamics of saying/showing deconstructs "common" and "current" speech. The paradox of said/shown, or a conception of language as *exteriority,* is related to that "dangerous game" Heidegger modeled when he asked if anyone can "hear what language really says when *it* speaks"?[11] Picturing, in Wittgenstein's extended sense of "to signify," must be ambivalent and dynamic, for there is always "otherness" at work in language itself.[12]

This shift to logical form brings together language, picture, and proposition around the consistent application of the principle of a gap between language and referent, saying and showing carried over to logic, to grammar, to figure, and to every linguistic usage. In addition to this fissure and slippage of the picturing function, in using a grammatical mode, we have great difficulty in noticing that our usage also embeds the grammatical within the rhetorical (as, for instance, an example). A consequence of this drift of meaning in language is the embarrassment that is ushered in toward philosophy and the humanities: The paradox of saying/showing makes referential discourse a fact of paradox. When an historian tells us that "Stalin was a Wolf," this picture cannot say how it can say just that without recourse to another discourse that authorizes it and, in so doing, ceases to say what it said. In the strongest terms: a given picture, "Stalin was a wolf," is rendered as a first-order meaning; it describes and its plausibility seems self-evident, as analogy and comparison, but the instant a question is put to it, it must lose its picturing status as standing for a fact and becomes a topic concerning its "rules of projection," that is, bias, theory, textual overcoding.

While the arguments of the *Tractatus* emphasized that we signify connections between language and events by assuming their common logical structure, this structure also takes into consideration that a sentence is not what it represents (for example, the concept of a cat is not the cat). Language has an indestructible aboutness or mediative function, not a grasping or possessive one. This implies that what sentences say are what we understand, not their references, which are turned into senses as the only way in which not-language can be presented. Here too we can understand why many traditional writing groups, historians especially, are embarrassed by Wittgenstein's arguments, why their "modernity" always lags behind the destructuration of the said/shown, or why Ginzburg's *The Cheese and the Worms* seems to experiment with history-writing, using abrupt and even cryptic figures for speaking of Menocchio the miller but collapsing into orders-for-reading, Menocchio oversymbolized instead of "shown." All sorts of skepticism are foreclosed if one asserts that reference is "outside" instead of noticing that the various reference-effects are discursive artifacts.[13] In fact, it may be suggested that language is in and of itself the termination of *reference,* just because of the rules of projection writing produces are institutionalized and often made undiscussable. If, as the *Tractatus* puts it, "the proposition is a picture of reality" and "the proposition *shows* its sense," then language can show only by the continuous destruction of the said: total war within language.[14] Once more: the idea can be conceived that *synecdochic error* allows one to shift from reference-as-code to reference-as-design, the latter blocking reflection of the skeptical type.

The affirmative and energetic conception released by these considerations suggests that *working a discourse is the only way to escape from the said of that discourse, and such work is not "mastery."* This involves the strong notion that every proposition be conceived as an experiment on both how language connects to world and how things within language are connected to our thoughts. The sense of any particular proposition requires another proposition, any particular proposition immediately transformed into a cognitive fact by yet another sentence. Any complicated text will use different kinds of models and connections to produce its effects; assertions are embedded in descriptive thickness, the latter in sequential notions (for example, causality), given dramatic emphasis, etc. In short, the said/shown brings with it the sense of force of passage, often unnoticed: all of a sudden the narrative becomes an admonition, all of a sudden an insight turns to intellectual mush, and so the question is why so many discourses close down saying/showing language's own game? Chapters one to four above suggest that it is at this point one might study the politics of discursive anti-intellectualism, the discursive codes of language *shut down*. Both the *Tractatus* and the *Philosophical Investigations* can be said to be adamant about the concept of *aidentity*, so that awareness of making pictures (propositions, descriptions) has a chance of dislodging the self-identification that comes when we lose ourselves in language construed as a medium of satisfaction.[15]

The *Tractatus* unsparingly adhered to the idea that philosophy, for which we can substitute any reflexive activity whatsoever, "will mean the unspeakable by clearly displaying the speakable." The conceptual existence of the "unspeakable" is not restricted to art, aesthetics, and ethics, as some readings of Wittgenstein have it (Stephen Toulmin's *Wittgenstein's Vienna* comes to mind), but is inclusive of experiences (life-forms) subject to the logic of picturing.[16] The unspeakable may be compared to the *virtuality* of signification, effected and created each and every time picturing occurs: the most rigorous application of language to a topic is less about settling a problem as it is about forcing to the surface of language what the "problem might be." Must we always repress this *extremism of signification,* that language cannot give possession, only perspectives?[17] Aesthetic, moral, and political disagreements show what remains to be said, this "remainder," as objectified, giving rise to more of the "unspeakable." Suspension of consensus competes with making consensus and, in this sense, conflict of and with language operates as a kind of limit on any discourse that claims to make language give possession of things. As the preface to the *Tractatus* puts it, there is

> a limit . . . to the expression of thoughts; for in order to draw a limit to thinking, we should have to be able to think both sides of this limit (we should therefore have to be able to think what cannot be thought). The

limit, can therefore, only be drawn in language and what lies on the other side of the limit will be simply nonsense.[18]

Thinking cannot be delimited, but every thought is precisely a limit in some way. What is shown in this exquisitely gnomic statement is that when we understand (apply a proposition), we are already practicing a rule of finality, which cannot be finalized except when passing over into *order-words*. Propositions that order in effect withdraw from the world, from activity, for they signify a suppression of the "rules of projection," effecting passage from language to "the way a world is," language projecting aesthesis over epistemic puzzles. In this sense, we should compare order-words to the hardening of thinking. And if we extend Wittgenstein's argument to a consideration of institutions, the latter are then *hard places,* with their own systems of escaping from self-elaborated constrictions. The proliferation of the discourses concerning "disaster" is paradigmatic here: apartheids, final solutions, Rwanda—millions of representations fail to express what such events show (what cannot be said). Language singles out, isolates, dramatizes, displays, spectrifies, these objects (*in their different realities*) and comes to the order-word/model type "African tragedy" so as to escape from showing/saying other things. Every act of signification releases potentially endless semantic conflagrations and recoding of order-words and models.

Moreover, the "unspeakable" of language exists because the "world is independent of my will"—that is to say, the events of the world are so diverse as to refute representation. Why do some groups think the modern city as "ruin" through the "rules of projection" offered by, say, Walter Benjamin and not, say, Celine's Bardamu in *Journey to the End of the Night?* No matter how many strings of models are linked to create plausible and credible "word pictures," what is said is immeasurably inferior to what the unsaid gives rise to—skepticism, query, puzzlement, stimulations. Brought back to a consideration of how we think about language, as the *Philosophical Investigations* put it, echoing yet flattening the *Tractatus'* gnomicisms (for instance, "Form is the possibility of the structure"), the "must" within signification, which always finds similarities and resemblances, "must" itself give way to suspension of name: "But if someone wished to say: 'There is something common to all these constructions [of the game-model]— namely the disjunction of all their common properties'—I should reply: Now you are only playing with words."[19] For example, in a vigorous defense of narrative history, an historian insists that there is indeed a model of narrative form which folds in and closes off skepticism toward narrative. He writes:

Narratives are historical in that they are not arbitrary, inasmuch as they are true, that is to say, historical. The "truth" or authenticity of a historical narrative—if we strip off the subjective categories and points of view of the narrator—is, like the *je ne sais quoi* of eighteenth-century aesthetic theoreticians, or like Kant's "intuition," evasive, incapable of isolation, yet ever present, triggered—we do not know how—by 'things in themselves' we cannot define except to say that they are, and are of necessity. [20]

The sense of this text asserts the continuity of an historical narrative with the "things in themselves," relying upon tautology, *vicariousness,* or what *je ne sais quoi* means, elimination of the "secondary." The force of this passage does not produce the unshowable but imposes it. Identity between "is" and "necessity," in matters as important as *je ne sais quoi* cannot be anything other than imposition. No one can possess such relations; language, if not following orders, can only enable more showings. The idea that identity is the ever-present condition of narration closes off an analytics of "showing," refusing to give its readers experimentation with meaning, just exactly as "African tragedy" cuts off discussion of something else, something unsaid.

Wittgenstein intended his schema to be in the service of science; philosophy stripped of content could survive only in becoming a critique of those signs that raised impossible metaphysical questions or word-spells (that is, "intelligence bewitched" by language), answers to questions of meaning suspended in favor of the production of more riddles about meaning. Wittgenstein, supposedly a "dry" philosopher, certainly gives us a way of conceiving language as "wet." The impossibility of there being an actual metalanguage, a "dry" and safe place of language, renders unnecessary all metaphysical beliefs (that the human "mind" is a "computer," "mother wit," or any other such identity), or that theories are the most significant products of intellectual creation.[21] Only a veritable explosion at the level of picturing allows for more to be conceivably shown. If what is said tends to reduce the showable to the sayable, then something like a "life of the mind" could be conceived as a footrace between signifying and consciousness of error, between what is said and shown. The great admonition of the *Philosophical Investigations*—"look and see" before you assume resemblance between any two things—also means "think and conceive" so as to not step into the trap of equating the said with transparency, perhaps the most seductive spell of all.

It is sometimes thought that Wittgenstein delivered the value laden aspects of human existence (are there any other?) to the inexpressible, which is the showable, if such things can be shown. Everyone is thereby deprived of any transcendental criterion made to apply to immanent situations: all phrases of the type "in the name of history" or "in the name of knowledge" can only be shown and are never shown finally. The politics of imposition makes use of metaphysical syntax. For example, we can say that "Capitalism is a devilish system" because assertion can perform this, but there is no ontological reality to the statement or proposition. Extreme propositions, however, are in a way more productive than representative ones: for if some way could be found to *show* "capitalism is a devilish system," what would happen to the rest of our picturings?

Gilbert Ryle has argued that theories of language, of which paradox is a limit-event, have been an "occupational disease of twentieth-century Anglo-Saxon and Austrian philosophy." Ryle believed he traced the concern with meaning in language to a fantasy, that words are names that make "us feel that what a word means is in all cases some manageable thing that that word is the name of."[22] To this sense of familiarity about words, word-friends, Ryle stressed the idea that "word-meanings do not stand to sentence-meanings as atoms to molecules or as letters of the alphabet to the spellings of words, but more nearly as the tennis racket stands to the strokes which are or may be made with it." Ryle replaced the fantasy of word-friend with the analysis of uses based on just that game. But every proposition that models "use" precisely models its conception of use and is not the use whereof it speaks. Ryle went on to claim that language meaning then "involves knowing a set of bans, fiats and obligations, or, in a word, it is to know the rules of the employment of that expression." "Knowing the rules" is undoubtedly a great thing, but this use-model reverts to a closed concept, assuming as it does the presence of "rule" in every language-use, which must suggest opening "rule" to the vicissitudes of its own disappearance as a model. Could one make a philosophical proposition that a concept such as *re* indicates antishowing?

The *initiative* out of Wittgenstein's propositions concerning language is inseparably related to showing, to exteriorization, without any chance of a "last use-model." In this sense, no such thing as finality belongs to language, unless it is the finality of what Pierre Bourdieu calls "that systematic principle of error which is the claim to a sovereign overview," manifested in language as the discourse of a censor, that is, "authorized statements" that are such only to the degree that we do not think about authorization.[23] There is a kind of existentialism here, for exteriorization of language is not necessarily symmetrical with truth and error. That is to say, one always has to choose what to *say more about*. One reads that a history of Los Angeles "shows" its "failures" of planning, what Los Angeles "lacks" by reference to other, better cities. What shows or demonstrates this if deeply embedded in such "lack" is a comparison to something incomparable; what models "failure"? What perspectives brought into language might legitimate the application of rules of importance here? To every statement that removes its own perspective from showability, such removal is betrayed by what is shown, if it can be, and Wittgenstein's texts suggest: experiment more with language. In this sense, connections can be made with Nietzsche's great essay, "Truth and Lies in a Nonmoral Sense," which emphasized how language is incessantly turned into a "prison-house."

Deleuze and Guattari's Implosion of Language

A Thousand Plateaus is an altogether different kind of radicalism then we find in Wittgenstein's texts. Instead of starting with formal concerns, as the picture-theory did by embedding "rules of projection" in notions of logical syntax, *A Thousand Plateaus* is explicit as to the politics of language. It asserts that the elementary unit of language, the statement, "is the order-word." Where Wittgenstein's concerns suspended an attempt to figure forth language as language, *A Thousand Plateaus* is not hesitant to take the plunge, which it does with glee: "Language is made not to be believed but to be obeyed, and to compel obedience."[24] Authors such as Gorgias and Vico can be heard in the resonance of this dissident claim, the inseparability of language and word-spell, language and imperative. What matters is the transformation of this "abominable faculty" we naively call language, a phrase undeniably horrific to the dominant western traditions of modeling language. Deleuze and Guattari are scathing toward the feature of redundancy built into language, which always undercuts the idealism of communication and meaning. In the ceaseless issue of grammatically and logically correct orders, what is "observed and retained" in the circulation of ideas and thoughts, are controls on sense-making. Our ceaseless invention of examples to confirm necessities of "an example" is a case in point.

In Deleuze and Guattari's account of language, statements of judgment, and expressions of feelings, covering subject-object relations of every type, presuppose a much more fundamental domain in which "a rule of grammar is a power marker before it is a syntactical marker."[25] What linguistics has said about language, emphasizing connections between sender and receiver, code and message, the isolation of proportions between information and redundancy, distinctions external and internal to language, is secondary next to the power to issue orders: "Language is not life; it gives life orders . . . Every order-word . . . carries a little death sentence—a Judgment, as Kafka put it."[26] Intellectual historians can see in this the continuation of Bakhtin's ideas of laughter and disruption toward "high culture," but there is a more intense existential pressure; expressive and interpretive uses of language as found in processes like hearsay tell us more about collective discourses than testing and polling, representative "case" studies, and the like. In the same way that the order-word moves a political category directly into formal territory, as in the example of Pinker's model of language as "engineering excellence," "hearsay" is not secondary but just as co-extensive with language as any other encoding, organization, more revealing of language than intralinguistic constructs such as metaphor. For example, *A Thousand Plateaus* works up indirect discourse as innovative *and* stereotypical responses,[27] in which language is made to pass from third parties to second parties to third parties claiming to be first-parties to . . . without there being any first involved. What de Man called prosopopeia is not just an imaginary subject of rhetorical/logical fusion but co-extensive with language, perhaps the latter at risk of being nothing but prosopopeic. For one group's "collective assemblage of enunciation" (roughly: medically trained psychiatrists as opposed to nurse practicioners), there are times in which that group appeals to the facts, because such appeal has a material support accessed and resourced, and times when another discourse used as strategy must be effected. For another group there is a specific trigger that tells them to "raise the ante" in negotiations over some matter, all such assemblages instances of wordedness or institution/group conjunctions. To speak is to participate and produce one's membership in other group's participation in their memberships, the respective order-words serving as boundary markers, with extraordinary fluidities and jumps from one terrain to another. The idea of a collective assemblage of enunciation affirms the social character of language, which does not mean public versus private, or critical versus descriptive, or pro-identity versus anti-identity, but only that discourse makes orders according to the most varied of purposes. We seem unable to deal with the fact that we are constituted by such multiplicity of language-functions.

Once they have radicalized or offended linguistic models of language, which is to say criticized the philosophy of language for overestimating metaphor as the figure of figures, Deleuze and Guattari turn to a consideration of the performative, the illocutionary and metaphor. Why such hostility to metaphor? In their system, metaphor works as a *syntactic obstruction,* making equivalences instead of hypotheses. *A Thousand Plateaus* treatment of metaphor makes it into a code of sacerdotalist word-magic, not in the affirmative sense but rather in the sense of castrating language, psychology over philosophy. Metaphorization and Oedipalization should be thought in their togetherness. Metaphor operates to withdraw semantic convolutions, serving "power-plays" in the control of local situations, or supporting the creation of "instant" governments and states that start to regulate the spillovers of sense. Considered as "inside" language, metaphor dissolves the imperceptibility of words and bodies, becomings of action and passion (surplus affects) and generalizes partial logics, destroying the time-becomings of events. In metaphor, the event is drawn back into a language that tells the time and dates the event, instead of adding simultaneities to language. For example, the application of "noir" metaphors to contemporary Los Angeles dates today as a time conceived of as *then,* reduction of difference to a failure of accounting for today, a continuous narrative line of the metaphor. When an historian writes that the last twenty-five years or so has involved "the Rusting of America," "rusting" carries with it a sense of decay transposed to social processes in such a way as to reduce and thereby control other processes, perhaps not so clear and recognizable. The consistency of metaphor leads discourse back to commanding discourse. Proper all the way through, metaphor expresses a death-within-discourse, which *A Thousand Plateaus* calls aesthesis, unity and resolution within language. Pragmatics teaches that the complicity of language and "timings" is not a secondary feature, a derivative relation, but co-extensive with language, with order-words, with indirect discourse. This shift to pragmatics, or separation from dependency on semantics and syntactics (for instance, rules of pertinence) is required because pragmatics "insinuates itself into everything," which is to say that hearsay, rumor, myth, and mixtures of the most varied types of causes are transferred into language.

But because the social and individual dimensions of meaning often blur, language is less than the perfect model for our comprehension of things social and institutional, and individual speech acts are more than subjective expressions.[28] Indeed, the very distinction between performatives (the doing of enunciations inseparable from actions) and constatives (language at a distance) begins to unravel, and the latter is dislodged as what constitutes the former. The constative certainly appears to be the very kernel of language relation, but the constative also presupposes a "collective assemblage of enunciation," what Brian Massumi describes as the power of meaning creating its own grounds. Students grumbling after a lecture, when someone says, "Did you see the speaker's yellowed paper . . . how many times has that talk been given before," renders the assemblage of alienated listeners where the comment, because immanent to language, connects with various "outsides." The pragmatic model asks that one treat every statement as diagrammatic, holding to the rise and the fall of the variables that are the enunciations along with their variables as well. A fuller elaboration of the order-word is then to be construed as not just a

> particular category of explicit statement, but the relation of every word or
> every statement to implicit presuppositions . . . to speech acts that are, and

can only be, accomplished in the statement. Order-words do not concern commands only, but every act that is linked to statements by a "social obligation" . . . The only possible definition of language is the set of all order-words, implicit presuppositions, or speech acts current in a language at a given moment.[29]

As with the *Tractatus,* language-as-such is emptied out: its phonological, grammatical, syntactical, and semantical pertinence is brought into existence by the acts that retrospectively constitute such domains (what semioticians might call code-making and code-switching—but that signs can be coded does not make of language a code). The contest is between order-words and the possibility of their undoing. Despite the fact that the order-word is the master-variable of a model of language that is all variable, new collective assemblages are created all the time and do not just react but set off stimuli rather than just interpreting at a distance. Active assemblages work through the distance under scrutiny by other order-words. Pragmatics focuses on the power-cuts that combine, prepare, and extinguish, that work up the immanent and the eternal, the now and to-be-taken-up-again, and enables the emergence of unknown times, "parenthetical imperatives" that diagram nonlinear interpretations and analyses.[30]

This positive "collective assemblage of enunciation" has intrinsic connections to "free indirect discourse" as well as to the "impersonal" quality of enunciation, and turns normative notions of discourse upside down: what matters is that what is said, heard, written, is already pluralized, already multiple in its concepts, affects, and functions; but the social demand to communicate, to subjectify oneself reduces these dimensions to redundancy, *uniforms*. Articulations of the most diverse sorts are stretched between these "uniforms" (broadly: markers of identification) and modes of discourse that work the multiplicity already available in favor of an "untimely" meaning. Thus, in their analysis of Kafka, Deleuze and Guattari argue that Kafka's immersion in the overcoded references and myths, archaicisms and symbolisms available in Czech or vernacular language and the high German of elite culture, allowed for taking Prague German to the desert: "to use syntax in order to cry, to give syntax to the cry."[31] Or the radio listener, attached to the seriousness of "listening for" (that song, that report) plunges into radio jumping, a different positioning of the listener, a different listener. In this model, there is no linguistic subject, only various subjectifications that, even though riveted to order-words, are interspersed with indirect discourse, "the whispering voices . . . the tribes and secret idioms from which I extract something I call my Self. *I* is an order-word."[32]

Acts "immanent to language" are called the "set of all incorporeal transformations current in a given society and attributed to the bodies of that
society."[33] Discourse is unthinkable without the notion of body, scattered
across linguistic materials and affecting every type of matter. When historians call for U.S. national education "standards" because Americans are so
"historically illiterate," they want the body of "historical knowledge" to
expand, they want reading bodies subjected to the mastery of a discourse,
so that actions will have the "body of history" to support the going "social
obligations." Drawing upon Oswald Ducrot's work on the enunciative act,
linkages between saying and social importance, incorporeal transformations, first modeled by Stoic logicians in their theory of *lekta,* are shown
in the juridical assemblage and its control of a body. There is a crime, an
accused, the trial, the penalty, each of which calls forth more bodies: the
property-body, victim-body, convict-body, prison-body; but the event that
turns accused into convict is said to be incorporeal, an "attribute that is the
expressed of the judge's sentence." Words don't convey resemblance and
identity unless they stick, mostly when they bring into existence an old existence (the accused into the convicted).

"An attribute that is the expressed" is the effect of a statement—what a
statement performs, whether a war declaration, a truce, an oath of love, a
dissimulation. Any body can receive incorporeal transformations, and each
reception can modify the actions and passions of other bodies: When we
say that there is abusive language such that children are often belittled by
their parents and peers, what this means is that the "body" called person,
with the predicate "self-respect," receives a wound and the wound immediately become an attribute of that body. Order-words "are precisely dated,
to the hour, minute and second, and take effect the moment they are
dated." The expressed always becomes an effect, seen in language thought
of as Way (Lao-Tzu), in which possible identifications are superimposed on
an event. One second someone is healthy and vigorous, the next one becomes a different person—an illness takes hold. It is a gross mistake to go
from Same to Same with language, when what actually occurs is the subjection of bodies and language to incorporeal effects. *A Thousand Plateaus*
asks us to listen more closely, read more acutely: there are always intensi-
ties, thresholds, degrees, and a quality of flux delivered by any statement,
even the ones serving a power set-up. These collective assemblages of
enunciation—financial, ideological, theoretical, psychological, sexual—are
in constant flux, but each has the quality of *la langue* at the instant orders
are registered. Order-words are a "marking of power" threaded to an "outside" that "brings to light variables of expression or of enunciation that are
so many internal reasons for language not to close itself off."[34] Such wordedness is also "instantaneousness . . . its immediacy gives it a power of vari-

ation in relation to the bodies to which the transformation is attributed." Orders to send troops co-occurs with a slew of other constants brought into play (for example, staging, feeding, securing), while orders in another assemblage may take years to be received or rather decoded (for instance, my colleagues are beginning to make strange use of their eyes when certain topics come up).[35]

Language, then, cannot be described in any univocal manner and it both does and does not belong to a genealogy of idealism; for there are affects and effects, endlessly constrained and reduced by the decoding and recoding of order-words, that nonetheless stall the nihilism of order-words. The representative function which subtends criticism and scholarship, namely *that* we give "sense" to others, educate, facilitate, is itself based on the "variation of the order-words and noncorporeal attributes linked to social bodies and effectuating immanent acts," not on an ideal we could know. When Lenin enunciates the slogan "All power to the Soviets," the vanguard is brought into existence. When Latour calls out "Are you not fed up with deconstruction," what counts are the "pragmatic implications . . . in relation to the implicit presuppositions, immanent acts, or incorporeal transformations," which is to say, the "new configurations of bodies" *called up*—as if language were itself a vast "army" of reserves (grammatical and figural stereotypes), each of us soldiering-figures in more than one situation, more than one conflict. When our contemporary sociobiologists such as Pinker try to prevent loss of faith "in" language by calling the latter "impression management," deglamorizing language as they make it a tactical machine, the model serves to represent "representation," this to conserve representation.

Because of the pressures of such conservations, the minimum condition of criticism could only be *passage* to something like "an evaluation of internal variables of enunciation in relation to the aggregate of the circumstances,"[36] evaluation standing for thinking through the implicit presuppositions of explicit statements, focus on "the cuer and the cued, of the song that always holds a tune within a tune in a relation of redundancy; a faculty that is in truth mediumistic, glossolalic, or xenoglossic."[37] Collective assemblages are the passing places of language, without which language would be nothing(ness). Language is both *inexistent* and a mixture of event/medium, a depurification of ideological stances. Although he rejects the rhizomic implications of the order-word, Eco also emphasizes what his own notion of semiosis shares with pragmatics: language is local and transitory before overcoded, where to speak is to position, an activity in which "meaning as synonymy and as essential definition" is not yet institutionalized.[38]

From here, *A Thousand Plateaus* takes up the thorniness of form and content, expression and formalization. Content is not opposed to form but has instead its own formalization: what Deleuze and Guattari call the "lesson of things," the infinity of pragmatic outcomes that have resulted from the treatment of bodies, including language. Formalized content can be seen when we say that a fact is established—unwithdrawable. Expression too has its own formalization: what they call the "lesson of signs." This can be seen when signifiers are given a stability or translatability function. Content and expression have their own forms and any duality between them is unraveled, since to grant to expression a form is to deprive it of the function of simply representing content. Relying on the Stoic distinction between action and passion of bodies and the incorporeal acts or expressed of statements, there is a form of expression (expresseds) and a form of content (what bodies become, undergo). A knife strikes a board, intermingling knife-hand-board; the statement "The knife won't cut this bread" produces a different event, the incorporeality of "to cut" as it has become will-not-cut. There is no question here of the detachment of the aspects, except for that "third-party" observer who obtains a benefit from commentary. The expressed of statements apply to bodies, not as representations, but as interventions—the expresseds "anticipate" contents, "move them back, slow them down or speed them up, separate or combine them, delimit them in a different way. The warp of the instantaneous transformations is always inserted into the woof of the continuous modifications."[39] Rather than consider the two forms as parallel or interpretants of the other, there is a "parceling"

> in which signs are at work in things themselves just as things extend into or are deployed through signs.

At any given moment, the "of" in "speaking of" can yield to a super-temporalization of discourse in which the incorporeal attributes given to bodies bring the datable, discourse as wound, as knife, as cut, in which after (saying, receiving) does not entail narrative and story, but differentiation, another now that is, in turn, to be cut. Enunciative assemblages (for example, this interpretation I am making now) are on the same level as states of things, states of content. Metalanguage is thoroughly destroyed. In a sense, the argument of *A Thousand Plateaus* asks us to think of the linkages between forms of expression and forms of content with our "between" taken out, an event in which we see

> the presence of the blue sky in and with the darkness of the clouds . . . clouds themselves then cease to be clouds—yes, they are there, and yet they cease to trouble us as such, as something veiling the blue."[40]

Neither content nor expression uncovers or represents the other but participates in each other's "otherness," by mutually contributing to what we somewhat lamely call an "event."

Here is where the terms machinic and collective really matter, or constitute a significant difference from standard models of representation and interpretation. These concepts suspend the need to make of language a motivation (to present intentions), to say what language is for, or to invent some design that modulates representation.[41] Bodies, actions, and passions are always the raw materials of a machinic assemblage, while statement-acts attribute incorporeal transformations to both bodies and other statements; taken together, there are constantly in formation discursive command-systems, some very long-lived and capable of astounding absorptions (law, grammar, narrative models), some datable to an instant (in 1995, the Mexican people "heard" the machine of devaluation "speak"). Order-words embedded in assemblages of enunciation produce divisions and joinings, when language effectuates or makes things move. When, say, in the very name of the "public," officials "retreat" to the closed doors of confidentiality, a controversy is dis-effected and new ones are started. "Machinic" relations are enunciated in all sorts of contested frames. For example, in considering academia as a bureaucratic institution, such devices as peer review, "outside" evaluators, and submission of one's bibliography for approval, are inseparable from the expressed (*lekta*) and serve to reterritorialize that institutional body. Any academic institution requires embodiment of its basic orders. A particularly instructive example is to be seen in considering such complexes as legal arrangements: rights are embedded in laws, but access to the law is also economic, and so just what a "right" *is* is perpetually tested by the system itself as subjects "test" themselves in exercises of perserverence as to the usefulness of their machinic and collective obligations. In the "canon wars," different machines compete directly over the erection of models of language and self in literary "classics" ("canons" of style, correctness, marginality). Or take a purely textual example. A prominent historian has insisted that despite the typical historian's "acuteness and obtuseness, fallacies and foresights," historical representation as a whole fulfills the responsibility never to suppress evidence: false misrepresentation by historians is infrequent, always watched for by comprehensive narratives and the sheer quantity of evidence.[42] The territory—historical responsibility—is protected from machinic breakdown (obsolescence), so that the wheels of representation will turn on more reterritorialization (evidence reworked). Here wordedness creates an indissolvable linkage between writing and instruction, representing and allocation of funds (research is expensive because it costs so much to accumulate evidence). But if the process of protecting us from "false" narratives is halted, what exactly are the *positive* benefits of "historical responsibility"? Much of what is machinic and collective belongs, unfortunately, to the conditions of passive nihilism, to overcoding treated as normal.

According to *A Thousand Plateaus,* a leading ideology concerning language is that there is an "abstract machine of language," that is, a black-boxed "treasury" or "endowment" of norms, from which, as in a mystical trance, we draw the waters of signification. But to language treated as assemblage, as "diagrammatic and superlinear," the standard issue of language as norm is not abstract enough, not inclusive enough of the extrinsics that permeate the "internality" of language nor extensive enough to consider the internality of pragmatics. Language as diagrammatic and superlinear involves the level at which language and the social can interpenetrate, to the point at which language can effect proposals, not yield to capture by order-words.[43] The diagrammatical and superlinear dimensions indicate conflict with the constancies, universals, binaries, competencies, homogeneities, and synchronies of language (for instance, transformativity, minimal constituents, contrariety, rigid judgments, integrality, and cohesion between subject/object). Required is a sense of language capable of manipulating "the singularity of abstract machines insofar as they are built around variables and variations."[44] For example, the "inherent variations" Labov emphasized in his analysis of Black English are not outside some system (as a stylistic peculiarity, as an historical constant); they are already systematic, a "de jure component affecting each system from within, sending it cascading or leaping on its own power and forbidding one to close it off, to make it homogeneous in principle." Labov did not investigate a deviation (from a norm); he simply demonstrated a different force field of effects and reciprocal presuppositions. The emphasis on affirmative pragmatics, then, involves *activating an excess, an explosiveness of language,* of reading even the most mundane prosaic code as the effectuation of one statement within other statements, as something "virtual, in other words, real without being actual, and consequently continuous regardless of the leaps the statement makes."[45] The more one listens and reads for the destinations and mixtures of the expressed, the more a pragmatics internal to language appears, a critical mix in which constants and continuous variations intersect:

> [a] continuous or discontinuous character of the variable itself: the order-word, a continuous variation for a discontinuous variable. . . . A variable can be continuous over a portion of its trajectory, then leap or skip, without that affecting its continuous variation; what this does is impose an absent development as an "alternative continuity" that is virtual yet real.[46]

The affirmative relations of this continuous variation of language are exemplified in experiences of reading that convey to us "secret languages, slangs, jargons, professional languages, nursery rhymes, merchants' cries," each having its own kernel of redundancy, each maximizing singular yet open effects of force. The issue is how to use language without bringing death-sentences, how to use order-words against themselves, in the service of flight rather than elimination.[47] When "atypical expression . . . produces the placing-in-variation of the correct forms, uprooting them from their state as constants," such atypical expressions operate as *tensors,* where language is deterritorialized, a nonplace within and without language at once, neither a "constant or a variable" but an event that conceives the "variation of the variable by subtracting in each instance the value of the constant $(n-1)$."[48] A close reading of the attributes and qualities given to the "expert" would want to show how the model makes its own constancy of this signifier, which requires separating "expert" from such proximate relatives as, say, an "expert criminal," for which sense of "perfection" connects them? If language is defined by its capacity to produce the most diverse relations between a "singular Abstract" and a "collective Concrete," then historiographic politics, for example, which returns to "facts" and a compulsive narrativizing, shows us how the atypical is disallowed.

Active writing is entirely differential. Deleuze and Guattari insist that it belongs to "transitional and limitrophe zones, zones of indiscernibility." Irreducible to the semiotic square, to grammaticality, they wish to consider thought opened up by a thought, not to its Other, but to something acute and even disruptive of that thought. In their terminology, active writing is a much more molecular notion than the traffic in generalizations that are delivered "on time" so as to "ground" and "anchor" basic propositions. Related to force and to the molecular, to what is "minor" in language, to "seeds, crystals of becoming," this active differential of writing "triggers uncontrollable movements and deterritorializations of the mean or the majority." The "minor" may be another way of specifying the separation from order-words, active when it tries to invent "a specific, unforeseen, autonomous becoming." While the order-word is itself a variable always turned into a constant of language, whose basis and limit is the sentence-figure conjugation, the atypic, minor, can also be "read" as something else, "like a warning cry or a message to flee." The continuous variation of atypical readings cannot transcend the sentence-figure but can reduce it "or make it a variation itself." The point is to increase the attributes of bodies, to add to the intensity of a metamorphosis such that texts "reach or overstep the limit of their figures." Here writing, speaking and acting are placed in a maximum of reciprocal presupposition such that the smallest distinctions can emerge with the work of the "cutting edges, tensors and tensions." Conjunctions replace identifications, judgment is stalled, and "matter has replaced the figure or formed substance." Not new answers to old questions, nor new questions; rather, the project here aims to respond positively "to the answer already contained in a question . . . one should respond with questions from another answer . . . pass-words beneath order-words."[49] In this sense, *A Thousand Plateaus* poses intensity as a challenge to order-words, an existentialism of the intense instead of the bureaucratization of commands, the "untimely" instead of historical culture.

De Man and the Love of Language

For left, right and center, de Man's European "past" is now an open order-word in the opportunity to moralize and trash certain aspects of deconstruction. Historians now regularly demand to know the "background of deconstructionism . . . to research the intellectual legacy and implications of deconstruction; to speculate on its place in the Romantic and Nietzschean tradition which led to, but not exclusively to, National Socialism," but can one ask the same questions of the critics?[50] Most of all, the negativity ladled on de Man and deconstruction is an opportunity for installing the signifier called "responsibility," giving the latter an unwithdrawable plus-value against deconstruction's skepticism. Here is a representative example of this "responsibility": Susan Buck-Morss upbraids de Man through that penultimate humanistic spellbinder, Walter Benjamin, and compares the program of deconstruction, anchored in de Man's personal irresponsibility, to Benjamin's, offered as authentic humanism. Where deconstruction is said to eschew any "image of the present as the moment of revolutionary possibility to arrest thought," Benjamin gave us the retrieval of "historical knowledge . . . buried within surviving culture," the writing here blind in the face of its contrast, to "arrest," to be "buried." Deconstruction isn't good for making "arrests," and Benjamin's work is good for unburying the dead; this is the figure of *antanagoge,* useful in political discourse, a contrast used to privilege an ideal. The past lives again when released by someone in the present who can

> bring to consciousness those repressed elements of the past which "place the present in a critical position." In the dialectical image, the present as the moment of revolutionary possibility acts as a lodestar for the assembly of historical fragments.[51]

Consider just the order-words here: Intellectuals today should "bring" the "repressed" to the present; as "lodestar," the present can receive these fragments, giving us unity. In this scheme of the present's obligation to the past and future, deconstruction is a barrier, it does not yield a "magnetic north pole." The writing does not attend to the construction "lodestar," this synecdochic command. Defined by what it is not ("lodestar"), deconstruction is "fashion that masquerades as politics." Buck-Morss's insistencies draw a share from that "collective assemblage" entitled scholarly idealism, closing with reactionary critics such as Lehmann and liberals such as Ginzburg who insist that deconstruction is irresponsible because it is not idealist. Again, the machinics are what matter: the intellectual in "nowtime" will "arrest thought" (police function), to give thought a meaning that will make good the sufferings of the past. Hence criticism is underwritten by a religious "implicit presupposition"—there is a "light" that we can follow. Effect: safety for dialectics from the ravages of "history" and language, safety from the risks of interpretation, from analysis. Here is history: it's yours forever to play with (since religious presuppositions are interminable)!

One of de Man's most interesting essays, "Shelley Disfigured," begins with questions that go to the paradoxes of interpretive culture, or cultures with high degrees of contention: "Is the status of a text like the status of a statue?" That is, do we locate Shelley's *The Triumph of Life* as a fragment of Romanticism and ourselves within Romanticism? How is Romanticism "historical" and not an "existential possibility," an ever-present choice? Is the play of status/statue the obligatory expression of a mimetic relation already there between text and world, the critic someone who finds connections so as to repair them? "What relationship do we have to such a text that allows us to call it a fragment that we are then entitled to reconstruct, to identify, and implicitly to complete"?[52] That is not a question often raised by academic discourse. The last part of the question is the thorniest: does the past need us? Why is there such mania for completion? Could the past have an interest, whether from collective agents or even stronger impersonal agents ("spirits," natural selection), in our having an interest? Further, why do we want to supply written substitutions, using ideas of continuity and discontinuity, of temporal succession, growth and degradation as figures of our "increased awareness" of the past? What justifies our corrections of the past and the belief that its energies would fall into oblivion—why, in short, do we want to historicize anything as complicated as a Shelley poem rather than using it for purposes we make explicit? Clearly, relations between the conditions of substitution and historicity are about as intimate and powerful as such relations could be: deeply grammatical, figural, and logical at once, provided that each of these zones is conceived as multiple and excessive. That is to say, dangerous.

De Man carefully shows how in the specific drafts and versions of Shelley's *The Triumph of Life,* so worked on by future commentators, Rousseau,

Plato, Wordsworth, and others are sometimes construed so as to deserve oblivion, made unhistorical, because of their status/statue parallel, this turning on the issue of evaluative hierarchies and critical values, "questions of origin, of direction, and of identity [that] punctuate the text without ever receiving a clear answer."[53] Shelley's "inquiry" is not that of a seeking hermeneut, shifting from the subject of history to the subject of poetry, nor is it a treatise in the genealogy of scholarship; rather, it moves in the atmosphere of a "question whose meaning, as question, is effaced from the moment it is asked. The answer to the question is another question, asking what and why one asked, and thus receding ever further from the original query." But to say Shelley's working of intellectual history can be compared "like a child from the womb, like a ghost from the tomb, I arise and unbuild it again," is too symmetrical for what Shelley has done. The thematics of the progress and regress of interpretation and artistic production are forestalled by Shelley's persistent disfigurations, to the point where the subjects of writing (history, poetry, evaluation) are immediately shown to be relations entirely provocative and thoroughly distorting. Questions of historical value, precedence, significance, and the like are not "normal" questions at all; their urgency is rather a symptom pertaining to the simultaneous reality and irreality of "crisis," but such "crisis" must be cast in misleading expressions of "normal language" so as to practice its own magical relation to the past. "Shelley Disfigured" opens up culture as a promise to deliver what cannot be delivered—"unresolved riddles" and "tangles" and "knots" claimed to be resolvable, more frightening and stimulating than terms like *irony*. Shelley, according to de Man, begins all these perplexities by modeling the human recording machine of "brain," soon replaced by the mind considered as "sand," as defacing of what we ordinarily think of as the normal human mind. "This trajectory from erased self-knowledge to disfiguration is the trajectory of the *The Triumph of Life.*" Shelley's text figures an epistemology of the truth of transitory knowledge, the feeling for mental surplus, a potentially unfathomable yet generative relation of self to its own enigmatic questions *of* and *to* the past.

Shelley's text carefully articulates Rousseau's mixture of a "delicacy of feeling" and "cunning and violence," often paralleling what occurs between "inner states of consciousness and acts of power," a mixture nowhere more revealing than in the "connivances" of words and deeds. De Man examines the permutations of these words and deeds, in which words issue from minds whose intentions are often unfathomable and where words are themselves actions in which they can neither be resisted nor accepted. This "discrepancy of action and intention that tears apart the historical world," what Lyotard once called "defaillancy," or internal distance of our thoughts concerning "history" that does not "mirror" any referential discrepancy, yields the constancy of an unwilled world, an absurdity perhaps, but one that interpretation cannot settle. De Man's reading gives its readers a "Shelley Disfigured" that cannot help ask as to how any mode of writing could be conceived of as *settling* language's relation to past. The concepts of "history," "self," and "continuity" acquire figures dissipating in the very act of using them; that is to say, Shelley has refigured Rousseauist *forgetting* and brought it to bear on any act of mind:

> The polarities of waking and sleeping (or remembering and forgetting) are curiously scrambled . . . with those of past and present, of the imagined and the real, of knowing and not knowing . . . For if . . . to be born into life is to fall asleep, thus associating life with sleep, then to "wake" from an earlier condition of non-sleeping into this "harsh world" of life can only be to become aware of one's persistent condition of slumber, to be more than ever asleep, a deeper sleep replacing a lighter one, a deeper forgetting being achieved by an act of memory which remembers one's forgetting . . . [that] necessarily hovers between a state of knowing and not-knowing, like the symptom of a disease which recurs at the precise moment that one remembers its absence. What is forgotten is absent in the mode of a possible delusion."[54]

The "scrambled polarities" of memory and forgetting suggest the actuality of their nonseparation; between language and consciousness, no amount of wish used to command thought can alter the fact that the instant one says "I know what (how) I remember" one has become possessed of the thought: possible delusion become intuitively true (for instance, the first words one says to oneself in moments of extreme tension). There is certainly "light" that permeates the territories of dream, sleep, and waking life, but where exactly is the precise cut that would render a purified clarity of the involved differences? Truth and error, epistemology and dream, consciousness and delusion are already inseparable when it comes to language. De Man's model, using Shelley's *The Triumph of Life* as its sounding, supposes that in areas as entangled as history and memory, clarity can veil, where "light covers light," where the giving of names is as much a model of ideological self-possession as it is our capture of the significance of meanings thrown up by the past.

It would be the most obfuscating thought of all to say that de Man follows Shelley, who follows Rousseau into the ambiguities of poetic language so as to arrive at the destination of "corrosive irony," referred to in a previous chapter. What is involved is the deterritorialization of those very precious boundaries and territories that protect our key faculties and powers—to desire, to know, to feel, to remember are opened up to "likenesses" in which their self-identity is entirely threatened, not confirmed. "Shelley

Disfigured" is a poem "shaped by the undoing of shapes," a condition for the possibility of the suspension of meaning, of interpretation; for even when Shelley allows for the flowing and glimmering waters of light and rainbow to illuminate the meaning of poetic ancestry, "this glimmering figure takes on the form of the unreachable reflection of Narcissus, the manifestation of shape at the expense of its possession."[55]

From a poetic perspective, the "shaped light of understanding" must always "wane away, layer by layer," leaving only the poem, that edifice "that serves to celebrate and to perpetuate its oblivion."[56] Figuration releases and contains forces, and self-obliteration is a necessary aspect of meaning. No poem is timeless, and figures of all types (sound, concept, synaesthesia) already contain "random and superficial properties of the signifier," (for example, accentuation and tone and conceptual "overload") which allow all uses of language to be potential experiences of satisfying failure. How can we know, concerning language and history, that a new truth is just an old lie made newly acceptable? De Man is unrelenting on this issue: improper signification is not responsible for the breakdown of "specular structures," as is said today when so many agree that "modernism is lost," a statement that then gives permission to nostalgia; rather, it is that no model of figuration is definitively constitutive of figuration. It is figuration itself that cannot in all cases be decisively analyzed, which allows us to bring to ourselves that force without which no figure of language itself is conceivable:

> The positing power of language is both entirely arbitrary, in having a strength that cannot be reduced to necessity, and entirely inexorable in that there is no alternative to it.[57]

Shelley's *The Triumph of Life* is then less a struggle with the ghosts of history and influence (*pace* Harold Bloom) as it is a remorseless self-contest with the "agonistic pathos of [a] dialectical battle" involving anthropomorphic forces, for it is the "sheer power of utterance" in and of itself that matters: "brusque" and "unmotivated," figuration should then be refigured as substitution, but a substitution for which there is nothing not already substitutive—except for an event of naming. And this event, this event of events, is both *not necessary and inexorable*. Nothing has to be said the way it is said; once said, it lives only outside what it said. In this sense, de Man's text works up an existentialism of the figure. When Archie (de)Bunker asks his wife Edith, "What's the difference?" in response to her question as to how to tie his bowling shoes, his "What's the difference?" is both a stick in the mind's eye and the potential truthful confession of a fool. It is also a superlinear commentary on language's own competence in specifying differences. "Shelley Disfigured" diagrams the most impossible dimension of this existentialism: "language posits and language means (since it articulates) but language cannot posit meaning; it can only reiterate (or reflect) it in its reconfirmed falsehood."[58] Metaphor or antimetaphor, it makes little difference: the eye as "light," the eye as "insight," the eye as that rendering Sense—all co-exist with the eye "as" and that is not antithetical to eye-as-darkening, for we know that "insight" can become the worst prejudice of all the instant that insightful words are misapplied.

With words and things, there are more forces than we might know; even so, the "blind force" of language is not an accidental feature of intersubjective relations, but neither is such an idea necessarily continuous with the "blind force" we can attribute to history or world. Not language behind our backs or beneath our feet or ahead or behind us: the "blind force" of language is ourselves, and belongs with the actions of others with which one has no choice but to contend. " . . . thought (i.e., figuration) forgets what it thinks and cannot do otherwise if it is to maintain itself."[59] Language and world, as Group Metaphor argued, are inseparable from the "autodestructive character of figured utterances," which no doubt accounts for our endless metalinguistic disputes, in which utterances less help settle things than they reconstitute the "euphoric" character of figural language. Figures must break down.[60] Blindness and insight. "Shelley Disfigured" closes with a complication of these matters as concerns the act of reading, here worth repeating:

> to read is to understand, to question, to know, to forget, to erase, to deface, to repeat—that is to say, the endless prosopopeia by which the dead are made to have a face and a voice which tells the allegory of their demise and allows us to apostrophize them in our turn. No degree of knowledge can ever stop this madness, for it is the madness of words.[61]

These phrases are a verbal model of the act differently called recoding, prosopopoeia, vicariousness, or mechanics in the politics of signification. They lay out, or diagram if you will, a character of a society layered with projections of memories and forgetting so entangled that no complete intellectual separation could be made, especially in the matters said to matter most. If "Shelley Disfigured" makes any sense at all, it is that making sense is dangerous, because the "madness of words" cannot be contained in any place. But the interpretation of that idea might just as easily lead to acceptance of the disfigurations of language, an *initiative* in the love of what we do to ourselves with language, the very antithesis of all those charges leveled at de Man's version of deconstruction.

Conclusion ◈

High Scholarship and the Politics of Writing

Following from what was said at the close of chapter five, or to continue in thinking the "madness of words," no doubt the order-words of this text have shown themselves, accounting for errors, blind spots, and other effects released by belief in criticism, or criticism turned into belief. Is it possible to make criticism of texts without making new orders?

The texts analyzed suggest a scholarship rigorously set against itself in the very act of narratively and discursively presenting final, definitive, absolute, certain, and aesthetically satisfying models of things. If the previous readings are at all plausible in accounting for connections between language, politics, and cultural historiography (*timings*), they indicate that a genealogy of contemporary scholarly writing might start naming and examining such conceptual entities as the "Momigliano effect," referred to in chapter four, which serves as a practical matrix for the issues involved. There, in the name of a cultural ideal, the scholar displaced questions of politics and epistemics onto questions of "taste" and connoisseurship, the rhetoric of scholarship unyielding in offering judgments by which rival discourses are discredited by misrepresentation giving itself the signifiers of authority. The dissension over the applicability and implications of concepts used by historiography were simply stopped in their tracks. We should give to scholarship what *properly belongs to it:* its aggressions, political and moral judgments that substitute for posing more, and possibly, insoluble problems no discourse can "master." In this sense, the humanities are not to be compared to the sciences because they cannot ever get off foundational issues; they are incomparable because so many texts "declare victory" instead of raising the ante on the nature of the work itself. For fifty years, from Milan to Chicago, "Momigliano words" were uttered within the academy, to presses and to editorial boards, to faculties and sponsors, words whose effects were decisive in ensuring the continuum of a certain kind of scholarship, a certain kind of academic politics, a certain "tone" and ethos that it was lethal to call into question.

Scholarly writing offers a precise contradiction: as discursive rivals are eliminated—the "hunter" rid of what could challenge its "rights," neopsychoanalysis's repetition of the metaphysics of the failure of desire— accomplished by many textual devices, these texts actually *subvert* the very epistemological ideals they claim to serve. Close reading asks epistemic questions in the face of texts that are aggressive toward such questions, and nothing can eliminate these epistemic meanderings, for they are defining of "high scholarship," especially the "new humanism" of today's academy. One can read one's contemporaries not "in the name of" historical claims, possession of history and culture, language and the present, but rather in *making names* for connections between text and institution, text and group, text and ideal, connections that would erode the careful boundaries of existing disciplinary structures. In the here and now, as concerns reading, closer readings favor linguistic proliferation rather than "mastery" of language by language, notions of which were given in chapter five, above. These subjects are irresolvable, and that does not mean the closest possible readings necessarily "fit" as models of existing arrangements of text and institution, especially if the purpose of such readings is to make more concepts, not fewer. The "madness of words" cannot be settled, but it can be worked with by the use of more concepts, not fewer.

There are so many works on the "new configurations" of university and society that one is hesitant to add to the existing misunderstandings, politics, or cultural historiographies of the university and social relations. Nonetheless, if it is plausible that there is a *nonseparability* of language, culture, and history, because of the *inseparability* of figuration from epistemology, epistemology from politics, culture from language, close reading may well be a symptom of what is *passing away* because it is a "tool" unwanted in many of the new configurations of scholarly writing.[1] All of the texts analyzed in the previous chapters are incontestably hostile to close reading: they want belief "in" their models, and if such texts are representative of a current transdisciplinary politics of language, then certain aspects of "high scholarly" writing point to a future calling for more and better criticism. Better in the sense that such criticism's point is not to make demands about what is "excluded" from discussion but to speak to the obligations of inclusion. Here is where the fiction called an "excessive reader" comes into play, for that reader "knows" that there is always more "fine print" to contend with. So rather than *repeat* the arguments as to the nihilistic effects of the writings critiqued, what follows offers a proposal, by way of theory and narrative, for how to intensify an actual politics of writing.

These remarks are, in part, derived from Gilles Deleuze's interpretation of Michel Foucault's elaboration of a dynamic concerning the cultural senses of infinitude and finitude, placed in the context of cultural production. In one way, the complex called "passive nihilism" indicates the persistence of a value attributed to "classical" writings, insofar as such texts submit to what they believe is a logic of infinitude to achieve a "share" in the culturally eternal, a "share" of value that cannot be withdrawn by the future. (This is not to say that writing of immediacy is more appropriate because of its "timeliness." The "timely" is a concept that should be radically evaluated whenever it appears in discourse). Whether through a resistance to death, dread of loss (not of the past, but of what one "knows" one has now to lose), or fantasies of what will "last," the texts that come to resolve use discourse against a politics of finitude. Appleby's text *is* representative of the belief that it is permissible, necessary, to *willfully misread* Nietzsche, so that such misreading will collaborate and prolong the "rightness" of their version of neoliberal humanism. In that way, a politics of writing is "covered by" a "share" in the cultural eternal. Politically informed misreadings are resistance to writing's utter finitude, of which deconstruction is the contemporary "outbreak." The aggressions toward skepticism indicate extraordinary textual and institutional energies set loose. Public life is riddled with demands for "cultural conversation" precisely because it is not allowed to take place other than by means of tightly controlled venues. Which means that writing is not allowed to produce its own finitude: "high scholarship" maintains the sense of writing "in the name of" the infinite ("truth," "humanity" "future," "memory"), rather than effecting transformation of its own archaicism's current plus-value. The latter concept delineates the presence, as language, of *recoding,* the textual consumptions that go by the name of cultural historiography.[2]

Ratcheting these words slightly tighter, consider what Alice Kaplan's *French Lessons,* discussed in the Introduction, helped to perform. Lauded in the media, in no small part because it made deconstruction scary and "over" in terms of embedding de Man the person/text in the politics of Romanticism blurred with fascism, it signals a purge of critical-linguistic interpretations of the politics of scholarly writing, one of many works written by new humanists, sophisticated versions sustaining the status quo. Cast in the rhetoric of a contemporary coming-of-age story of the scholar's love of the objects of study become one's life (the scholar's "my work is my life"), *French Lessons* offered a *spectacle* of order-words, politics, and cultural historiography. Her own *ressentiment* concerning her education and professional life was "cured," she tells us, only when the "real history" of de Man's notorious "past" made her writing, a literary history of fascism, into an "insider" text, so that just as she had to come to terms with "history," now the deconstructionists had to as well. Her self-declared "happiness" at getting out from under de Man's influence is rendered this way: "the moment of my greatest glee, the moment when I finally had something on my most enigmatic, famous teacher—just what I had always longed for!"[3] These words model aggression toward epistemology since they connect "history" directly to *ressentiment* in ways potentially unfathomable to anyone, and they also then tell us about the politics of circulating the rhetoric of intellectual "responsibility," especially given the media's participation.[4] To whatever extent, and without any finality ("infinite") to this, scholarship lives off such nihilisms of language and cannot be said to separate from its own nihilism.

Leaving off from what is clearly irritation with the *lessons* of *French Lessons,* Avital Ronell has taken great pains to demonstrate the history of *ressentiment* is a factual affair, a not-simple matter of circulating errors "in thinking [that] could mess us up for hundreds of years . . . history gone bad," and so it is a question of working the finitude of writing even harder, trying to stretch what can be interpreted psychosocially or self-referentially to the limits, maximizing writing, writing harder, a hyper-production of criticism, one that does not serve existing interests so much as creatively theorize word/institution relations, both within academia and without.[5] Contrary to Kaplan's "mastery" of *ressentiment by ressentiment,* perhaps one can start in a place that does not serve existing alliances. On reading Kaplan's carefully constructed use of words, one might compare her book to another autobiographic work, on matters intrinsic to *French Lessons.* In his remarkably understated *My Life In Germany Before and After 1933,* the philosophical historian Karl Lowith calmly suggested, in the face of the obvious horrors of early Nazi Germany, that the scholarly "communities" that made up the humanistic German intelligentsia did indeed recode their own multifaceted relations to the "new politics" of the times. The image perpetuated in the United States of the destruction of Euro-scholarship has helped to destroy alternatives here, and helps us to forget the typical aspects of the "time." Interestingly, Lowith interpreted that it was as an anonymous statement of the form that even though things were bad for intellectual life, the intellectuals could live with the idea that "things would have been much worse yet . . ." The logic of the acceptance of the least negative was a protective barrier against their "unthinkable," the disappearance of themselves, *terror at the very heart of scholarship.* They gave themselves an order-word: things *will get* worse if we do anything.[6] That specific situation, that "now of recent times," Lowith concluded, is as "old as history itself." Ironic, to be sure, but since irony is something to work on and not necessarily work "in," one might think of Lowith, kicked out of Germany and writing *From Hegel to Nietzsche* in Sendai, Japan, still one of the best works on nineteenth-century thought, and then think of our scholars in America and the American fear of things critical.

The demand for an economy of explanation—political moral interpretations cast as absolute truths—requires the concoction of objects increasingly rendered incredulous, like "connoisseur," "narrative satisfaction," or "soul craving," concepts that no doubt operate on different levels of sense production but that always congeal around certain hallucinatory effects. They may or may not be derived from "folk psychology" as Arthur Danto recently put it, but the orders and cultural timings analyzed in the previous chapters refer to scholarship in which politics, desire, exclusions, and much more are joined in verbal artifacts that are prosopopeiac, clearly text-aggressions in the name of ideals.

Michel Foucault argued that an important component in the genealogies of scholarship is what goes by the name "fellowships of discourse." The main elements of such "fellowships," he argued, were ritual, speakers invested with truth (code) and secret (for example, Jameson's "single white lie"), and the ensuing "strict regulation" of signification in which discourse would be produced and preserved as it was transmitted by apprenticeship (the new university press editors, *rivals* instead of *friends of texts*).[7] Made to become true discourse, or ritual inflected by positivisms and scientisms of all sorts, by work permits, credits of name and recognition, resumes, connections, Latour's ubiquitous *networks,* this conjunction of secret and truth, discourse and its transmission, is now called "public intellectual life"; there, cult-like groups work their dogma into fashion and overcoding, such cults rising and falling according to the logic of the least negative: incessant recoding of the negative, passive nihilism normalized. These groups work in disembodied signifiers that belong to "all" and "none"—that is, the stock of previously encoded systematic distortions of words. Foucault proposed that the persistence of "fellowships of discourse" or competing dogmas has come to "effect a dual subjection, that of speaking subjects to discourse, and that of discourse to the group, at least virtually, of speakers."[8] Out of this passive nihilistic continuum, where ideals freely circulate as commands, discourse over subject, dogma over discourse, now routed into management functions, Foucault drew a conclusion: such politicization of the epistemic bases of humanistic discourses results in a "muzzling of paradox." Such "muzzling of paradox" indicates oversupply of order-words, subjects of discourse whose overt logophilia as members of "fellowships of discourse" is undone by its own logophobia:

> a sort of dumb fear . . . of this mass of spoken things, of everything that could possibly be violent, discontinuous, querulous, disordered even and perilous in it, of the incessant, disorderly buzzing of discourse.[9]

Could scholarship exist, in its present form, as we know and are now un-knowing it, if we really complicated it, rendered unto it the status of its own textual complexity, which is to say, read it for the mixed genealogies that make it "timely"? What are strong readings to do with the persistent arrogance of "taste" set against epistemic questions which, in the humanities, has now made it all but impossible for such discourses to have the very credibility they claim except on the grounds of readers *not* reading very closely?

Notes

Introduction

1. Friedrich Nietzsche, *Philosophy and Truth* (London: Humanities, 1979), 51–52.
2. See Mario Biagioli, "Tacit Knowledge, Courtliness, and the Scientist's Body," in *Choreographing History,* edited by Susan Foster (Bloomington: University of Indiana, 1995), 72ff.
3. Gilles Deleuze and Felix Guattari, *Anti-Oedipus* (Minneapolis: University of Minnesota, 1977), 250.
4. Are these remarks "historical" in that they date this work in relation to a narrative (for instance, scholarship's undoing) or are they something else, a layout of thinking a text?
5. Paul de Man, *The Resistance to Theory* (Minneapolis: University of Minnesota, 1986), 49–50.
6. J. Hillis Miller, "An Open Letter to Professor Jon Weiner," in *Responses: On Paul de Man's Wartime Journalism,* edited by Werner Hamacher, Neil Hertz, and Thomas Keenen (Lincoln: University of Nebraska, 1989), 339.
7. Jacques Derrida, *Specters of Marx* (New York: Routledge, 1994), 97.
8. Joyce Appleby, review of "History Wars," *Los Angeles Times,* August 4, 1996, 9.
9. See chapter 1.
10. Deleuze and Guattari, *Anti-Oedipus,* 250ff.
11. Gilles Deleuze and Felix Guattari, *A Thousand Plateaus* (Minneapolis: University of Minnesota, 1980), 6.
12. Alice Kaplan, *French Lessons* (Chicago: University of Chicago, 1993), 172.
13. Kaplan, *French Lessons,* 172.
14. Martin Jay, *Downcast Eyes* (Los Angeles: University of California Press, 1993), 15.
15. This idea of intervention is drawn from the remarkable book by Jean-Jacques Lecercle, *The Violence of Language* (New York: Routledge, 1990), 226.
16. In a sense, this entire book is a probe of texts with de Man's insight in mind: it is the relations of language and intuition that are the most difficult to state clearly. See below for specific references to more precise aspects of de Man's arguments.

17. This concept is drawn from chapter 4 of Deleuze and Guattari's *A Thousand Plateaus*. See chapter 5 for a discussion.

18. Richard Rorty, "Solidarity or Objectivity?," in Cornel West and John Rajchman, *Post-Analytic Philosophy*, (New York: Columbia, 1985), 12. The extremely *repressive* aspects of Rorty's ideas can be seen in an essay in the *Chronicle of Higher Education (April 3, 1998, B5),*with the lurid title "The Dark Side of the American Left," in which Rorty claims the "cultural left" is just not concerned with the average American's interest in taxes and the welfare state. This "cultural left" "prefers not to talk about money" and is said to be obsessed with "mind-sets." The very attempt of "problematizing concepts" is declared worthless. Rorty's simply asserts that nationalism is the criterion of political relevancy, a rigid anti-intellectualism. So much the worse for what passes as "public intellectual" work.

19. I owe this characterization of this argument to the close reading of John Tagg.

20. These remarks are based on Paul de Man's *The Resistance to Theory* (Minneapolis:University of Minnesota, 1984), 10.

21. These remarks are drawn from Cynthia Chase, "Trappings of an Education," in *Responses,* edited by Werner Hamacher, Neil Hertz, Thomas Keenan (Lincoln: University of Nebraska, 1989), 60.

22. Friedrich Nietzsche, *The Genealogy of Morals* (London, 1913), section 26.

23. Interview with C. West by A. Stephanson, *Art and Philosophy* (Milan: Politi, 1991), 158.

24. Nietzsche, *The Genealogy of Morals,* part 3, section 18.

25. A catalogue of events for the Los Angeles County Museum of Art's "Emigres and Exiles" exhibition lists sponsors from universities to television stations to wealthy donors; a lecture at a school is tied to a slide show at a gallery, the German model of emigre serving as a model of all "diasporic" relations (the show appropriates Latin and Iranian exiles, in particular). The show—spectacle is more correct—is indebted to scholarship, but also serves as a massive fundraising effort for the Museum. What do we call these new extravaganzas?

26. The phrase "bittersweet" was used by professor Gary Nash, of UCLA.

27. "How Like a Goddess," Thurza Goodeve and Sandy Stone, *Artforum* (September 1995), 121.

28. Paul de Man, *Allegories of Reading* (New Haven:Yale University, 1979), 111.

29. Fredric Jameson, "On Cultural Criticism," *Social Text, 1993,* 39–40.

30. A vast literature now exists on university downsizing, increases in illiteracy, the collapse of readers for difficult books, the superstar syndrome, strange accounting procedures, etc.

31. G. A. Kelly, *Idealism, Politics and History* (Cambridge, 1969), 11. If we turn from the polite mode of aggressive idealism that subtends Professor Kaplan's writing, what do we find in the area of accessible criticism, the kind everyone claims to want to read? In a recent arts magazine, "popular music" is said to be the "dominant art form of this American century." Nothing is offered

by way of evidence. "Rock" is said to have replaced "jazz" as this dominant form of the popular, jazz an idiom of "nice," "free" and "autonomous," the slave's dream, "rock" ushering in "get it to-fucking-together, man" signifying "a fractal filigree of delicate distinction." Apart from the dubious interpretation (it suppresses punk, for instance the Dead Kennedy's refrain "Is my brain small enough is my cock big enough for you to make me a star?"), the writing profits from the discourse of alliteration, ushering in a spiritualization of the everyday. What has happened here? *Faux populism?* Fake proletarianization? Nostalgia? The "hip" taking charge of the popular? Dave Hickey, "The Delicacy of Rock and Roll," in *Art Issues* (Sept-Oct., 1995), 10.

32. Idealism often goes berserk, for instance, when Andrew Ross, director of the American Studies program at New York University, denounces the "cult of artistic freedom" and demands that criticism "seed the future" in the name of "cultural justice" and "cultural rights," an idealism that cannot be fulfilled, cannot here even be specified, though the demand remains. *Artforum* (1995).

33. Kelly, *Idealism,* 357.

Chapter 1

1. Jean-Jacques Lecercle, *The Violence of Language* (London: Routledge: 1993), 22.

2. Keith Jenkins, *On What Is History?* (London: Routledge, 1995), 6

3. Jenkins, *On What Is History?,* 176.

4. Jenkins, *On What Is History?,* 14.

5. Paul de Man, *Blindness and Insight* (New York: Oxford, 1971), 182.

6. Vivian Sobchak, "Introduction: history happens," in Sobchak, (ed.) *The Persistence of History* (New York: Routledge, 1996), 3.

7. Sobchak, "Introduction," 14.

8. Sobchak, "Introduction," 4.

9. Sobchak, "Introduction," 4, 6.

10. Frank Ankersmit, "Statements, Texts and Pictures," in Kellner, *New Philosophy,* 213. All further references to this work will be made parenthetically in the text.

11. Umberto Eco, *A Theory of Semiotics* (Bloomington: Indiana UP, 1976), 200ff.

12. de Man, Resistance to Theory, 16ff.

13. See Norman Bryson, *Vision and Painting* (New Haven: Yale, 1983), 42ff.

14. Jeremy Gilbert-Rolfe, *Beyond Piety* (Cambridge: Cambridge University, 1995).

15. Joyce Appleby, Lynn Hunt, and Margaret Jacob, *Telling The Truth About History* (New York: Norton, 1994), 1. All further references to this work will be made parenthetically in the text.

16. Jacques Derrida, *Specters of Marx* (New York: Routledge, 1994), xviii. All further citations from this text will be given in the chapter.

17. "*Differance* is literally neither a word nor a concept." *Margins of Philosophy* (Chicago: University of Chicago, 1982), 3. To differ and to defer are the standard renditions of *differance,* coded by Derrida to mean the "unnameable" play "which makes possible nominal effects."

18. Pierre Nora, "Between Memory and History: *Les Lieux de Memoire,*" in *Representations* (26: 1990), 9.

19. See the work of Reinhart Koselleck in *Futures Past* (Cambridge: MIT, 1985).

20. Rodolphe Gasche, *Tain of the Mirror* (Cambridge: Harvard, 1986), 205, has it that differance "promotes the plurality of difference, of a conflictuality that does not culminate in contradiction but remains a contradiction without contradiction." Rhetorical analysis sees in this the affirmation of a paradox, no longer paradox then, a way of sustaining what Gasche calls the "quasi-transcendental" status of differance.

21. See the brilliant remarks by Karl Lowith, *Meaning in History* (Chicago: U. of Chicago, 1949), 18ff.

22. These remarks are drawn from Vincent Descombes' *Modern French Philosophy* (Cambridge: University of Cambridge, 1980), 145ff.

23. The historian L. P. Curtis once wrote that the English psycho-image control over things Irish consistently played off the confusion of "guerilla"/"gorilla" in the imagery of nineteenth-century newspapers.

24. Lowith, *Meaning in History,* 44–46.

25. See the work of Emile Benveniste, *Indo-European Language and Society* (Coral Gables: University of Miami, 1973), 410ff.

26. This interpretation may appear harsh, seeming to put Derrida's work into a black box that distorts it. But statements of the type "it is necessary is necessary" should be taken at face value, especially since Derrida insists he is not making figures.

27. Carlo Ginzburg has repeatedly denounced Derrida by name as writing trash—and Ginzburg's own major contribution to historiography has been the elevation of the model of hunting as the basis of narrative and inquiry. See below, chapter four.

28. See Deleuze and Guattari, *Anti-Oedipus,* 17ff.

29. Michel Haar, "Nietzsche and Metaphysical Language," in David Allison, ed., *The New Nietzsche* (Cambridge: MIT, 1990), 14.

30. Umberto Eco, *The Role of the Reader* (Bloomington, IN: Indiana University, 1979), 33.

31. Henri Birault, "Beatitude in Nietzsche," in Allison, *New Nietzsche,* 221.

32. These remarks are based on Gilles Deleuze, *Nietzsche and Philosophy* (New York: Columbia, 1983), 144ff.

33. See Biagioli, "The Scientist's Body."

34. Greimas and Fontanille, xxiv.

35. All these remarks are drawn from Roland Barthes, *S/Z* (New York: Hill and Wang, 1972), 11.

36. Arthur Danto, "The Decline and Fall of the Analytical Philosophy of History," in Kellner, *New Philosophy,* 82–84.

37. Nietzsche, *Genealogy of Morals,* 43; Eco, *Role of the Reader,* 33.
38. Deleuze, *Nietzsche and Philosophy,* 73–74.
39. Massumi, *Deleuze and Guattari,* 12.
40. Massumi, *Deleuze and Guattari,* 15.
41. Greimas and Fontanille, *Semiotics,* 3; Goux, *Symbolic Economies,* 14.
42. Richard Kaplan, "The Economics of Family and Faith," *L.A. Times Book Review,* 30 July, 1995, 5.
43. See Evelyn Keitel, *Reading Psychosis* (New York, 1989).
44. See Roland Barthes, *Elements of Semiology* (New York Hill and Wang, 1968), 32–33.
45. See the crucial essay by Michel de Certeau, "The Historiographical Operation," in *The Writing of History,* translated by Tom Conley (New York: Columbia, 1988).
46. Quoted in Joan Stambaugh, *Nietzsche's Thought of Eternal Return* (Baltimore: Johns Hopkins, 1972), 53, 55.
47. Nietzsche, *Philosophy and Truth,* 85.
48. Nietzsche, *Philosophy and Truth,* 88
49. Nietzsche, *Philosophy and Truth,* 99.

Chapter 2

1. Michael Geyer, "Multiculturalism and the Politics of General Education," *Critical Inquiry* (Spring 1993).
2. Geyer, "Multiculturalism," 531.
3. Geyer, "Multiculturalism," 529.
4. Cf. Steven Pinker, *The Language Instinct* (New York: Morrow, 1995), 32–33.
5. Timothy Bahti, *Allegories of History:Literary Historiography after Hegel* (Baltimore, 1992), 11. For a much stronger view of related matters, see Reinhart Koselleck, *Futures Past* (Cambridge: MIT, 1985), in particular Koselleck's argument that enlightened historiography is, semantically considered, stretched between "the alternatives of progress or conservation, catching up or delay," which, in turn, is related to "history in emergence," a rewriting-machine that blocks consideration of "constant surprise," even if the "surprise" is itself a reminder of repetition. Koselleck, p. 250, 253. See also Sande Cohen, *Academia and the Luster of Capital* (Minneapolis, 1993), chapter four.
6. Geyer, "Multiculturalism," 531.
7. This is such contentious material that anything said in a note is bound to be inadequate. Geyer argues (p. 526) that the ontology of monoculturalism, universalism, etc. is threaded to the loss of academic autonomy (p. 527); the new "subjects" of history/pedagogy are then associated with a globalism defined as "the domain of financiers, entrepreneurs, entertainers, soldiers, professions like lawyers or medical doctors and the occasional politician or (natural) scientist . . . no longer local knowledge-systems with universalizing claims, but they are a multitude

of very tangible networks that shape local experience" (p. 528). Geyer has obliterated, through affirmation, all the contentious senses and dislocations pertaining to "network," for instance, that it is part of the superdetermination of every aspect of contemporary life but also that it is a direct expression of the concentration of power *tout court*. The "network" model is a part of the new elitism of institutions. For a critique of the "network" as it has resulted in dubious systems of academic ranking, exclusionary practices, explicit anti-intellectualism, and some of the filthiest politics imaginable, see my *Academia and the Luster of Capital* (Minneapolis, 1993), chapter two.

8. Paul de Man *The Rhetoric of Romanticism* (New York: Columbia, 1984), 117–18.

9. Jean-Jacques Lecercle, *Philosophy Through the Looking Glass* (LaSalle, 1985), 69–71.

10. Geyer, "Multiculturalism," 512.

11. Donna Haraway, for example, embeds "material-semiotic actors" in "world," in "generative nodes," in "conversations" and in "agency," among other terms. She, quite properly in my opinion, wants us to think of the "world" as "witty agent and actor," but she appropriates as the cultural model for this "new world" the "Coyote or Trickster . . . searching for fidelity, knowing all the while we will be hoodwinked." The logic and semantics of the proposition are highly questionable: "searching for" is a piece of classical idealism now co-coded with a theory of absence; the object, "fidelity" is pulled into the implied narrative necessity and is attached as the missing; but "fidelity" is itself a wavering concept, since it means an absolute promise and also the testing of its "fidelity." "Fidelity" is moralizing-identitarian. "Hoodwinked" either works as irony or as self-correction, and it is undecidable. Furthermore, the "coyote or trickster" is a logic of equivalence challenged, for example, in Deleuze's suggestion that the trickster is a cultural figure of *too much identity or likeness,* in that the trickster "claims to take possession of fixed properties, or to conquer a territory, or even to introduce a new order . . . The priest, the soothsayer, is a trickster, but the experimenter is a traitor." The first clause does not apply to Haraway's argument, but the second and third seem to. Finally, the "coyote" is not defamiliarizing. It is too explicitly still "us": why not "The termites . . . searching for fidelity"? Because we cannot mediate them? Because there is no translation? See Donna Haraway, *Simians, Cyborgs and Women* (London: 1991), 201, and Gilles Deleuze and Claire Parnet, *Dialogues* (New York: 1987), 41.

12. I am using modernism as a synonym for the perpetual recoding of capitalism (which is always neocapitalism), cultural issues of autonomy vs. legislation, the relevance of the Kantian-Nietzsche line in art (the sublime is an "outrage" vis-à-vis imagination), technology unbounded by social rules, the excessive pressure of conformity, the calling into question of language as communication.

13. Bruno Latour, *We Have Never Been Modern* (Cambridge: Harvard, 1993), 14. All further references to this text will be given parenthetically in the text.

14. Bruno Latour, *Science in Action* (Cambridge: Harvard, 1987), 16.

15. A passage from Latour's *Science in Action* is indicative of what I mean. There he asserts "we need to get rid of all categories like those of power, knowledge, profit or capital, because they divide up a cloth that we want seamless in order to study it as we choose." The phrase "get rid of" is a piece of symbolic violence, euphemism, just as is "we want seamless," which installs a demand. See Jean-Jacques Lecercle, *The Violence of Language* (London: Routledge, 1990), 179 and Pierre Bourdieu *In Other Words* (Cambridge: Polity, 1990), 84.

16. I am presupposing the adequacy of Deleuze's notion of transcendence, in which political idealism tries to establish criteria of legitimation and exclusion on the basis of an idea or value or thought's *participation* in an Idea.

17. Paul de Man, *The Resistance to Theory* (Minneapolis: University of Minnesota, 1986), 15.

18. De Man, *Resistance to Theory,* 11. I have changed de Man's citation; the original specified that it is not certain that "literature is reliable." I believe his argument holds for prose.

19. I am drawing upon the remarks of Tzvetan Todorov in *The Poetics of Prose* (Ithaca: Cornell, 1977), 146. The literariness of "a weaver of morphisms" implies super-idealism, every "network" a new thread.

20. A. J. Greimas and J. Fontanille, *The Semiotics of Passions* (Minneapolis: University of Minnesota, 1993), 8.

21. One of the most interesting discussions of this topic is found in Deleuze and Guattari's *Anti-Oedipus.*

22. Latour's plea for holistic anthropology, or integrative writing, can lead to some amusing examples. Another anthropologist has written that "No one buys a Big Mac for the simple reason of eating it . . . the behavior is part of an entire *gestalt* in which the consumer participates on a subliminal level . . . The purchase of a Big Mac involves a "deep" interior perception of self, family, country and socioeconomic status . . . a consumer "buys" a well deserved break; a vision of family cohesiveness . . . a particular type of patriotism." Latour would call the Big Mac a hybrid-network! Quoted in the *Los Angeles Times,* Thursday Dec. 30, 1993, A1, A18.

23. These remarks are drawn from Jean Baudrillard, *Fatal Strategies* (New York: Semiotext(e), 1990).

24. For instance, as when neopsychoanalysis installs the universality of recognition-claims as its special expertise, Zizek's assertion that the realization of desire can never be its fulfillment but rather only "the reproduction of desire as such, with its circular movement." See chapter 3.

25. Baudrillard argues that liberation is normative, a requirement, for example, of contemporary art in which what matters is not the production of images that resist repression (art as negation, as criticism) but images that give

the illusion that art is still "an outside." Not artist versus world, but art in which "subjectivity . . . endeavors to reconcile itself with its own image," or art liberated for a greater consumption than resistance ever promised. See Jean Baudrillard, "Gesture and Signature," in *For a Critique of the Political Economy of the Sign* (St. Louis: Telos, 1970), 109–11.

26. This is an amazing section: The moderns "capitalized" everything, but science studies will reign over the right to "give credit" to what the moderns could not recognize about themselves. Ethnography and anthropology converge with dogmatic elements of post-Freudian psychoanalysis in taking charge over the sorting and ranking operations of the signifier, practices, and institutions.

27. On modern art as hybrid—translation, mediation—any of the works of T. J. Clark are relevant. I might add that it is quite telling that WHNB is silent on the matter of art.

28. What WHNB renders, unconsciously, is a model of time as closed loop: eternality.

29. The plus-value of "resource" is unquestioned by WHNB. Nonetheless, the term is not so neatly "filed away" on the side of positive virtues. James Adler, chairman of the L.A. County Public Social Services Commission, which is about as fiscally "tight" as a "network" can get, calls for treating "welfare programs themselves" as "resources"—that is welfare to be replaced by "payment for work performed." *Los Angeles Times,* B7, Jan. 4, 1994.

30. Latour's remarks echo the reading of Manfred Frank's *What Is Neostructuralism?* (Minneapolis: University of Minnesota, 1989).

31. See Mario Biagioli, "Hoarding Telescopes: Galileo's Discoveries and the Moral Economy of Credit," forthcoming.

32. De Man, *Resistance to Theory,* 98.

33. Roland Barthes, *Mythologies* (New York: Hill and Wang, 1972), 152.

34. De Man, Resistance to Theory, 64.

35. De Man, *Resistance to Theory,* 16; de Man, *Rhetoric of Romanticism,* 118, 275.

36. De Man, *Resistance to Theory,* 10–11.

37. De Man, *Rhetoric of Romanticism,* viii.; de Man, *Allegories of Reading,* 10.

38. De Man, *Rhetoric of Romanticism,* ix. Reflection on these matters might consider "Shelley Disfigured," discussed more fully below, chapter five, in which de Man singles out the emphatic mode, imposition, which becomes a "positional act," and "which relates to nothing that comes before or after . . . How does a speech act become a trope . . . which then engenders . . . narrative sequence . . . It can only be because we impose, in our turn, on the senseless power of positional language the authority of sense and meaning." *Rhetoric of Romanticism,* 117–118. One could compare this formulation of a metaphysics of discrepancy, discrepant to itself, with, first, Deleuze and Guattari's notion of order-words in *A Thousand Plateaus* and then Baudrillard's use of the concept of objective irony.

39. In the writings about de Man's supposed use of deconstruction as an alibi for poor choices made in 1940, the most amazing is a letter to the *London*

Review of Books (November 4, 1993) by V. Richardson, who charges that "every mind that [de Man] seduced to his own emptiness was a mind that had thrown away the instruments by which he might be judged." cf. *London Review of Books,* November 4, 1993.

40. De Man, *Blindness and Insight,*11.
41. De Man, *Resistance to Theory,* 12–13.
42. De Man, *Blindness and Insight,* 18.
43. See David Lodge's comments in *Modern Criticism and Theory* (New York, 1988), 354.
44. Edward Said, *The World, the Text and the Critic* (Cambridge: Harvard, 1983), 163–64.
45. De Man, *Resistance to Theory,* 69–70. Modern criticism, according to de Man, is very much suggested as the production of a "grammatical subject cut off from its consciousness, the poetic analysis cut off from its hermeneutic function, the dismantling of the aesthetic and pictorial world . . . the dismemberment of the aesthetic whole into the unpredictable play of the literary letter."
46. De Man, *The Rhetoric of Romanticism,* 105. Thanks to Hayden White for reminding me of this essay.
47. De Man, *Resistance to Theory,* 70–71.
48. Said, *The World, the Text and the Critic,* 26.
49. Jean-Jacques Lecercle, *Philosophy Through the Looking-Glass* (La Salle, 1985), 38. My thanks to Gary Kibbins for this reference.
50. J.F. Lyotard, *The Differend* (Minneapolis: University of Minnesota, 1988), 5; Jean Baudrillard, *For A Critique of the Political Economy of the Sign* (St. Louis: Telos,1981), 101.

Chapter 3

1. I am drawing upon A. J. Greimas and J. Fontanille, *The Semiotics of Passions* (Minneapolis, 1993).
2. Vincent Leitch, *Deconstructive Criticism* (New York 1983), 11.
3. Slavoj Zizek, *Tarrying with the Negative* (Durham, Duke: 1993), 20–21.
4. Kaja Silverman, *The Subject of Semiotics* (London, 1983), 3.
5. Silverman, *Semiotics,* 150.
6. Silverman, *Subject,* 152.
7. Cf. Ernst Gellner, *Legitimation of Belief* (London: Cambridge, 1973), 99–100.
8. Thomas Pavel, *The Feud of Language* (London: Blackwell, 1989),133.
9. Quoted in Silverman, *Semiotics,* 157–58.
10. Slavoj Zizek, "It Doesn't Have to be a Jew," in *Lusitania,* v. 1, #4 (1993), 51.
11. Silverman, *Semiotics,* 166.
12. Quoted in Silverman, *Semiotics,* 178.
13. Jean-Joseph Goux, *Symbolic Economies* (Ithaca: Cornell), 22.

14. Jacques Lacan, *Ecrits,* (New York, Norton: 1977), 50.

15. Gayatri Spivak, *The Spivak Reader* (New York: Routledge, 1996), 112–13.

16. Here I am borrowing from Deleuze and Guattari, *Anti-Oedipus* (New York: Pantheon, 1977), 28.

17. Deleuze and Guattari, *Anti-Oedipus,* 83.

18. Jean-Francois Lyotard, *The Lyotard Reader* (London: Oxford, 1989), 30.

19. Lacan, *Ecrits,* 157.

20. J. F. Lyotard, *Libidinal Economy* (Bloomington: Indiana, 1993), 122.

21. Felix Guattari and Gilles Deleuze, *politique et psychanalyse* (Paris, 1977).

22. Deleuze and Guattari, *A Thousand Plateaus,* 114–15.

23. Slavoj Zizek, *Looking Awry* (Cambridge: MIT, 1993), vii.

24. See Clement Greenberg, "Avant-Garde and Kitsch," in *Pollack and After,* ed. by Francis Frascina (New York: Harper, 1986), 25.

25. Zizek, *Looking Awry,* viii.

26. Zizek, *Looking Awry,* 4.

27. Zizek, *Looking Awry,* 5.

28. Zizek, *Looking Awry,* 5.

29. Zizek, *Looking Awry,* 6.

30. Zizek, *Looking Awry,* 8.

31. Zizek, *Looking Awry,* 12.

32. Erich Auerbach, Mimesis (Princeton: Princeton University Press, 1953), 439.

33. From the catalogue's frontpiece, "Disembodied Militarism, Preface 1988." *Catholic Tastes* (New York: Whitney, 1993).

34. David Ross, "Director's Foreword, *Mike Kelley,* 9.

35. A point made by Jean Baudrillard in *Simulations.*

36. Ross, *Mike Kelley,* 9.

37. See J. L. Talmon, *Romanticism and Revolt* (New York: Harcourt, 1967), 162–63.

38. Elizabeth Sussman, "Acknowledgments," *Mike Kelley,* 11.

39. Elizabeth Sussman, "Introduction," *Mike Kelley,* 16.

40. Sussman, *Mike Kelley,* 16.

41. Sussman, *Mike Kelley,* 20.

42. Sussman, *Mike Kelley,* 20.

43. Sussman, *Mike Kelley,* 32, 38.

44. In *Future of an Illusion.*

45. Howard Singerman, "Charting Monkey island with Levi-Strauss and Freud," *Mike Kelley,* 102- 103.

46. Colin Gardner, "Let It Bleed," *Mike Kelley,* 112.

47. Mike Kelley, "Plato's Cave, Rothko's Chapel, Lincoln's Profile," *LAICA,* Fall 1985, 18.

48. Kelley, "Plato's Cave," 20.

49. Gilles Deleuze, *The Logic of Sense* (New York: Columbia, 1990), 83–93.

50. Mike Kelley, 'The Poltergeist," *LAICA,* no. 3 (1980).

51. Mike Kelley, "Three Projects," n.d.

52. Mike Kelley, "Three Projects," 10.
53. Mike Kelley, "Three Projects," 12.
54. Mike Kelley, "Foul Perfection: Thoughts on Caricature," *Artforum,* (27), 1989, 94.
55. Kelley, "Foul Perfection," 95.
56. Kelley, "Foul Perfection," 97.
57. Kelley, "Foul Perfection," 99.
58. Mike Kelley, "In Youth is Pleasure," *Flash Art* (164, May-June, 1994), 86.
59. Judith Butler, *Bodies That Matter* (London: Routledge, 1993), 189.
60. Butler, *Bodies That Matter,* 190.
61. Butler, *Bodies That Matter,* 204.
62. Butler, *Bodies That Matter,* 209.
63. Butler, *Bodies That Matter,* 218.
64. Butler, *Bodies That Matter,* 219.
65. Butler, *Bodies That Matter,* 219.
66. Butler, *Bodies That Matter,* 221.
67. These remarks are based upon Deleuze, *Nietzsche and Philosophy,* xii–xiv.
68. Fredric Jameson, "On Cultural Studies," *Social Text* (1993), p.33. All further references to this essay will be given parenthetically in the text.
69. Karl Lowith, *From Hegel to Nietzsche* (New York: Holt, Rinehart and Winston, 1964), 197.

Chapter 4

1. As Kant puts it in his "Idea for a Universal History."
2. See Roy Harris, *The Origin of Writing* (London, 1986), 46, who carefully articulates this "scriptist bias which is deeply rooted in European education," and where "respect for the written word . . . for the book above all as a repository of both the language and the wisdom of former ages" allows for writing to be thought of as continuous with nature, the natural.
3. Carlo Ginzburg, "Witches and Shamans," in *New Left Review* (v. 200, 1993), 76.
4. Carlo Ginzburg, "Checking the Evidence: The Judge and the Historian," *Critical Inquiry* (Autumn 1991), 92.
5. W.V. Harris, "The Silences of Momigliano," *Times Literary Supplement* (12 April, 1996), 7–8.
6. Carlo Ginzburg, "Just One Witness," in Saul Friedlander, ed. *Probing the Limits of Representation: Nazism and the "Final Solution"* (Cambridge: Harvard, 1992), 89–92.
7. Arnold Davidson, "Carlo Ginzburg and the Renewal of Historiography," in *Questions of Evidence* (Chicago: U of Chicago, 1994), 310.
8. Davidson, "Ginzburg," 314.
9. Friedlander, "Introduction," *Probing the Limits of Representation: Nazism and the 'Final Solution,"* 6.
10. Friedlander, "Introduction," 7.

11. Ginzburg, "Just One Witness," 84. See my discussion of *The Cheese and the Worms* below.

12. Does "echo" mean "return" or does it mean rhetorical repetition, that is, that Quinoni and Josephus were producing cliches?

13. Reality, then writing; something, then interpretation. What is blocked is the idea that layer after layer of interpretation often comes before, especially when readers of history texts are unfamiliar with the documentation.

14. Ginzburg, "Just One Witness," 89.

15. Ginzburg, "Just One Witness," 91.

16. The concept of "discipline" seems to be giving way to a more entangled, if unanalyzed, notion of "enclosure," in which the sense of "wall" obtains. For a somewhat "blind" defense of such "enclosures," see David Hollinger's "The Disciplines and the Identity Debates, 1970–95, *Daedalus* (Winter 1997, v. 126, #1).

17. An association Alice Kaplan made in *French Lessons* (1994), as pointed out in my introduction.

18. Ginzburg, "Just One Witness," 93.

19. Ginzburg, "Just One Witness," 94.

20. Ginzburg, "Just One Witness," 94.

21. Emile Benveniste, *Indo-European Language and Society* (Coral Gables, 1973), 527.

22. Dominic LaCapra, *History and Criticism* (Ithaca: Cornell, 1985), 51.

23. LaCapra, *History and Criticism,* 54.

24. LaCapra, *History and Criticism,* 56.

25. LaCapra, *History and Criticism,* 62.

26. LaCapra, *History and Criticism,* 63.

27. LaCapra, *History and Criticism,* 69.

28. Davidson, "Renewal of Historiography," 305.

29. Davidson, "Renewal of Historiography, 307–08, emphasis mine. I should say that at one point, Davidson quotes Ginzburg's mother, Natalia Ginzburg, as a source for this truth-ideal, without suggesting to the reader their relation. Fuel for LaCapra!

30. Cf. Umberto Eco, *A Theory of Semiotics* (Bloomington: Indiana, 1976), 61.

31. Davidson, "Renewal of Historiography," 310.

32. Davidson, "Renewal of Historiography," 314, emphasis mine.

33. Davidson, "Renewal of Historiography," 315.

34. Ginzburg, *Cheese and the Worms,* xii.

35. Ginzburg, *Cheese and the Worms,* xii, xvi.

36. Mikhail Bakhtin, "From the Prehistory of Novelistic Discourse," in Lodge (ed.), *Modern Criticism and Theory* (Essex, 1988), 132.

37. Ginzburg, *Cheese and the Worms,* xix, xxiii, 9, 10, 17, 19, 28, 36, 38–39, 45, 51, 51, 54, 57–59, 61, 64, 66, 68, 77, 80, 82, 86, 91, 99, 104, 105, 107, 112–115, 117, 123.

38. Ginzburg, *Cheese and the Worms,* 105.

39. Ginzburg, *Cheese and the Worms,* xxiii, 19, 36, 58, 59, 64, 86, 112.

40. Ginzburg, *Cheese and the Worms,* 19, 28, 45, 47, 51, 61, 68, 107.

41. This conjunction is particularly aggressive, since what is attributed here to "instinctive peasant materialism" was described by Orpheus—so originary that no writings survive—as rewards and punishments; for the just "in the next world . . . a life of feasting and everlasting drunkenness," and "mud" for the unjust. Kathleen Freeman, *Ancilla to the Pre-Socratic Philosophers* (Cambridge, 1969), 1. Orphic "drunkenness" is hardly the same as "feast."

42. Gerhard Ladner, *The Idea of Reform* (Cambridge, 1959), 21–29.

43. Friedrich Nietzsche, *The Genealogy of Morals,* First Essay, sections 15–16.

44. Lucretius, *On the Nature of Things* (Baltimore, 1971), 79, writes that myths, such as the conjunction of putrefaction = origin, evoke an "immortal existence in utter tranquillity, aloof and detached from our affairs . . . free from all pain and peril, strong in its own resources, exempt from any need of us, indifferent to our merits and immune from anger." Instead of celebrating Menocchio's mythologizing, another interpretation could make it out as part of a non-instinctive passivity. On an alternative reading to Ginzburg's insistence that Menocchio's discourse before the inquisition indicates "obscure peasant mythologies," see Herschel Baker, *The Image of Man* (New York, 1947), 121.

45. In "Witches and Shamans," cited above, Ginzburg writes of his shift to the study of "the victims of persecution" (Menocchio). As his father was persecuted by fascists and Nazis, the decision to study a peasant society long vanished was to bring the victims—now his father and Menocchio—out of "shadows." Here again is the figure of communicating with the dead, the fairy-tale and populism idealized to the point at which they are undiscussable in terms of critical evaluation. His statements as to "discovering" the 1591 interrogation of Menocchio is put this way: "I remember perfectly that after reading this document (not more than three or four pages) I fell into a state of excitement so strong that I had to interrupt my work . . . an extraordinary stroke of fortune . . . as if I suddenly *recognized* a document which was perfectly unknown to me." This "ecstasy" of course is itself a model of the "ecstasy" then "found" as that stratum of peasant culture long suppressed: it is impossible to tell what is from the document and what is from the writing.

46. Ginzburg, *Cheese and the Worms,* 58. The other, most relevant, uses are to be found on pp. 49, 57, 66, 68, 71, 79, and 113. If I were making LaCapra's case for psychoanalysis, the discussion of "echo" should be brought into alignment with this citation from "Witches and Shamans": "To know . . . is always to recognize. It is only what we already know, what is part of our baggage of experience, that permits us to know the new, isolating it from the mass of disordered and casual pieces of information which continually rain down on us." (p. 81). His father's death and the lack of communication of the benandanti, incomprehensible to the inquisitors, "brings to the surface a layer of deep and hidden beliefs: an ecstatic cult centred on fertility." Isn't this a displacement/restatement of the death of the father,

whose fertility is now sought for in the *benandanti?* All of the tags of continuity between the historian and his object—aren't they confirmed in this
weaving of the autobiographic and the continuous narrative? Is this not
desire in writing, writing as desire?

47. C. Ginzburg, "Introduction," *Clues, Myths and the Historical Method* (Baltimore, 1989), x–xi. But in an essay published with C. Poni, "The Name of
the Game: Unequal Exchange and the Historiographic Marketplace," in
Microhistory and the Lost Peoples of Europe (Baltimore, 1991), 2, 4, Ginzburg
insists that historical knowledge "needs" anthropology so as to speak of the
relationships implied by discrete documents, for the "unpredictable data,
such as criminal or inquisitional proceedings . . . are the closest thing we
historians have to the modern anthropologist's field of study." This "proso-
pography from below" involves anything but "chance and curiosity." It requires cases from below which are "normal exceptions." And what are
these? "Marginal cases that bring the old paradigm back into the arena of
discussion . . . to create a new paradigm," as "clues . . . of a hidden reality."
What is not-here is asserted as hidden. Such cases "throw into disarray the
superficial aspect of the documentation," that is "unimportant crimes" by
"unimportant individuals" allow historians to study the "rules of the game"
or where an "invisible level" is grasped. "Real life" and "invisible structures"
are thus linked, Marx and Freud thrown together by means of Saussure:
Thus, this ideal synthesis will have to resist Barthes and poststructuralism.

48. Ranke, quoted in George Iggers, *The German Conception of History* (Middletown, 1968), 78. "The historian . . . finds an infinity in every existence,
an eternal element coming from God in every being . . . For this reason
the historian inclines to turn to the individual. He makes the particular interest count. He recognizes the beneficent and enduring. He opposes dis-
integrating change. He acknowledges a portion of truth even in error." See
note 102 for Ginzburg on Derrida.

49. Ginzburg, *Clues,* 98.

50. Ginzburg, *Clues,* 101.

51. Ginzburg, *Clues,* 101.

52. Ginzburg, *Clues,* 101.

53. The continuism of the Double requires, according to Freud, "unbounded
self-love," at first "an assurance of immortality," later "the ghastly harbinger
of death." Freud, "The 'Uncanny,'" in Sigmund Freud, *On Creativity and the
Unconscious* (New York, 1958), 5.

54. Roland Barthes, "The Old Rhetoric, an aide-memoire," in *The Semiotic
Challenge* (New York: Farrar, Straus, Giroux, 1988), pp. 55–56.

55. Freud, *On Creativity and the Unconscious,* 144.

56. Barthes, "Old Rhetoric," 60.

57. Ginzburg, *Clues,* 102.

58. Ginzburg, *Clues,* 102.

59. Louis Marin, *Portrait of the King* (Minneapolis: University of Minnesota,
1988), 48.

60. Ginzburg, *Clues*, 102. For only one quite different reading of the hunter, see Rene Grousset, *Empire of the Steppes* (Brunswick, 1994), 195, 224, who notes that among the Turko-Mongol peoples, the hunter was never separate from sorcery, theft, and power relations, was as much a stalker as a "reconstructor" and almost never hunted alone. Ginzburg's hunter is irreducibly the ideal *generic European*.

61. See Friedrich Nietzsche, *The Genealogy of Morals* (Edinburgh, 1913), 184, 186, 192.

62. Friedrich Nietzsche, *The Use and Abuse of History* (Macmillan, 1957), 58.

63. See Rodolphe Gasche, *The Tain of the Mirror* (New York, 1986), 159–60.

64. Page duBois, *Torture and Truth* (New York: Routledge, 1991), 41.

65. Ginzburg, *Clues*, 103.

66. Ginzburg, *Clues*, 103. This section of *Clues* is highly reminiscent of J. T. Shotwell's *The History of History* (New York, 1939), which emphasized the "exhilarating sense of direct contact with a living past," in which the historian was to resolve "the absence of a guide" for the "adventure" of historical thought (ix). Shotwell goes on to add that the "earliest historical narrative is the myth . . . The long canoes are swept to sea by the northeast hurricane and year by year in the winter nights at the campfires of those who go by long canoes the story is repeated. . . ." Are "those who go by" comparable to Ginzburg's "someone [who] passed this way"? Shotwell also noticed the violence of storytelling, that such writing congeals into "creed," in which "the unbeliever is ostracized or put to death" (p. 18).

67. These issues are given an excellent treatment in Koselleck's *Futures Past*, cited above.

68. Ginzburg, *Clues*, 104.

69. Ginzburg, *Clues*, 105.

70. Herbert Butterfield, *The Origins of History* (New York, 1981), 133.

71. Ginzburg, *Clues*, 105.

72. Ginzburg, *Clues*, 106.

73. Ginzburg, *Clues*, 106.

74. R. G. Collingwood, *The Idea of History* (London, 1946), 234–35.

75. Ginzburg, *Clues*, 108.

76. Ginzburg, *Clues*, 115.

77. Ginzburg, *Clues*, 115.

78. Ginzburg, *Clues*, 115.

79. Ginzburg, *Clues*, 117.

80. Ginzburg, *Clues*, 120.

81. Ginzburg, *Clues*, 122.

82. Ginzburg, *Clues*, 123.

83. Ginzburg, *Clues*, 124.

84. Gilles Deleuze, *Proust and Signs* (New York: Braziller, 1972), 16.

85. Ginzburg, *Clues*, 124.

86. Ginzburg, *Clues*, 124.

87. Collingwood, *The Idea of History*, 255.

88. Ginzburg, *Clues,* 125.
89. Ginzburg, "Microhistory," 24.
90. Ginzburg, "Microhistory," 26. This reading of the painting is incredibly selective. As Koselleck points out in *Futures Past,* 6, Altdorfer's painting was commissioned for its "eschatological status," as part of Luther's belief in the "signs of the End of the World," Altdorfer himself dabbling in astrology and active in the expulsion of Jews from Regensburg.
91. Ginzburg, "Microhistory," 33.
92. Carlo Ginzburg, "Killing a Chinese Mandarin: The Moral implications of Distance," in *Critical Inquiry* (Autumn 1994, v. 21, n. 1), 48.
93. Ginzburg, "Killing," 52.
94. Ginzburg, "Killing," 56.
95. Ginzburg, "Killing," 57.
96. Ginzburg, "Checking the Evidence," 80.
97. Ginzburg, "Checking the Evidence," 83.
98. The argument here is that Ginzburg's "specific code" reduces what was written to decipherability and evades interpretability—first of the documents, then of the reading of them. It assumes disambiguation as a given of reading, a practice which de Man emphasized as one of the most embedded illusions of writing and reading, assuming *an* interpretation is *the* interpretation.
99. L. Canfora, "Analogie et histoire" *History and Theory* (v. 22, #1), Autumn 1983, 23. Canfora notes that the index, to which Ginzburg's "hunter" is always sensitive, served as the basis of to "find, that is to say, to evaluate in language the 'grandeur' . . . of an historical fact." The resources devoted to "research" of the past—by the ancients themselves—were to make memorable and to "permit the recognition of superior grandeur (of duration, number of battles, villages destroyed, populations reduced to slavery)."
100. Carlo Ginzburg, "Montrer et citer," in *Debat,* n. 56 (1989), 43.
101. Ginzburg, "Montrer et citer," 44.
102. "I am really convinced that you have to use philology in order to understand the right meaning of a text or of a work of art. I am deeply interested in catching the right meaning . . . I am deeply against every kind of Derrida trash, that kind of cheap skeptical attitude." Carlo Ginzburg, "Interview," *Radical History Review* (#35, 1986), 100.
103. Ginzburg, "Montrer et citer," 46.
104. Clark, *Rhetoric,* 20–23. Gerard Genette, in his *Figures of Literary Discourse* (New York, 1982), 53, points out that this figure of description is also part of a "passion to name which is a mode of self-expansion and self-justification: it operates by increasing the number of objects in one's purview," which he calls *abruption.*
105. See Koselleck, *Futures Past,* 23.
106. Ginzburg, "Montrer et citer," 48.
107. As quoted in George Nadel, "Philosophy of History Before Historicism," in *History and Theory* (v. 3, n. 3, 1964), 295.

108. See C. Perelman and L. Olbrechts-Tyteca, The New Rhetoric (Notre Dame, 1969), 438.

109. Ginzburg, "Montrer et citer," 53. But note that Baronius "antirhetoric" was also a defense of the medieval church, a refutation of Protestantism. Annalism was a rhetoric of continuism, and was answered by Casaubon who insisted upon its many errors of interpretation of Greek, Hebrew, and Latin writings. Cf. Ernst Breisach, *Historiography, Ancient, Medieval and Modern* (Chicago: University of Chicago, 1983), 167–68.

110. Ginzburg, "Montrer et citer," 54. Here too Ginzburg has it that this "effect of truth" is still "truth," but an "effect" is always an interpretation, a "truth on truth," if one likes, in which the data is subservient to the "effect,"if "data" can be even "thought" at that point.

111. Arnaldo Momigliano, *Studies in Historiography* (New York: Harpers, 1966), 19.

112. Momigliano, *Studies in Historiography*, 69.

113. Momigliano, *Studies in Historiography*, 110.

114. Momigliano, *Studies in Historiography*, 111.

115. G.W. Bowersock, "Momigliano's Quest for the Person," in *History and Theory Beiheft* 30, v. 30, #4, 1991, 35.

116. Mikhail Bakhtin, "From the Prehistory of Novelistic Discourse," in *Modern Criticism,* 135.

117. Umberto Eco, *Semiotics and the Philosophy of Language* (Bloomington: Indiana, 1984).

118. See the analysis by Jacques Derrida, "Economimesis," in *Diacritics* (Summer, 1981), 12. Thanks to Andrea Loselle for this reference.

119. On this point, see Hans Georg Gadamer, *Philosophical Hermeneutics* (Berkeley, 1976), 83, who emphasizes that the substitution of one expression for another stops at poetic creation-untranslatability.

120. Umberto Eco, *Semiotics and the Philosophy of Language* (Bloomington, 1984); Bakhtin, "From the Prehistory of Novelistic Discourse," in *Modern Criticism,* 135ff.

121. R. Koselleck, *Futures Past* (Cambridge: MIT, 1979), 170.

122. Barthes, "Old Rhetoric," 85.

Chapter 5

1. A rebus contains elements of the past that survive in concepts Derrida has worked extensively, like "nonlinear and "nonsuccessive."

2. Vincent Descombes, *Objects of All Sorts* (Baltimore: Johns Hopkins, 1986), 41.

3. For example, in rejecting "essentialism" as a help in overthrowing "gynophobia," the cultural critic Emily Apter asserts that "90's feminism endorses antiessentialism by jettisoning gender stereotypes, theorizing the body, queering sexual difference, and plugging the ears to the maternal recidivism of friends ('But now that you have a boy . . . ')." Three of the terms,

"jettisoning," "theorizing" and "queering" refer to existing, declared aims of feminism. They are goals of scholarly feminism—its "antiessentialism." The fourth term, however, or "plugging the ears" refers to an internal voice, autobiographic, and is strange just for its *paratactic* relation to the first three goals. Is this openintg of the autobiographic space ("maternal recidivism") a solidarity with other academics who have decided to write autobiographies or ? See *October* (Winter, 1995), #71, p. 9.

4. Stephen Pinker, *The Language Instinct* (New York: Morrow, 1995), 28.

5. See Bill Reading, *Introducing Lyotard,* 107.

6. Ludwig Wittgenstein, *Philosophical Investigations* (New York: Macmillan, 1968), 13e.

7. See Zygmunt Bauman, *Intimations of Postmodernity* (London, 1992), 105–06.

8. See Arthur Danto, *Analytical Philosophy of Knowledge* (Cambridge: Cambridge University, 1968), 235.

9. Ludwig Wittgenstein, *Tractatus Logico-Philosophicus* (London: Routledge, 1922), 61.

10. Wittgenstein, *Tractatus,* 67.

11. Martin Heidegger, *What Is Called Thinking* (New York: Harper, 1968), 119.

12. See the remarks by Samuel Weber, "Afterword: Literature—Just Making It," in Jean-Francois Lyotard and J. L. Thebaud, *Just Gaming* (Minneapolis: University of Minnesota, 1985), 108.

13. This is perhaps where Wittgenstein's model of language moves away from "humanist" concerns.

14. Wittgenstein, *Tractatus,* 67.

15. See the remarks by C. A. van Peursen, *Body, Soul, Spirit* (London: Oxford, 1966), 144.

16. Van Peursen, *Body,* 147.

17. Wittgenstein, *Tractatus,* 77.

18. Wittgenstein, *Tractatus,* 27.

19. Wittgenstein, *Philosophical Investigations,* 32e.

20. Amos Funkenstein, "History, Counterhistory, and Narrative," in Saul Friedlander, *Probing the Limits of Representation* (Cambridge: Harvard, 1993), 67–68.

21. Jonathan Bennett, *Kant's Analytic* (Cambridge: Cambridge University, 1966), 4.

22. Gilbert Ryle, "The Theory of Meaning," in Thomas Olshewsky, ed. *Problems in the Philosophy of Language* (New York, Holt, 1969), 132, 134.

23. See Pierre Bourdieu *In Other Words* (London: Polity, 1990), 179ff.

24. Deleuze and Guattari, *A Thousand Plateaus,* 76.

25. Deleuze and Guattari, *A Thousand Plateaus,* 76.

26. Deleuze and Guattari, *A Thousand Plateaus,* 76.

27. Labov, *Sociolinguistic Patterns,* 250.

28. Deleuze and Guattari, *A Thousand Plateaus,* 78.

29. Deleuze and Guattari, *A Thousand Plateaus,* 79.

30. Massumi, *User's Guide,* 33.
31. Gilles Deleuze and Felix Guattari, *Kafka* (Minneapolis: University of Minnesota, 1986), 23–25.
32. Deleuze and Guattari, *A Thousand Plateaus,* 84.
33. Deleuze and Guattari, *A Thousand Plateaus,* 80.
34. Deleuze and Guattari, *A Thousand Plateaus,* 82.
35. Deleuze and Guattari, *A Thousand Plateaus,* 82
36. Deleuze and Guattari, *A Thousand Plateaus,* 83.
37. Deleuze and Guattari, *A Thousand Plateaus,* 84.
38. See Eco's *Semiotics and the Philosophy of Language,* 34.
39. Deleuze and Guattari, *A Thousand Plateaus,* 86.
40. D. T. Suzuki, *Zen and Japanese Culture* (New York: Pantheon, 1959), 156.
41. See Anthony Wilden, "Changing Frames of Order: Cybernetics and the Machina Mundi," in *The Myths of Information* (Madison: Coda Press, n.d.), 232.
42. Perry Anderson, "On Emplotment: Two Kinds of Ruin," in Friedlander, *Probing the Limits,* 64.
43. Language as imposition, to posit, modalized as the effect of assertion, is here very close to arguments stressed by Paul de Man.
44. Deleuze and Guattari, *A Thousand Plateaus,* 93.
45. Deleuze and Guattari, *A Thousand Plateaus,* 94.
46. Deleuze and Guattari, *A Thousand Plateaus,* 95.
47. Deleuze and Guattari, *A Thousand Plateaus,* 109.
48. Deleuze and Guattari, *A Thousand Plateaus,* 99.
49. Deleuze and Guattari, *A Thousand Plateaus,* 110.
50. Thomas Pavel, *The Feud of Language,* (London: Blackwell, 1989), 155–56.
51. Susan Buck-Morss, *The Dialectics of Seeing* (Cambridge: MIT), 338.
52. Paul de Man, "Shelley Disfigured," in *The Rhetoric of Romanticism* (New York: Columbia, 1984), 94.
53. De Man, "Shelley Disfigured," 98.
54. De Man, "Shelley Disfigured," 102–03.
55. De Man, "Shelley Disfigured," 109.
56. De Man, "Shelley Disfigured," 112.
57. De Man, "Shelley Disfigured," 116.
58. De Man, "Shelley Disfigured," 117–118. Perhaps an example is necessary here. Zygmunt Bauman, cited earlier, writes in his *Intimations of Modernity* (1992),105–06, that the discipline of sociology can become relevant again only by means of an affirmation of the plural, of the many: the "skill of interpretation" is today more important in sociology's capacity for "self-reproduction," since sociology is losing its connections to state management (as the latter is reduced to issues of law and order). The plural and the many replace sociology's provision of order and direction (teleology) for societies that are already overordered and overdirected. But this turn is cast by Bauman in language which is at once necessary and frightening:

The only reasonable cognitive strategy is therefore . . . recovery of the meaning of the alien experience through fathoming the tradition (form of life, life-world, etc.) which constitutes it, and then translating it, with as little damage as possible, into a form assimilable by one's own tradition . . . the expected "enrichment" of one's own tradition, through incorporating other, heretofore inaccessible, experiences, which is the meaning bestowed upon the exercise by the project of "'interpreting sociology'."

But what does "fathom" involve? What is "recovery" here? What is "translation"? What could "enrichment" of ourselves mean, and how would such meanings be separate from colonizing and economizing sememes: "with as little damage as possible" begs the question—how much damage is little?

59. De Man, "Shelley Disfigured," 119.

60. See Group Metaphor, *A General Rhetoric* (Baltimore: Johns Hopkins, 1981), 228–29.

61. De Man, "Shelley Disfigured," 122.

Conclusion

1. To take one example, editorials in the *New York Times* have, over the past few years, repeatedly emphasized the *reconcentration* of academia around a few dense centers, while the runaway elimination of positions goes bemoaned amidst endless hand-wringing. A purging of the professoriat, carried out by the professoriat against itself, has already occurred in the United States.

2. See Gilles Deleuze, *Foucault* (Minneapolis: University of Minnesota, 1988), 126–27.

3. Alice Kaplan, *French Lessons* (Chicago: University of Chicago, 1993), 169–73.

4. Someone should do a study of the editorials published by the *Los Angeles Times* concerning the University of California and deconstruction, in particular the editorials by UC historians. It doesn't have to be deconstruction: any contentious movement, thought-form, etc. would suffice.

5. Avital Ronell, "A Note on the Failure of Man's Custodianship," in *Public*, #8, 1993.

6. Karl Lowith, *My Life in Germany Before and After 1933* (Chicago: University of Illinois, 1994), 60.

7. Fashion and overcoding, among other forces, are at work here. The replacement at university presses by Ph.D.'s indicates a number of operative factors or causes, but the result is that these editors serve the interests of those who appoint and support them, often their own mentors. Lists at university presses increasingly show this type of control and channeling. The circulation of "prestige" is not the only issue. When the University of California press recently published Michael Wood's psycho-pop "repetition" of the "journey" of Alexander the Great, the "message" to authors

with difficult works is chilling. If university presses compete, as they do, for popular texts to defray the expense of publishing scholarship, they drive the market. The result is the university press as *designer scholarship* in which the editors not only compete with their authors over positions and prestige, but also actively create prestige value. At what point are *private* editorial decisions of *public* value? The presses, in other words, have been recaptured by neoconservatives, whose discourse is often "avant-garde" or "timely."

8. Michel Foucault, "The Discourse on Language," in *The Archaeology of Knowledge* (New York: Pantheon, 1972), 225ff.

9. Foucault, "The Discourse on Language," 229.

Bibliography

Abel, Elizabeth. "Black Writing, White Reading." *Critical Inquiry.* (v. 19, n. 3, Spring 1993).

Anderson, Perry. "On Emplotment: Two Kinds of Ruin." In *Probing the Limits of Representation,* edited by S. Friedlander. Cambridge: Harvard, 1993.

Ankersmit, Frank. *Narrative Logic.* The Hague, 1983.

Appleby, Joyce. "History Wars," Los Angeles Times, August 4, 1996.

Appleby, Joyce, Hunt, Lynn and Jacob, Margaret. *Telling the Truth About History.* New York: Norton, 1994.

Apter, Emily. "Questions of Feminism: 25 Responses," *October.* no. 71 (Winter 1995).

Auerbach, Erich. *Mimesis.* Princeton: Princeton University, 1953.

Bahti, Timothy. *Allegories of History: Literary Historiography After Hegel.* Baltimore, 1992.

Baker, Herschel. *The Image of Man.* New York, 1947.

Bakhtin, Mikhail. "From the Pre-History of Novelistic Discourse," in David Lodge, ed., *Modern Criticism and Theory.* Essex, 1988.

———. *Rabelais and His World.* Bloomington: Indiana, 1984.

Barthes, Roland. *Mythologies.* New York, 1970.

———. *The Semiotic Challenge.* New York, 1988.

———. *Elements of Semiology.* Boston: Beacon, 1967.

Baudrillard, Jean. *Fatal Strategies.* New York: Semiotext(e), 1990.

———. *For a Critique of the Political Economy of the Sign.* St.Louis: Telos, 1981.

———. *Simulations.* New York: Semiotext(e), 1983.

Bauman, Zygmunt. *Intimations of Postmodernity.* London, 1992.

Bennett, Jonathan. *Kant's Analytic.* Cambridge: Cambridge University, 1966.

Benveniste, Emile. *Indo-European Language and Society.* Coral Gables, 1973.

Bernstein, J. M. "Introduction" in T. W. Adorno, *The Culture Industry.* London, 1991.

Biagioli, Mario "Hoarding Telescopes: Galileo's Discoveries and the Moral Economy of Credit." forthcoming.

———. "Tacit Knowledge, Courtliness, and the Scientist's Body," in *Choreographing History,* ed. by Susan Foster. Bloomington: Indiana University, 1995.

Birault, Henri. "Beatitude in Nietzsche," in David Allison, *The New Nietzsche.* Cambridge: MIT, 1990.

Bloom, Harold, ed. *Romanticism and Consciousness.* New Haven: Yale, 1970.

———. *A Map of Misreading.* New York, 1975.

Bourdieu, Pierre. *In Other Words.* London: Polity, 1990.

Bowersock, G. W. "Momigliano's Quest for the Person." *History and Theory Beiheft 30* (1991, #4)

Breisach, Ernst. *Historiography, Ancient Medieval and Modern.* Chicago, 1983.

Buck-Morss, Susan. *The Dialectics of Seeing.* Cambridge: MIT Press, 1989.

Burke, Kenneth. *A Grammar of Motives.* Berkeley: University of California Press, 1969.

———. *Language as Symbolic Action.* Los Angeles, 1968.

Butler, Judith. *Bodies That Matter.* London, 1993.

Butterfield, Herbert. *The Origins of History.* New York, 1981.

Canfora, Ludovic. "Analogie et histoire," in *History and Theory.* v. 22, #1, (Autumn 1983).

———. *The Writing of History.* New York: Columbia, 1987.

Chase, Cynthia. "Trappings of an Education," in *Responses: On Paul de Man's Wartime Journalism,* ed. W. Hamacher, N. Hertz, and T. Keena. Lincoln: University of Nebraska, 1989.

Clark, D. L. *Rhetoric in Greco-Roman Tradition.* New York: Columbia, 1957.

Cohen, Sande. *Academia and the Luster of Capital.* Minneapolis: University of Minnesota Press, 1993.

———. *Historical Culture: On the Recoding of an Academic Discipline.* Berkeley: University of California Press, 1986.

Collingwood, R. G. *The Idea of History.* London, 1946.

Danto, Arthur. *Analytic Philosophy of Knowledge.* Cambridge: Cambridge University, 1968.

Davidson, Arnold. "Carlo Ginzburg and the Renewal of Historiography." in *Questions of Evidence.* Chicago, 1994.

de Certeau, Michel. "The Jabbering of Social Life," in *On Signs,* edited by M. Blonsky. Oxford, 1985.

Deleuze, Gilles. "Active and Reactive,"in The New Nietzsche, edited by D. Allison. Cambridge: MIT Press, 1985.

———. *The Logic of Sense.* New York: Columbia, 1990.

———. *Nietzsche and Philosophy.* New York: Columbia University Press, 1983.

———. *Proust and Signs.* New York: Braziller, 1972.

Deleuze, Gilles, and Guattarti, Felix. *Anti-Oedipus.* Minneapolis: University of Minnesota Press, 1983.

———. *A Thousand Plateaus.* Minneapolis: University of Minnesota Press, 1987.

———. *Kafka: Toward a Minor Literature.* Minneapolis: University of Minnesota Press, 1986.

———. *Qu'est-ce que la philosophie?* Paris, 1991.

———. *politique et psychanalyse.* Paris: des mots perdus, 1977.

Deleuze, Gilles, and Claire Parnet. *Dialogues.* New York, 1987.

De Man, Paul. *Allegories of Reading.* New Haven: Yale, 1979.

———. *Blindness and Insight.* New York: Oxford University Press, 1971.

———. *Resistance to Theory.* Minneapolis: University of Minnesota, 1986.

———. *The Rhetoric of Romanticism.* New York 1984.

Derrida, Jacques. "Economimesis," in *Diacritics* (Summer 1981).

———. *Specters of Marx.* New York: Routledge, 1994.

Descombes, Vincent. *Modern French Philosophy.* New York: Cambridge University Press, 1988.

———. *Objects of All Sorts.* Baltimore: Johns Hopkins, 1986.

de Spinoza, B. *Theological-Political Treatise.* New York: Dover, 1951.

Donato, Eugene. "The Two Languages of Criticism," in *The Languages of Criticism and the Sciences of Man,* edited by R. Macksey and E. Donato. Baltimore: John Hopkins, 1970.

DuBois, Page. *Torture and Truth.* New York: Routledge, 1991.

Eco, Umberto. *A Theory of Semiotics.* Bloomington: Indiana University, 1976.

———. *Semiotics and the Philosophy of Language.* Bloomington: Indiana University, 1984.

Feyerabend, Paul. *Killing Time.* Chicago: University of Chicago, 1995.

Foster, Hal. "What's Neo about the Neo-Avant Garde?," *October* #70 (Fall 1994).

Foucault, Michel. *Language, Counter-Memory, Practice.* Ithica, 1977.

———. *The Order of Things.* New York: Pantheon, 1970.

———. *The Archeology of Knowledge.* New York: Pantheon, 1972.

Frank, Manfred. *What is Neostructuralism?* Minneapolis: University of Minnesota Press, 1989.

Freeman, Kathleen. ed. *Ancilla to the Pre-Socratic Philosophers.* Cambridge: MIT Press, 1978.

Friedlander, Saul, ed. *Probing the Limits of Representation: Nazism and the "Final Solution."* Cambridge: Harvard, 1993.

Freud, Sigmund. *On Creativity and the Unconscious.* New York, 1958.

Funkenstein, Amos. "History, Counterhistory, and Narrative," in *Probing the Limits of Representation.* edited by Saul Friedlander. Cambridge: Harvard, 1993.

Gadamer, Hans-Georg. *Philosophical Hermeneutics.* Berkeley, 1976.

Gardner, Colin. "Let it Bleed," in *Mike Kelley, Catholic Tastes,* edited by Elizabeth Sussman. New York: Whitney, 1993.

Gasche, Rodolphe. *The Tain of the Mirror.* Cambridge: Harvard, 1986.

Gellner, Ernest. *Legitimation of Belief.* London: Cambridge, 1973.

Genette, Gerald. *Figures of Literary Discourse.* New York: Columbia, 1982.

Geyer, Michael. "Multiculturalism and the Politics of General Education," in *Critical Inquiry* (Spring 1993).

Gilbert-Rolfe, Jeremy. *Beyond Piety.* Cambridge: Cambridge University, 1995.

Ginzburg, Carlo. "Interview," in *Radical History Review* (#35, 1986).

———. "Checking the Evidence: The Judge and the Historian," in *Critical Inquiry* (Autumn 1991).

———. *The Cheese and the Worms.* Baltimore: Johns Hopkins, 1978.

———. *Clues, Myths and the Historical Method.* Baltimore: Johns Hopkins, 1989.

———. "Killing a Chinese Mandarin: The Moral Implications of Distance," in *Critical Inquiry* (v. 21 #1, Autumn 1994).

———. "Microhistory: Two or Three things I Know about It," in *Critical Inquiry* (v. 20 #1, Autumn 1993).

————. "Montrer et citer," in *Debat* (#56, 1989).

————. "Witches and Shamans," in *New Left Review* (v. 200, 1993).

Goodwin, Charles and Sandro Duranti. "Rethinking Context: An Introduction,"in *Rethinking Context: Language as Interactive Phenomenon*. Cambridge: Cambridge University, 1992.

Gorgias. "Encomium on Helen," in *Ancilla to the Pre-Socratic Philosophers*, edited by K. Freeman. Cambridge, 1978.

Goux, Jean-Jacques. *Symbolic Economies*. Ithaca: Cornell, 1990.

Greenberg, Clement. "Avant-Garde and Kitsch," in *Pollack and After*, edited by F. Franscina. New York: Harper, 1986.

Greimas, A. J. "The Love-Life of the Hippopotamus," in *On Signs*, edited by M. Blonsky. Oxford, 1985.

————. *Structural Semantics*. Lincoln, 1983.

Greimas, A. J., and Fontanille, Jean. *The Semiotics of Passions*. Minneapolis: University of Minnesota Press, 1993.

Group Metaphor, *A General Rhetoric*. Baltimore: John Hopkins, 1981.

Grousset, Rene. *Empire of the Steppes*. New Brunswick, 1994.

Grube, G. M. A. *The Greek and Roman Critics*. London: Metheun, 1965.

Guattari, Felix. *Chaosophy*. New York: Semiotext(e), 1995.

Haar, Michael. "Nietzsche and Metaphysical Language," in *The New Nietzsche*, edited by D. Allison. Cambridge, 1990.

Haraway, Donna. *Simians, Cyborgs and Women*. London, 1991.

Harris, Roy. *The Origin of Writing*. LaSalle, 1986.

Harris, W. V. "The Silences of Momigliano," *Times Literary Supplement*, 12 April 1996.

Heidegger, Martin. *Basic Writings*. New York, 1977.

————. *Being and Time*. New York 1962.

————. *What is Called Thinking*. New York: Harper, 1958.

Hickey, Dave. "The Delicacy of Rock and Roll," *Art Issues* (Sept.–Oct., 1995).

Hjelmslev, Louis. *Prolegomena to a Theory of Language*. Madison, 1969.

Hoesterey, I. *Zeitgeist in Babel*. Bloomington, 1991.

Iggers, George. *The German Conception of History*. Middletown, 1968.

Jameson, Fredric. "On Cultural Studies," in *Social Text* (1993).

Jay, Martin. *Downcast Eyes*. Berkeley: University of California, 1993.

Jenkins, Keith. *On "What Is History"* New York: Routledge, 1994

Johnson, Barbara. *The Critical Distance*. Baltimore: John Hopkins, 1980.

Kant, Immanuel. *The Critique of Judgment*. London, 1931.

Kaplan, Alice. *French Lessons*. Chicago: University of Chicago, 1993.

Kaplan, Richard. "The Economics of Family and Faith," in *L.A. Times Book Review* (30 July 1995).

Keitel, Evelyn. *Reading Psychosis*. New York, 1989.

Kelly, George Armstrong. *Idealism, Politics and History*. Cambridge: Cambridge University, 1969.

Kelley, Mike. "Foul Perfection: Thoughts on Caricature." *Artforum*. (#37, 1989).

————. "Plato's Cave, Rothko's Chapel, Lincoln's Profile." *LAICA* (Fall 1985).

————. "The Poltergeist." *LAICA* (no. 3, 1980).

————. "Three Projects." n.d.

Kneale, William and Mary. *The Development of Logic.* Clarendon, 1957.

Koselleck, Reinhart. *Futures Past.* Cambridge, 1985.

Krauss, Rosalind. *The Optical Unconscious.* Cambridge: MIT Press, 1994.

Labov, William. *Sociolinguistic Patterns.* University of Pennsylvania, 1972.

Lacan, Jacques. *Ecrits.* New York, 1977.

————. "Of Structure as an Inmixing of an Otherness Prerequisite to Any Subject Whatever," in *The Languages of Criticism and the Sciences of Man.* Baltimore: John Hopkins, 1970.

LaCapra, Dominick. "The Cheese and the Worms," in *History and Criticism.* Ithaca, 1985.

Laclau, Ernst and Chantal Mouffe. *Hegemony and Socialist Strategy.* London, 1985.

Ladner, Gerhard. *The Idea of Reform.* Cambridge, 1959.

Latour, Bruno. *Science in Action.* Cambridge: Harvard, 1987.

————. *We Have Never Been Modern.* Cambridge: Harvard, 1993.

Lecercle, Jean-Jacques. *Philosophy through the Looking Glass.* La Salle, 1985.

————. *The Violence of Language.* London, 1990.

Leitch, Vincent. *Deconstructive Criticism.* New York, 1983.

Lodge, David. *Modern Criticism and Theory.* New York, 1988.

Lowith, Karl. *From Hegel to Nietzsche.* New York: Holt, 1964.

Lucretius. *On the Nature of Things.* Baltimore, 1971.

Lyotard, Jean-Francois. *The Differend.* Minneapolis: University of Minnesota, 1988.

————. *Libidinal Economy.* Bloomington, 1993.

————. *The Lyotard Reader.* Oxford, 1989.

Marin, Louis. *Portrait of the King.* Minneapolis: University of Minnesota Press, 1988.

Martinet, Andre. *A Functional View of Language.* Bloomington, 1984.

Massumi, Brian. *A User's Guide to Capitalism and Schizophrenia.* Cambridge, 1993.

Miller, J. H. "Dismembering and Disremembering in Nietzsche's 'On Truth and Lies in a Nonmoral Sense'" in *Boundary 2.* (v. 9, #3 and v. 10 #1, Spring-Fall 1981).

————. "An Open Letter to Professor Jon Weiner," in *Responses: On Paul de Man's Wartime Journalism,* edited by Werner Hamacher, Neil Hertz, and Thomas Keenan. Lincoln: University of Nebraska, 1989.

Momigliano, Arnaldo. *Studies in Historiography.* New York: Harper, 1964.

Nadel, George. "Philosophy of History Before Historicism," in *History and Theory* (v. 3, #3, 1964).

Nietzsche, Friedrich. *Genealogy of Morals.* London, 1913.

————. *Joyful Wisdom.* New York, 1960.

————. "On Truth and Lies in a Nonmoral Sense," in *Philosophy and Truth,* edited by D. Breazeale. London, 1979.

————. *Philosophy and Truth.* New Jersey, 1978.

————. *The Use and Abuse of History.* New York, 1957.

————. *The Will to Power.* New York: Vintage, 1975.

————. *Ecce Homo.* New York: Random House, 1927.

Nora, Pierre. "Between Memory and History," in *Representations* (Spring 1989, #26).

Olbrechts-Tyteca, L. and C. Perelman. *The New Rhetoric.* Notre Dame, 1969.

Pavel, Thomas. *The Feud of Language.* Cambridge, 1989.

Pinker, Stephen. *The Language Instinct.* New York: Morrow, 1995.

Poni, G. "The Name of the Game: Unequal Exchange and the Historiographic Marketplace," in *Microhistory and the Lost Peoples of Europe.* Baltimore, 1991.

Putnam, Hilary. "After Empiricism," in *Post-Analytic Philosophy,* ed. by Cornel West and John Rajchman. Reading, Bill. *Introducing Lyotard.* New York: Routledge, 1990.

Ricoeur, Paul. *The Rule of Metaphor.* Toronto, 1977.

Robins, Robert. *A Short History of Linguistics.* Bloomington, 1970.

Ronell, Avital. "A Note on the Failure of Man's Custodianship," in *Public,* #8, 1993.

Rorty, Richard. "Solidarity or Objectivity," in Cornel West and John Rajchman, eds. *Post-Analytic Philosophy.* New York: Columbia, 1985.

————. "The Dark Side of the American Left," *Chronicle of Higher Education* (April 3, 1998).

Ross, Andrew. "Culture Vultures," in *Artforum* (December 1995).

Ross, David. "Disembodied Militarism," in Mike Kelley, *Catholic Tastes,* edited by E. Sussman. New York: Whitney, 1993.

Ryle, Gilbert. "The Theory of Meaning" in *Problems in the Philosophy of Language,* edited by T. Olshewsky. New York: Holt, 1969.

Said, Edward. *The World, the Text and the Critic.* Cambridge, 1983.

Shotwell, John. *The History of History.* New York, 1939.

Silverman, Kaija. *The Subject of Semiotics.* London, 1983.

Singerman, Howard. "Charting *Monkey Island* with Levi-Strauss and Freud," in *Catholic Tastes.* New York: Whitney, 1993.

Sobchak, Vivian. "History happens," in *The Persistence of History.* New York: Routledge, 1996.

Spanos, William. *Heidegger and Criticism.* Minneapolis: University of Minnesota, 1993.

Spivak, Gayatri. *The Spivak Reader.* New York: Routledge, 1996.

Stambaugh, Joan. *Nietzsche's Thought of Eternal Return.* Baltimore: Johns Hopkins, 1972.

Stone, Sandy. "How Like a Goddess," in *Artforum* (September 1995).

Suzuki, D. T. *Zen and Japanese Culture.* New York: Pantheon, 1959.

Tarski, Alfred. "The Semantic Definition of Truth," in *Problems in the Philosophy of Language,* edited by Thomas Olshewshy. New York: Holt, 1969.

Todorov, Tzvetan. *The Poetic of Prose.* Ithaca: Cornell University Press, 1977.

————. *Theory of the Symbol.* Ithica: Cornell University Press, 1982.

Turkle, Sherry. *Life on the Screen.* Cambridge: MIT, 1995.

Tyler, Stephen. *The Unspeakable.* Madison: University of Wisconsin, 1987.

Van Peursen, C. A. *Body, Soul, Spirit.* London: Oxford, 1966.

Vico, Giambattista. *The New Science.* Ithaca, 1968.

Weber, Samuel. "Afterwork: Literature-Just Making It." in J. F. Lyotard and J. L. Thebaud. *Just Gaming.* Minneapolis: University of Minnesota, 1985.

West, Cornel. "Interview with A. Stephanson," in *Art and Philosophy,* Milan: Politi, 1991.

White, Hayden. *Metahistory.* Baltimore: Johns Hopkins, 1973.

Wilden, Anthony. "Changing Frames of Order: Cybernetics and the Machina Mundi," in *The Myths of Information.* Madison: Coda Press. n.d.

Wittgenstein, Ludwig. *On Certainty.* London: Blackwell, 1969.

———. *Philosophical Investigations.* New York: Macmillan, 1968.

———. *Tractatus Logico-Philosophicus.* London: 1921.

Wollen, Peter. *Raiding the Ice-Box.* London: Verso, 1993.

Zizek, Slavoj. "It Doesn't Have to be a Jew," in *Lusitania* (v. 1, #4, 1993).

———. *Looking Awry.* Cambridge: MIT, 1993.

———. *Tarrying with the Negative.* Durham: Duke University, 1993.

Index